EFFECTIVE MANAGEMENT OF FOREIGN EXCHANGE

A CORPORATE TREASURER'S GUIDE

ERRATUM

The diagrams for Figures 6.1 and 6.2 (page 55) have been transposed. Figure 6.1 shows a straddle option and Figure 6.2 represents a bull call option.

Effective Management of Foreign Exchange

Effective Management of Foreign Exchange

A CORPORATE TREASURER'S GUIDE

BRIAN MAPLETOFT

McGRAW-HILL BOOK COMPANY

London · New York · St Louis · San Francisco · Auckland
Bogotá · Caracas · Hamburg · Lisbon · Madrid · Mexico
Milan · Montreal · New Delhi · Panama · Paris · San Juan
São Paulo · Singapore · Sydney · Tokyo · Toronto

Published by
McGRAW-HILL Book Company (UK) Limited
Shoppenhangers Road, Maidenhead, Berkshire, SL6 2QL, England
Telephone 0628 23432
Fax 0628 770224

British Library Cataloguing in Publication Data
Mapletoft, Brian
Effective management of foreign exchange: a corporate treasurer's guide
1. Foreign exchange
I. Title
332.45

ISBN 0-07-707329-0

Library of Congress Cataloging-in-Publication Data
Mapletoft, Brian
Effective management of foreign exchange: a corporate treasurer's guide/Brian Mapletoft.
p. cm.
Includes index.
ISBN 0-07-707329-0
1. Foreign exchange. 2. International business enterprises--Finance. I. Title.
HG3851.M295 1991
658.15'5--dc20 91-37

Typeset by BookEns Ltd, Baldock, Herts.
and printed and bound at the University Press, Cambridge

Contents

Foreword

Readers of company reports will be familiar with references to the impact of exchange rate movements on results. Strangely, such references almost invariably describe an adverse effect—surely, on occasions, profits will have been aided but this is rarely mentioned! In fact, given the extent of exchange rate movements in almost every year for the past ten years or more, there can be few businesses of any size that are totally immune to exchange markets.

Once the sensitivity of profits is appreciated, it is clear that a policy is needed to manage exchange risk, but considerable debate exists over the extent to which the policy should be risk averse or, at the other end of the spectrum, should seek to make an additional profit centre from dealing.

Brian Mapletoft has faced this key issue and advances detailed reasoning to answer the question 'Why deal?' He then describes the various techniques that might be employed, ranging from orthodox spot and forward operations, leading on to the newer, more flexible techniques, especially options, which, in the right hands, come near to allowing treasurers to have their cake and eat it, with only the small matter of a premium to spoil the fun!

Ever conscious of the need to convince senior management of the value of a professional approach to exchange rates, Brian includes suggested reporting formats in his practical and well-documented guide to an area of risk that has for too long been neglected or seen as sharing the famous inevitability of death and taxes.

All those who work in the stimulating environment of the foreign exchange market will welcome this contribution to the treasurer's library. Even if rates still move erratically or perversely, at least the available management techniques can now be studied and applied so that no surprises emerge at the year end.

Alan E. Moore, CBE
Director of Corporate Banking and Treasury
Lloyds Bank plc

Preface

This work originated in the revision of my *Corporate Management of Foreign Exchange* (1988 Eurostudy), and was originally to be simply the second edition. However, the author's involvement with systems for foreign exchange management prompted the inclusion of two significant sections which augmented and changed the structure of the original work. Also a change in publishers was the occasion for the new title, which incidentally appeals to the author's penchant for value-added as a motivator.

Firstly, the section dealing with Financial Control explains a concept (the CUF—currency usage fee) which had its origins in Plessey and was transmuted for APV plc, courtesy of Chris Beenham and the late Bill Webb. Its application is mainly for multi-country sourced enterprises where the divisional and functional mix can cause managerial and control problems in individual business units, and where the control of cash is crucial to the survival of the business.

Secondly, the Jonathan Robin Dealing System was derived from ground-breaking work at Amersham International plc, performed by Tom Triggs and Colin Tyler. This is a sterling-based single-company forex computer system which provides a practical insight into the controls and mechanisms required for a stand-alone, professional system for foreign exchange management.

Apart from corrections and amplifications, the book contains several changes. The chapter dealing with currency options has been rewritten to include further strategies that have developed, plus some particular examples. The chapter on charts has been updated and the style of the charts has changed with the development of the trigger concept for actions, rather than the more cerebral concept of momentum.

Given the rapidly changing environment, both within the treasury discipline and in markets generally, future changes to the content and presentation will be unavoidable. The introductory chapter has been updated to take into account the unification of Germany and the collapse of communism in eastern Europe, the Gulf crisis and the entry of sterling into the ERM of the EMS. Owing to the requirement to terminate data at a particular point (end 1990 being chosen), significant events like the 1991 recession and the Gulf War are not covered. The decision to go ahead and publish is taken in the certain knowledge that other parts of the work would only require further amendment in turn, and in confidence that the readers will be charitable in their consideration of the author who acknowledges that all faults and omissions are his alone.

Brian Mapletoft
Hong Kong, February 1991

CHAPTER 1

The changing role of the financial officer

The periodic financier

During the period 1945–70, exchange rates were generally stable, with fixed parities against the dollar and the dollar freely convertible against gold at $35 an ounce. Therefore it was conventional that an organization's financial officer should be concerned with the raising of finance, the investment of surplus cash at advantageous interest rates, and the general monitoring of the financial evolution. This was the era of the comforting security of certainty. Administration was the name of the game, and clerical activities in the manual control on invoices and payments occupied the minds of most financial officers. In this people-related function, it was not uncommon for staff numbers to be very large indeed.

In so far as nascent treasurers were recognized at all, they were the financial accountants and specialists in cashiers' sections, interested in economics, taxation and comparative trade flows, and fascinated by the beginnings of the break-up of the fixed exchange regime at the Smithsonian conference in the early 1970s. They were bright yet peripheral creatures, seeking a role but yet to find one. Over the next twenty years their function was to advance and evolve, so that by the 1990s every significant company, and certainly every multinational, now has its own treasurer with very diverse remits that touch on the financial flows of the business, its strategy in risk management and drive to the heart of decision-making that can affect the survival of the company itself.

The purpose of this book is not to chart this transformation, but to focus on some of the outstanding issues in the area where this new discipline impacts on the organization most visibly—namely, in foreign exchange.

The changed status and role for the treasurer has been accompanied and influenced by the macro-economic changes in the world at large, as fixed exchange rates have given way to floating, and as the old certainties of the past have been replaced by the volatilities of today. This introductory section traces some of these currents.

With both foreign policy problems and the worsening of its balance of payments in the late 1960s, the US position of centrality in the world financial system came under increasing strain. By 1971, the old situation was untenable and the US could not fulfil its obligations under Bretton Woods to convert the dollar into gold at the agreed rate. The gold price rose, and currencies floated. Domestic economic policies were freed from the artificial constraints of the fixed exchange rate regime, and companies began to feel the pain and pleasure of foreign exchange losses and windfall gains.

The 1970s were characterized by the oil price shocks of 1973 and 1979 and the requirement to recycle petrodollars to the less developed countries (LDCs). Meanwhile the USA's temporary retreat from the international stage in the mid-1970s was followed by the new-found self-assertiveness of the Reagan administration. Rearmament was accompanied by a deficit spending policy funded by high interest rates and a strong dollar. Size and growth took precedence over solvency.

This provided the basis for the later 1980s and 1990s, where overall financial fragility is accompanied by the United States now being the largest debtor nation in the world. One was used to 'non-bankable' countries of eastern Europe and South America being a cause for anxiety of central bankers and chief executive officers (CEOs) of city institutions. To find the United States of America wholly reliant on insurance and pension funds from Japan for the funding of its central government was disturbing for economists and commentators accustomed to thinking that the USA was the repository of the ethic of conservatism, financial prudence and prosperity.

The counterpoint to the decline in economic influence of the USA has been the growth of three competitive areas—Europe, Japan and the Pacific rim—having significant creditor nations in world terms, notably the UK, Japan and Taiwan. Indeed, in their growth from obscurity to financial prominence, the new industrialized countries (NICs) of the Pacific rim, (Taiwan and South

Korea) and the 'Asian' countries (notably Thailand and Singapore) are a motor for the world economy in the late 1980s in a similar way to Japan and Germany in the 'miracle' 1960s. The significant creditor nations of the next generation, barring unforeseen catastrophes, are expected to be these countries, whose investments are already welcomed by their neighbours (e.g., Philippines, Indonesia).

After the generation of Brezhnev-inspired stagnation, in 1989 eastern Europe discarded the political shackles that were restraining market development. The opportunities opened up for investment and expansion are enormous, but are matched by the practical problems resulting from over forty years of neglect and poor resource utilization. In the problems of underinvestment, pollution, and energy inefficiency, eastern Europe demonstrates the magnitude of the task of reconstruction. The 1990s could see the expansion of the free-trade area of the EC to include some of the former communist countries of eastern Europe as their economies are restored and their populations seek the stability of a larger trading bloc. However, the problems of German monetary union in July 1990 illustrate that, though such a process has an element of inevitability, the rebuilding of infrastructures involves more than currency transactions and changes in laws. The position of Germany as the main economic driving force in Europe, as well as its geographical and historical position in the centre of Europe, determines its direction of expansion in political and economic influence over the next decade. German capital will be attracted to this reconstruction process in eastern Europe, and not to the USA, which has been the destination of much of the surplus investment capital of the UK and Japan.

The larger scene shows the long-term decline of the United States from world dominance in the decades after the Second World War towards significant influence only, with the currencies of the rest of the redeveloped world being revalued accordingly. The second stage, the revaluation of the currencies of the NICs, has partially taken place as a by-product of the efforts of the US administration to correct the dangerous twin deficits in the mid-1980s. For short-term and export incentive purposes, such revaluations have been resisted by the countries themselves since cheap exports, particularly to the USA, help their industry. This is a modern replay of the German and Japanese situation in the 1960s when, to a larger degree than in the 1980s, the USA could afford the luxury of imports subsidized by uncompetitive exchange rates.

However, as might be expected, the larger scene does not depict an undisturbed dollar decline, but mirrors the decline in influence of the UK in the devaluation of sterling over the last century (and even in the 1970s), which was not a straight-line process. There have been periods—1983–84 being a case in point—where the US dollar seemed to defy gravity. Looking at the macro-economic picture, it was easy for commentators and pundits to forecast the decline of the currency to a more stable level, but it was not so easy to predict the timing of this, with most predicting a decline of the dollar in 1983 or 1984 rather than 1985.

The fact that the decline from an overbought situation in spring 1985 was then followed up by significant central bank intervention in the Plaza accord, illustrates not only the power of central bankers in influencing markets but that, for the first time, international monetary authorities were perceived to act together to change expectations. Whatever the side-effects of such action—and these could be interpreted to include the Tokyo stock market adjustment of spring 1990—it was now clear that, apart from the trade and capital flows and the speculative movements in currencies, a new force was at work in forex markets that would need to be watched closely. Where, in the past, the trade numbers affected the markets, it would now be the verbal submissions of the Chairman of the Federal Reserve in reports to the Open Market Committee of Congress.

The variability of nominal rates of exchange against the US dollar over the last twenty years can be read for three currencies on Figure 1.1. Sterling is egotistically quoted as US dollars to the pound, in deference to convention, while all other currencies are quoted at their number to the US dollar. Even if sterling were inverted the chart would still be a jumble. To make sense of this, the numbers need to be scaled and expressed logarithmically. Figures 1.2 and 1.3 make the data somewhat more intelligible.

From a base of 100 in 1969, it will be seen that the yen almost reached 300 in 1988 before subsiding to 2.5 in 1990, while the deutschemark, which had lagged the yen in appreciation against the dollar, has caught up following its rise in the light of the opening up of eastern Europe in 1989 and the possibility of reconstruction under German leadership in the 1990s. Sterling has predictably

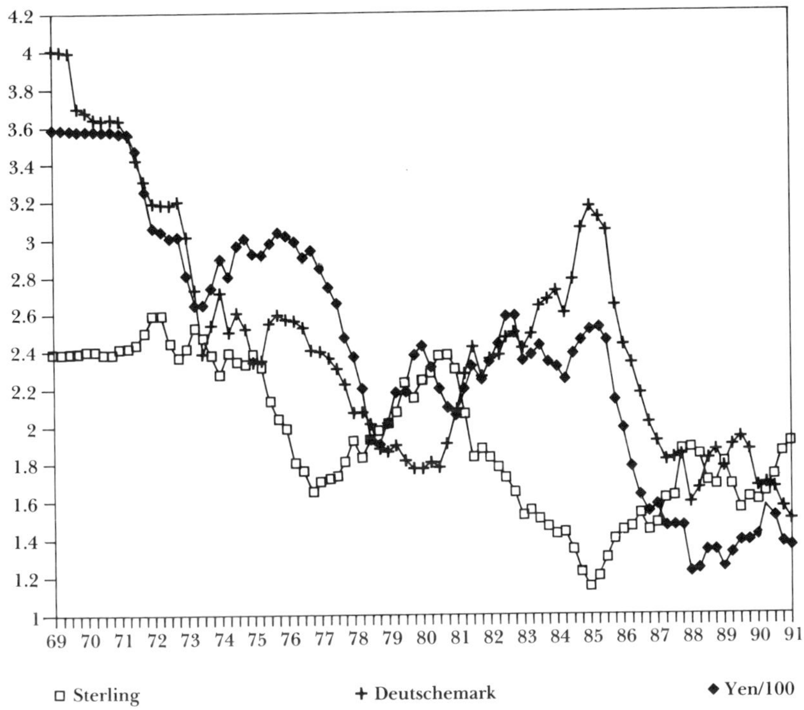

Figure 1.1 Exchange rates v US dollar

lagged all these currencies, including the dollar, achieving at its peak in 1988 only 80 per cent of its 1969 value of $2.4.

In logarithmic terms, the scale of advance by Germany and Japan is somewhat more modest, and the cyclical effect of the declines and temporary resurgences of the dollar (and the pound) is more clear. Sterling, in particular, is perceived to have recovered dramatically from two cyclical troughs, in 1976/7 and 1984/5. The comparative decline of sterling against the yen and deutschemark is perceived to be less than the straight comparison of rebased rates would imply, but its restitution has been tempered by economic limitations.

Where, then, does this leave organizations that have seen their profitability expanding and declining as a result of exchange rates, with no influence having been brought to bear by themselves? There have been two main reactions: strategic and tactical.

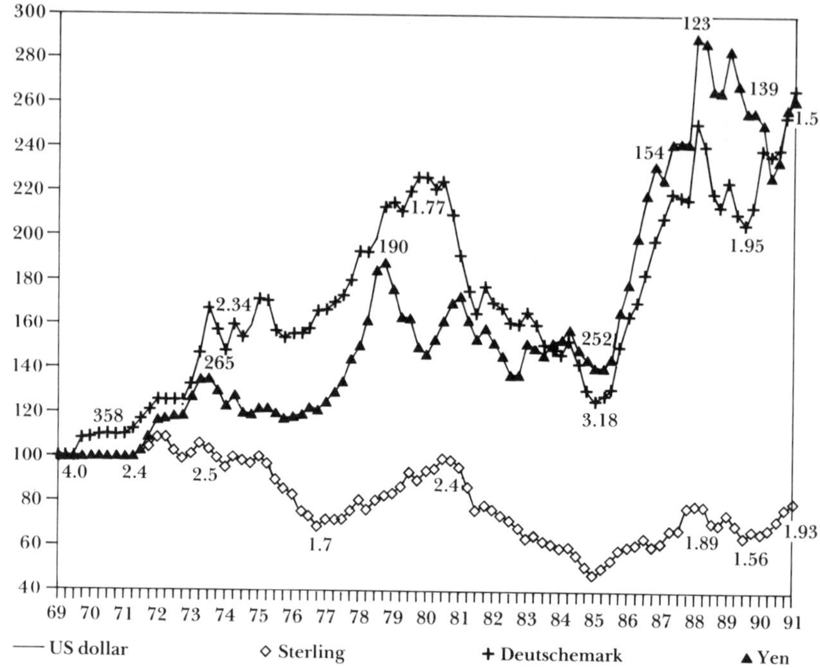

Figure 1.2 Exchange rates v US dollar (1969 = 100 (end quarter data))

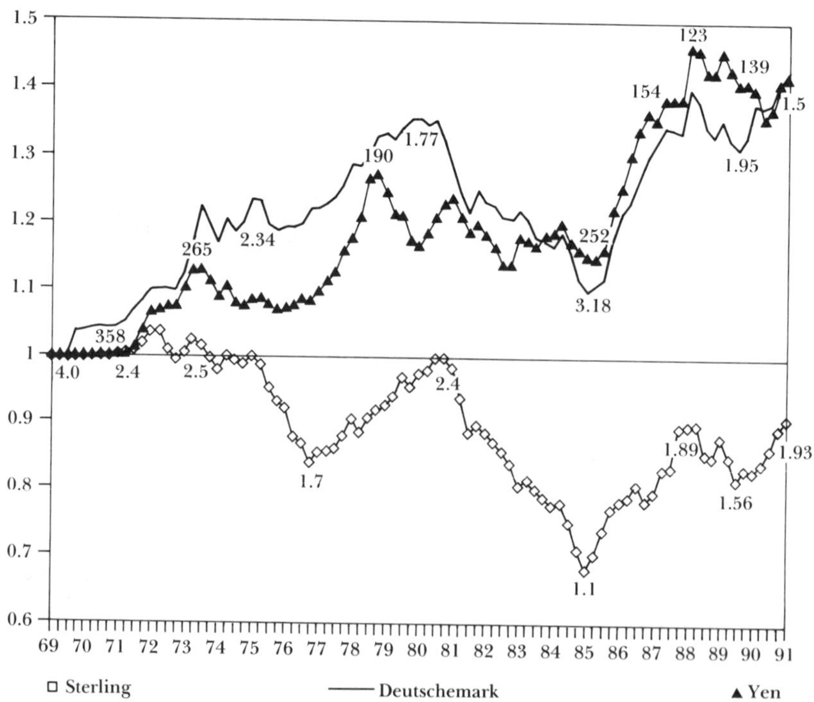

Figure 1.3 Exchange rates v US dollar

Strategic

More attention has been directed to the strategic location of manufacturing capacity. For example, in the light of the strong yen and the perception of increased protectionist sentiment - notably in the USA—there has been, in the late 1980s, a significant disinvestment by Japanese industries out of Japan into the USA and the UK on the one hand and into NICs on the other. Motor transplants into the US and European car markets can avoid the problems of quotas on imports. Production of audio and electronic equipment in NICs can take advantage of cheap labour and relatively competitive exchange rates. Paradoxically, legislators in the USA are beginning to be worried about these transplants, even though the domestic effect is to increase employment and spur the efficiency of local producers. The political reaction in the UK, where the need for inward investment has been felt more acutely, has been somewhat more mature and welcoming. A workable compromise on the sale of such home-produced transplants in the EC is being negotiated.

Tactical

Organizations are taking their treasury operations (which, in the early 1970s, they hardly recognized) very seriously indeed. The decisions on whether to cover significant exposures are taken at senior level, and the post of director of treasury, group treasurer or treasury manager is now realized as being vital for the company. Should the treasurer either not be empowered to put a given action into operation or fail to take the necessary steps when currencies move beyond a particular point, the consequences can be dire for that organization.

In the last ten years there has been a general awakening in the corporate sphere of the consciousness of the need to manage risk in a professional way. Corporates had been accustomed to dealing with the business risks of the enterprise—its manufacturing, products and market mix, and competitive pressures. In the modern environment they also need to manage the financial risks—those deriving from changes in interest rates, and particularly exchange rates. With modern instruments, these are controllable within prescribed limits.

The risk manager

The professional risk manager has appeared—perhaps not recognized by that title in many locations, but nevertheless someone whose prime concern is to safeguard the interests of the organization in the various currency and financial markets. Generally, in contrast to, say, the financial controller, the risk manager only requires a small departmental team but needs plenty of computer support to analyse data, to store records, to advise, to deal, to control and to account for the myriad banking services of the corporate. The functions of the risk manager are various:

- protection of the company from adverse movements in exchange rates
- management of short-, medium- and long-term interest rate risks
- structuring funding and treasury activities to minimize adverse taxation consequences
- establishment of necessary controls, accounting structures and systems support to manage the function properly.

Sensible actions can be taken to reduce the risk profile of the group and to economize on banking flows. These can be regarded as being within the domain of the company and need not necessarily involve outside parties, and include such items as:

- netting of payment flows
- invoicing in strong currencies
- leading and lagging receipts and payments.

Netting of payment flows

In a group situation, there are cash flows between subsidiaries and parent and also between subsidiaries. Clearly, if these are not adjusted, there is a duplication of transactional charges and total flows. Several banking packages are available allowing such payments to be netted multilaterally in order to economize on transaction costs and to enable attention to be concentrated on the fundamental flows of the company rather than on the administration of the detail.

Invoicing in strong currencies

This is a quite logical approach where a multinational has the choice of billing in a variety of currencies. The concept sounds a little patronizing to the modern ear. While, in theory, it is sensible to invoice in preferred currencies with upward potential, in practice, the choices are limited to the availability of currencies and the ability and wish of the customer to pay in the currency chosen.

Leading and lagging receipts and payments

Occasionally, if the debt due from a subsidiary to a large multinational parent is sufficiently significant, it may be worth considering whether to delay payment in anticipation of a devaluation or realignment. While this might seem a clever and cheap method of protecting the short-term position, it is not particularly significant for the company because of this short-term nature. Furthermore, for every successful attempt to forecast the required devaluation that makes this worth while, there would in all probability be a number of occasions on which such devaluation did not materialize.

Therefore these internal methods of hedging might be regarded as simply good house-keeping or as an attempt to seem to be active without affecting the real world. However, they are in no way a substitute for a considered and effective programme of hedging, which is where the risk manager can really have an impact on the enterprise.

Conclusion

Given the rapidity of change in world financial markets in the last twenty years, it is not surprising that corporates and institutions have developed their own responses to the threats and opportunities available. Some corporates that have been 'street-wise' and confident—generally those with a large portfolio of foreign exchange—have also ventured into the area of trading their positions. Some have established formal finance companies, some in tax havens, to manage this either as an adjunct to their conventional business or as a separate trade. Others have simply managed according to their more limited circumstances, by developing a respectable profile and reputation in the markets. Alternatively, some corporates, unable to deal with the mental anxieties in this area, have labelled foreign exchange 'banking' and steered a wide berth.

Clearly, if one responds to the threats of a storm simply by battening down the hatches, one is also prevented from benefiting when the storm is over. To take advantage of opportunities one must also undergo a degree of risk. The risk manager is the corporate's response to financial threats and opportunities; and the market-traded and bank-derived instruments are the tools of the trade. The risk manager must learn to use them wisely.

CHAPTER 2

Impact of foreign exchange on the business

For a complex multinational, the easiest way of simplifying the company structure would be simply to stop selling overseas. It is possibly a truism that the requirement to trade in many different countries is a prime reason for the intricacy of accounting and systems in multinational organizations. But to avoid selling overseas would clearly be to eliminate the *raison d'être* for such a company. The need to transact, deal and think in a variety of different languages and currencies—that is, foreign exchange—is the aspect that sets the multinational corporate apart from a simple company.

Foreign exchange, therefore, has an effect on the environment and attitude of a company, making the ethos more subject to diverse influences, and tending to add a cosmopolitan flavour. Often such companies are open to ideas and approaches from diverse origins and almost by definition are interesting and exciting places in which to operate. Of itself, foreign exchange may seem a little remote as a motivating element in the direction of a company. However, the requirement to think and plan in a variety of currencies gives the possibility of extraneous gains and losses and the need to manage the risks and opportunities associated with this additional dimension.

The corporate culture is affected by foreign exchange in a variety of ways, ranging from the trivial requirement to travel and appreciate the risks of currency conversion, to the important need to price in local currency and compete internationally. Among the diverse aspects of the company that are affected by foreign exchange are:

1 sales in currencies, with need to transact, record, and move funds;

2 selling organizations located abroad, often in local subsidiary companies, implying the need for:
   (a) international sales and marketing management, enabling the company to appreciate the impact of foreign competition on those markets;
   (b) purchases in foreign currency, clearly often a requirement even for completely domestic companies, but providing a rationale for:
      (i) exchange management, in terms of the purchase of currency for foreign supplies, the receipt of currency from sales, and the management of the net exposures, developing into
      (ii) treasury strategy, involving the establishment of the company's philosophy and approach to exchange risk.

The serious commitment of the company to an international policy of selling and commerce leads automatically, via the establishment of an overseas presence, to the creation of overseas subsidiaries with a potential manufacturing capability. This generates a further layer of complexity in the ability provided to the company to source from multiple locations, with the associated problems of international transfer pricing and the location of profits. Each company has the capability, and often the need, to borrow locally and to manage an international balance sheet.

The dynamics of the business determine the asset mix and location of centres of production and marketing. However, treasury considerations are uppermost in the decisions to hedge, borrow locally, establish group banking structures and otherwise manage the net asset mix of the group. Taxation considerations also have an impact, notably where offshore structures are employed.

The impact of foreign exchange is therefore seen as a cultural issue for the corporate. It is also a management issue. The resolution of the structural problems associated with the transition from a simple national company to a complex international or multinational corporate leads the company to think differently and act in a more considered and less parochial way. National companies are established, each of which has its own ethos and contribution to the parent company, and their control leads to the development of marketing and sales organizations that are primarily international in character. Add to this the diversification of production outside the parent country and the stage is set for a truly multinational company. The need and even desirability to use expatriates to establish and run overseas selling and distribution is superseded by the employment of wholly indigenous staff, leading ultimately to the nomination of non-nationals of the home company to the board of the parent.

Given the transition of the company from its insularity to its awareness that it has developed from a national to a multinational company, are its problems then solved? In some senses they are only just beginning.

From an accounting perspective, the more complex the company, the more sophisticated the systems needed to underpin the transactions. For example, consider a matrix organization involving a string of manufacturing companies, and selling individually to a group of overseas selling companies. Each company will require information in its own currency and in the foreign currency involved in its sales through each of the selling companies and agencies. Likewise, each selling company will be required to report the make-up of its own mix of products sold, together with stocks held. Control and reporting are needed, both in the relevant currencies and in the home currency, for each company and each specialist division. Similarly, plans, forecasts and budgets must be prepared for the entire range of requirements. Statutory and periodic accounts need control and systems, and action has to be taken to ensure that local reporting constraints are met (e.g., SEC requirements in the US). The planning and administration of taxation and customs duties has also to be managed.

However, even if the relatively straightforward accounting issues are settled, there are significant financial points that require resolution, mainly in the area of treasury management as it has evolved over the last few years. These include structural and policy issues that take the company into the area of philosophy—notably, the need to recognize the kind of business it is in, the level of exposure cover that is appropriate, the commitment it should provide to the internal systems that control the cash aspects of the company, and its entire approach towards financing. Such issues are symptomatic of the impact of foreign exchange on the practical workings of the treasury department, and to a large degree are the rationale for its existence.

The impact of foreign exchange

The impact of foreign exchange can be seen particularly on treasury items within balance sheets and profit and loss accounts and cash flow.

The balance sheet

Evidence of the influence of foreign exchange can be seen in an examination of the balance sheet.

Firstly, the denomination of assets of the company, structurally where to locate centres of production and distribution, including stocking points, is a decision as much linked to long-term views on comparative long-term economics of manufacture and competition as to exchange rates *per se*, but requires similar thinking on the assets of preference and their management.

The decision to lease or to buy the assets of overseas companies is determined not just by the calculation of the short-term effect on the profit and loss but also by the longer term view of currencies.

Secondly, the structure of the liabilities side of the balance sheet can be affected by currency considerations. The decision of equity listing is linked to the availability of international capital, and to the desire of companies to ensure adequate availability of their stock, liquidity and share price support. Company image and esteem linked to perceptions of the international nature of the business will also be motivating factors. Currency borrowing is a business-related decision and also one determined by central strategy. This incorporates not only borrowing for business requirements, where often local loans are efficient to achieve maximum tax deductability, but centralized and strategic borrowing where the choice of currency and location of debt are interlinked decisions. In this area, too, lies the concept of 'matching' liabilities to assets in order to eliminate the risk of an unhedged asset impacting adversely on reserves on consolidation.

Thirdly, short-term asset management is an area in which there are structural considerations of a foreign exchange nature, apart from the hedging and off-balance-sheet obligations that will be a significant consideration elsewhere. Debts are incurred in a variety of currencies, and it is clearly possible for the company to elect not to invoice in, say, Turkish lire or Columbian pesos, and when exporting to such countries to do so in US dollars. The effect of such a decision will eliminate some complexity in the handling of exotic currencies within the company and, potentially, will provide windfall exchange gains at the centre if the local currency loses value. The cost of such a decision is the rigidity that this can build into the trading relationship—particularly acute where US dollars are in short supply in the paying country and where central banking authority has to be sought for the export of hard currency.

The decision to police longer or shorter periods of credit allowed to debtors of different countries is another policy that impacts on the structure of the balance sheet. It may be that the general requirement to allow as little credit as possible on debtors and to take as much credit as possible on payables is a little too simplistic for an international operation. Local custom and practice might enable rapid payment of debts in strong currency centres such as Germany and Holland, but may delay payment in Latin countries for instance. However, the perception that poor credit performance equates also to periodic exchange losses as currencies devalue can impact on the decision to enforce tighter credit policies to the 'mañana' countries.

Profit and loss

Influences of foreign exchange decisions are very evident in an examination of the profit and loss account.

Firstly, the conversion of foreign currency denominated receipts and payments is the major variable against which hedging actions are often recommended. Mainly such conversion is done at spot rates, but where forward contracts have been undertaken the relevant forward rate is used. As treasury dealing becomes more sophisticated it is possible to appraise the two activities separately, and thus treasury's own contribution is soon regarded as an activity to be appraised independently.

Secondly, the translation of overseas subsidiaries' local profits to the home currency, which is sometimes regarded as outside the control of the central treasury since no cash flows are made for this variable until dividend payments are made. There is a perceptible trend for such profits to be regarded as within the purview of treasury operations at a group level, and therefore capable of being managed. Two developments are sharpening the debate in this area: namely, the increasing trend towards 'average rate accounting' superseding 'period end accounting', which automatically removes the uncertainties of reported performance depending on the accidental rate of exchange applying at year-end; and also the development of average rate options, which allows such average rates still to be managed within certain parameters.

Thirdly, currency movements on short-term assets and liabilities are revalued into the profit and loss account at accounting period ends, rather than into reserves, which is the treatment for long-term balance sheet items. The implication for treasury management is that the balance of foreign currency denominated debtors and creditors should be taken into account in currency management decisions.

Finally, protective actions taken by treasury or some other relevant department in the company to avoid or soften the effect on the business of movements in the foreign exchange markets are, of course, profit and loss items just like the items they are there to control. These include the attributable gain or loss resulting from treasury action, whether from the difference in exchange rates recorded (e.g. forward v spot at maturity) or from the payment of premia on options.

Cash flow

The cash flow of the company must clearly exhibit the impact of foreign exchange decisions on the financial operations of the company.

Business-related foreign exchange cash flow items are, clearly, the supplies of imported raw materials and machinery and the export of finished product, their timing and pricing terms and conditions. Other financial flows include interest payments on loans and deposits and dividend flows in currency.

The impact of foreign exchange actions designed to address these cash flow items, and the profit and balance sheet items above, is felt finally on the cash flow of the company. A low-key and simple enabling policy of foreign exchange will be evidenced by a level of activity that simply mirrors the relevant cash flows related to the business. A more adventurous or comprehensive policy will be exhibited by significant cash flow effects that are generated by such cover strategies: for example, the cash flow effects of foreign exchange gains and losses resulting from profit cover activities, or the costs and benefits of options, or the 'rolling cover' of a comprehensive forward cover strategy.

Treasury management

Treasury management is evolving as a discipline, and it can be argued that no one approach is correct for all types of company. For example, a low-margin engineering company may be risk-averse (and therefore opportunity-blind) for the cultural reason that money is hard to make and that the expertise of the engineers is in their widgets and valves, and they want their cash simple—in pound notes (forgetting the note has given way to the coin, which has even less purchasing value)! A high margin speciality manufacturer or service company might be able to regard foreign exchange as a nice addition to an already lucrative underlying business, and therefore ideal to exploit or even establish as a second-line business, with its own budgets and performance measures. However, the philosophy underlying the approach might not be more than a prejudice of the chairman or senior executive and no more relevant to the future of the business than their own job tenure!

It is therefore unsurprising that a variety of conventions has grown up to address the philosophy and thinking of what action is appropriate for businesses. For convenience, these are categorized broadly as 'safety first', 'limited management' and 'total management'.

Safety first

While this is an attitude of mind rather than a well-expounded philosophy, there are several aspects that provide clues to the concept of this approach. Management under 'safety first' tends to adopt an approach that is designed to achieve a low profile, and the latter is deemed to be conducive to personal and corporate survival. A low profile can mean different things to different audiences, and therefore both extremes of zero action or unquestioning activity can fall within this approach. Disasters in, for example, full cover of foreign exchange receivables which produce mammoth opportunity (and cash) losses can paradoxically be praised by analysts and commentators as being 'prudent'.

Balance sheet risks are treated either as uncontrollable, with borrowing to finance the ongoing multicurrency assets being drawn down only in the parent company, or as strictly apportioned in relation to the currency assets. The former approach avoids the inconvenience of local currency borrowing and the requirement to hedge the balance sheet. The latter approach accepts balance sheet hedging as a requirement, but avoids the requirement to exercise judgement on those currency assets that should be hedged and those that should not, therefore sidestepping the issue of the inadvisability of borrowing strong currencies. This latter comforting philosophy was a factor in the conscientious borrowing of Swiss francs in the early 1970s by some corporates at the bargain rate of 3 per cent; only on repayment of the loan in later years did they calculate the real rate after exchange impact at much higher than the average sterling cost of borrowing of around 10 per cent.

New instruments are shunned by the safety first manager because they are novel and might result in a requirement for some future action that is not known at the outset (the option might need to be exercised, and what then?), and because there is a risk that the banks might not have thought through all the implications of their use. There is some justification in the latter area, notably opposite taxation requirements, but uncertainties in this area are rapidly being resolved as case law builds up and as changes in legislation catch up with market developments.

Therefore, only conventional instruments are used for foreign exchange management. The approach of the safety first manager is to be as distant as possible from the decision of whether or not to cover. The optimal approach for the manager is to have a specific policy, either always to cover, or, just as logically, never to cover. In these cases, the job of the safety first manager is just to run the shop, not to make decisions. The end results, whether good or bad for the company, will be attributed to market circumstances and will always be outside that manager's control and influence.

This approach is risk-averse, but also judgement-averse. It recognizes structures rather than opportunities. It regards the limits of delegated authority as very restrictive, and the requirement to maintain dictated policy as sacrosanct. It defines the limits of treasury authority very strictly, and treasury discretion is almost completely denied. The results of the policy can clearly be either excellent or dreadful, but are quite likely to be merely indifferent since, as the name implies, certain underlying aims of the corporate are achieved and the minimum aim of survival is achieved. More than the minimum aim is unlikely to result.

The defence of this policy can be twofold: either the company is small and an active management policy would be a diversion of senior effort and a distraction for the main business, or the company is large but not profitable, when the risks from an active approach (even if successful) are too high for the company to contemplate.

Since reasonable affluence is not the aim under this policy, it would be surprising if good all-round and consistent performance were assured.

Limited management

This style of management is appropriate to a large multinational, where the advisability and even ability of any individual to do more than influence the management of foreign exchange is doubtful. A risk-averse policy can be quite appropriate, but there is too much applied and even surplus intelligence around for a passive or non-reactive policy to be viable, even should it be felt desirable by the manager, treasurer or director. Therefore, a high degree of activity and thought might be given to the management of exposures, with early morning think-tank sessions, or parliamentary-style monthly committee meetings to decide actions; but the net effect of the actions decided in relation to the magnitude either of the task or of the enterprise itself might be very small.

Looking at balance sheet structure, it might be seen as entirely appropriate simply to borrow locally where there are local needs, irrespective of the long-term thoughts of the direction of the exchanges. It is no one's responsibility actually to address balance sheet exposure *per se*, the magnitude of the task militating against it, particularly where there is a local subsidiary stock exchange quotation. Thoughts on the currency denomination of central borrowings, either through the parent company or, more often, through offshore finance companies, centre on the efficiency of local sources of finance and the competitiveness of interest rates in the local markets. Funds thus raised are then commonly swapped into the parent currency, leaving a requirement to repay in the future the same currency liability.

If thought is given to the matching of central borrowing to local assets, then action to restructure the book might well take place over a period of years, long after the original motivation has disappeared. For example, one company with significant dollar borrowings found itself in 1984 very concerned at the growth in the sterling value of the liabilities it had accumulated. Over the next three years the treasurer's attention was concentrated on a series of swap transactions to borrow a whole range of deutschemarks, yen and sterling in lieu of dollars. This was hailed as a significant achievement, which technically it was. The long-term cost of the exercise will be calculated, however, when the loans are repaid. Should the dollar not recover in the meantime, then the all-in cost of the move to currency borrowing will have been very expensive.

Similarly, the use of sophisticated instruments may not be abjured, since only the foolhardy or supremely confident would reject out of hand developments that are the epitome of market advancement, and which the corporate would like to be seen to espouse. However, it can be correspondingly very difficult to convince the large corporate that, for example, futures or options have a significant role to play in their foreign exchange cover strategy. There is to some degree a touch of arrogance in the large multinationals—after all, are they not the Everest which it is the duty of every self-respecting merchant banker and broker to climb? Are large corporates not a little too proud to condescend to enter the hurly-burly of the traded exchanges, even though it is clearly respectable to enter into intellectual banter with option strategists? It is probable that for not only a few large multinationals, the foreign exchange option for example will be regarded as a rather interesting but remote instrument, of little perceived relevance to their needs. Options might be seen as providing an opportunity for ambitious lieutenants to win their spurs, but very much in the category of peripheral and 'nice-to-have' rather than essential and relevant.

For the limited manager, cover strategy might also be a little semidetached, suburban and urbane. Who is going to stick out a neck if an index-linked pension and wall-to-wall carpet are at stake? Committee decisions have the advantage of being compromises, and therefore of having the benefits of pooled wisdom, experience, seniority and somnolence. The security of strength in numbers provides adequate insurance against both an incorrect decision and also the courageous one—indeed corporate street-lore often equates the two.

Very occasional forays into strategic cover for the occasional currency might be taken, but these are exceptional, and therefore are unlikely to have any signficant long-term effect on the company. A retreat into tactical buying and selling is the only course left. These can, of course, be profitable; but since the company is not a broker, and since the *raison d'être* of the corporate treasurer is to protect the underlying business (even though, in reality, by a lack of direction this duty is not being performed properly), there is no conviction behind these tactical moves, which are therefore relatively ineffectual. Therefore, regrettably, such a treasury structure is the Shakespearian 'much ado about nothing', since it is designed in point of fact so to be.

Limited management is the halfway house between a completely battened-down policy and one completely open. Decisions are often delayed but almost always adequately documented. Authorities are carefully delineated, and decisions are often made by committee. Parameters for action are carefully laid out, and the exposure under management is properly defined—if in some cases in a restricted way, ignoring for instance all or part of economic exposure. This system is symptomatic of an aspiring wheeler-dealer trying to get out, but attempting at the same time to avoid the charge of being avant-garde, gung-ho or irresponsible. Internal politics rather than the survival of the company is the name of the game being played. Points scored are on the wording of the minutes documenting the actions rather than the *post factum* evaluation of the desirability of the recommendations made.

In defence of 'limited management' is the requirement of the central treasury to provide a service to the units. Therefore a book might be maintained to each division or operating company, guaranteeing relevant exchange rates for particular transactions. In feeding the total of these individual deals to the market there is scope for the central operation to pool deals, take advantage of the yield curve and tactically time deals to improve the rates of exchange achieved for the company. The correctness and attention devoted to the maintenance of positions is for such operations a good part of their rationale, and therefore profit potential for treasury and the company at large may be a secondary though welcome bonus, recognized at the appropriate time by financial compensation to the commanding officer.

Total management

In this scenario, the treasury is recognized as being a senior and sensitive area of management. Decisions are reactive and often involve the top management of the group. Clearly, banks and finance houses are amenable to this approach, but certain corporations, notably smaller and more dynamic companies, can also utilize such a style. The term 'total management' is coined to describe the complete dedication of the resources of the treasury team to the solution of the balance sheet, profit and loss and cash flow problems of the corporate. Conceptually this describes a situation where the constraints on management freedom are relaxed and where judgement is encouraged for decisions to be taken on the profile of exposures, on balance-sheet hedging, and on the instruments to be used for exchange management.

On balance sheet exposures, a non-dogmatic approach is the prerequisite. In certain circumstances, hedging is seen to be the most appropriate way of reducing balance sheet exchange risk. However, this is employed only where the long-term view is that it would be profitable to do so. Some balance sheet exposures are good. Yen assets (particularly properties in central Tokyo) have been excellent investments that it would have been most unwise to hedge. Dollar assets are ideal candidates for long-term borrowing as 'matched loans' (to use the terminology of SSAP20, the UK accounting standard for foreign exchange). For the active and non-dogmatic corporate with the freedom to decide, a careful choice of balance sheet hedges should enable positive revaluations of net assets to accrue to reserves at the year-end. Balance sheet management is part of 'total management'.

For financial instruments, the choice for total management is not 'whether' but 'how' and 'when', since it will be acknowledged that all methods of effecting cover have their rationale and appropriateness for given circumstances. The motivation might be vanity and the desire to try something new, but should really be the correctness of a given strategy or approach for a given set of circumstances. One is reminded of the clearer who was approached by a particular ambitious treasurer for a currency loan. A simple conventional loan was deemed to be the best, but he objected because it was not complicated enough! A reasonable precept for the total manager is that there are no preconditions except that prejudices are unacceptable. An open mind and enquiring disposition, plus an ability and strength to reject the inappropriate but try the novel where it is right, are the attitudes required to fulfil the challenge of total management.

Looking at cover strategy, the timing of forward contract maturities is less important than the fact of the cover, but the timing of the commencement of cover is as important as the principle of taking cover action at all. The motivation, apart from the protection of the underlying business, is to make profit both for the company and for the treasury function. The concept of a profit centre is not anathema, and the treasury section as thus constituted can be grafted onto virtually any style of underlying company—commodity broker, property dealer, multinational company—either as an integral department delineated only perhaps by a separate budget, or as a completely separate legal entity responsible for its own salaries and overheads.

Total management implies both an open approach and a deep and active commitment to the success of the enterprise. It requires ongoing thought, and the application of a range of decision making parameters, both long and short term. The appropriateness of the action for the circumstances is the major motivation, and a major difference from both other styles is the ability to change one's mind and the responsibility to recognize and act to correct mistakes in judgement or in the sense of the direction of the market. A reactive and responsive policy implies both flexibility of mind and a degree of short-term action. While the former is acceptable as a constructive management approach, the latter should not be overstressed since, for balance sheet and long-term strategic cover actions, there is every need to balance short-term decisions with long-term actions.

Total management is not risk-averse, but can be very successful. It is not a policy for the faint-hearted, and the object is to do more than survive. It can be very creative, and the object is to put treasury in the forefront of achievement for the corporate.

It is not implied that the other styles of management are worse than total management, just that their ambitions are less—often for good institutional or business reasons. But it is alleged that they are more limiting for the treasury function, both in the range of operations and in the instruments deemed appropriate for utilization. Nor is it implied that total management is superior in achievements, since there can be bad as well as good decisions. At worst, a poor decision can threaten the organization as a whole, so 'total management' is not performed in a vacuum but with the support and involvement of the senior members of the company—certainly the finance director, and in some instances the chief executive. As a matter of note, the chairman would become involved only in the event of something being deemed to have gone wrong!

CHAPTER 3

Why deal?

The act of dealing in foreign exchange is a sombre transaction which, by the spoken word over the telephone, commits the corporate to a specific—and often large—obligation. This will be to deliver a given volume of currency to a specific place at a specific time, in exchange for another volume of another currency delivered to another place at (normally) the same time. There is a risk to the company at several layers:

- *Delivery risk* The bank might make a mistake and deliver the wrong amount of currency, or the right amount on the wrong day or to the wrong location.
- *Credit risk* The financial intermediary might (unusually) default on its obligations as the result of a financial crisis.
- *Transaction risk* There might be a mistake in the verbal understanding between the corporate and bank, undiscovered until the checking of confirmations or the (non)delivery of the relevant currency, resulting in the cancellation of the deal.
- *Management risk* Each transaction will be open to scrutiny on its validity and rationale, and will be capable, either separately or in aggregate, of being appraised for its merit.

The first three risks are normally met by established controls within the corporate and bank. The creation of agreed credit lines within specific parameters (known within banks as 'dealing limits') provides a level of sensitivity for the maximum size of particular deals and of total deals on the books. The establishment of rapid and efficient systems for the confirmation of verbal instructions by letter, facsimile or telex enables the process of back-up and control to work routinely. The separation of duties of dealing from such support activities as bank account reconciliations and confirmation-checking, and (for banks rather than corporates) in the recording of all telephone conversations between dealers and corporates, provides a clear audit trail and acceptable framework for relationships.

However, management risk is the risk that many corporates find most difficult to accept as this strikes at the very rationale for a dealing and treasury operation. Management risk may be defined as the propensity of a given course of action to expose management to a criticism of its effect. Whether there is a decision to sell a currency receivable in advance of receipt or to leave the exposure until the cash arises, management can be criticized for sub-optimizing the result for the company. Of all motivations for dealing, the in-house resolution of this problem—i.e., of the containment of management risk—is probably the most potent.

There are three main reasons for dealing in foreign exchange:

1 To sell receivables or purchase payables, mostly in fulfilment of business commitments opposite customers or suppliers, or financial commitments opposite banks and other institutions—e.g., interest flows.
2 To manage currencies as part of a comprehensive ongoing currency management position, where, for example, maturing forward deals need to be rolled forward to future periods.
3 To take positions where distinct views have been taken within the company on the desired composition of its future flows of currency payables and receivables, and these views differ from the company's 'natural' or unamended position.

While the first two reasons flow from the company's practice in dealing for its ongoing requirements—the first being common to all companies, and the second more attributable to the more sophisticated companies—the third reason is the one that most interests the treasurer, the bank and the markets. Relative currency moves take place as a result of conscious decisions about which currency to buy and sell, rather than the standard flow of currency-related business (which is essential but does not in fact change anyone's perceptions of the relative strengths or merits of different currencies).

It is therefore to this third area that most commentators address their attention, either to recommend (as a bank), or to hear and perceive as a means to increasing understanding (as a corporate), or to appraise and evaluate (as an analyst), or simply to comment (as a newspaper). Owing to its understandable interest for the involved and the observer, this is the area to which the majority of comments in this section will be directed.

Why take a view?

It may be supposed that by deciding to sell one currency in advance of another, the corporate is favouring the latter at the expense of the former. Should a sufficient number of other corporates do likewise, at a reasonably similar time, then pressure might well build in the foreign exchange (forex) markets against the currency sold. Assuming that the long-term effects of intermediaries (banks and brokers) in this process are self-cancelling and, for the purposes of this argument, that the combined effects of either central bank management or investment money flows are zero, the final arbiter of relative currency strengths is the combined economic force exerted by these financial transactions presaged and caused by other physical trading but not for this purpose time-dependent on them.

Such a view on the causes of underlying changes in foreign exchange rates can impact on the market in several different ways, not all involving relatively glamorous forex dealing but involving electronic communications, computers and hi-tech paraphernalia. The business decision to invoice in dollars instead of pesos is immediately relatively bullish for the dollar: the sum total of dollar-denominated assets will rise. The purchasing decision to pay in dollars rather than yen provides a dollar liability, increasing one's requirement to settle in dollars in the future and, long term, is a sign of pessimism for the dollar rate. Likewise, timing changes to accelerate receivables or defer payment can affect the demand for the relevant currency, and at times of currency crisis can be a tangible reason for a currency's further decline. This is most clearly seen in the EMS where payments of (say) French francs may be delayed pending a realignment, and the cumulative effect of this freeze in short-term demand for the soft currency may be enough to precipitate the timing of the realignment itself. Indeed, the inverse of this process, the acceleration of payments overseas by some multinationals, has in the past been specifically outlawed in Italy when the process was regarded as destabilizing the already weak currency.

However, the most visible way in which the power of choice is exercised in foreign currency management is the operation of the foreign exchange market itself—the physical trading of the currencies in an economically almost perfect market. The mores, jargon and accoutrements are rapidly becoming commonplace, but the way in which decisions are taken is still the subject of debates, seminars and articles, and it is this area that is the source of most fascination.

There are many levels of consciousness within the corporate organization that have an impact, direct and indirect, on the corporate decision to act. There are different constraints impacting on the decision-making process; these vary between companies, with some encouraging disciplined activity in managing risk, while others are more averse to the visibility inherent in an overt risk-management strategy. There are many different levels of management that might have a bearing on the approach and even detailed decisions that might be taken. The board may well have a view on the various vulnerabilities of the company, and unless they have delegated authority to act they are the final arbiters of whether moves should take place to protect the company. The board is often influential in the magnitude and time period for the cover action recommended. The dealer might be more influenced by short-term considerations, such as the potential impact on exchange rates of the latest trade figures or money supply data, which impacts on the direction and timing of shorter term actions, including intra-day timing. But at the end of the process is the conscious or unconscious desire to act in a way that actually helps the company to achieve better performance.

The motivations to act may be codified, may be routine, may be institutional or may even be merely a reflex action. The rationale is mostly characterized by a range of requirements, involving one or more objectives, e.g.,

1 to increase certainty—for example, the sale forward of a debt in order at least to ensure a given (say dollar or sterling) equivalent value, for reasons of costing or return on sales, or to safeguard budget exchange rates for the transaction;

2 to provide for an element of smoothing—somewhat more sophisticated and recognizing the volatility of exchange rates, this desire is perhaps not to sell or purchase at necessarily the best rates, but to time the transactions in order to even the exchange gains and losses over time and between budget periods;
3 to improve on market rates—the most difficult task since all market participants would like to achieve this, but nevertheless the final arbiter of the comparative success of the treasury operation.

These rationales for action may be regarded as a hierarchy, with certainty being the least difficult but also, in some respects, the least valuable. Certainty may be the best course of action since it presupposes a 100 per cent secure position. However, it may also be the worst, particularly if the result is to lock in place exchange rates that are wholly uncompetitive when the deals mature. Smoothing is the middle road, where the corporate has appreciated that 'you cannot win them all', but that periodically one is happy, on a precautionary basis for example, to sell receivables in the event of the currency's decline. If the currency rises, then one will have suboptimized, producing opportunity and dealing cash losses, so cutting off the peaks. If the currency falls, then one will have the security of some better rates than those obtainable in the market at maturity, and therefore some support above the worst of the troughs, although if one has not sold everything one will not be fully protected. Smoothing of forex gains and losses between periods will be the result, which is more ambitious than mere certainty. This is also of long-term use for the corporate in levelling returns (*ceteris paribus*) between accounting periods, and therefore contributing to the stabilization of profits and consequently, in principle, the share price of the company. However, the benefit of this course of action is somewhat theoretical, even though it does give senior management the satisfaction of feeling that the situation is being managed according to a set of understood parameters.

The real and long-term benefit to the corporate of a properly managed treasury position is its propensity to beat the market over time. This may be seen as an elusive 'holy grail' for which many strive, but few achieve. Conversely, it could be argued that if the entire market is viewed by some (rather fatalistically) as a closed system and a zero-sum game, then the constitutents of the market will be a wide range of levels of expertise, and in logic those with the greatest 'feel' (or application, or reactivity or even luck) will prosper. There will be winners and losers, and it is not necessarily a throw of the dice or the number of London Transport buses crossing Lambeth Bridge (to use an ICI Millbank expression) that will determine the correct decisions. Against each tale of the unravelling of the mysteries of motivation, reaction, management and decision, can be quoted opposite cases of disappointment, underperformance, consternation and disaster. Studies have shown that intensive professional fund managements have actually underperformed the market over a period of years—and what is true for one market should in principle surely apply to another. Nevertheless, if this third albeit ideal and ambitious goal is the long-term rationale for the existence of treasury departments (acknowledging that the trappings of authority and responsibility hardly attach to the mundane tasks of merely moving and clearing cash—the financial equivalent of a petrol-pump attendant), it surely merits close consideration, whether or not the goal of consistently (within reason) beating the market is realistic.

If one is trying to improve performance over time, this needs to be related to the underlying business, which both provides the rationale for entry into the market and provides a measure of the effectiveness of the actions taken. The rationale for action is the probability that certain transactions will be required in the future, so one can anticipate them by choosing the timing of one's activity, i.e., by dealing forward. Such a forward deal can be the result of a chosen policy or, more responsibly, the result of a careful decision-making process. Generally the activity in the forex market is designed to address the question of risk management—and one is taking a view on the currencies in which one is dealing.

The measurement of the effectiveness of the action taken is something from which some treasurers shy away because (a) they have had a bad experience in the past from appraisal after the event by the uninvolved, or the tactless, or (b) they are sitting on poor positions and would rather have them expire quietly, or (c) they believe their action is always 'future-based' and that the scrutiny of the past is unprofitable or misleading or irrelevant. However, such views—based on a mixture of mistrust, caution and arrogance—are becoming less fashionable. Indeed, the enlightened treasurer can regard the appraisal of his or her actions as a worthy exercise for a variety of reasons: it can reassure senior management of the effectiveness of the treasury function; it can provide a useful caution to ill-advised activity; more materially it can provide the basis for an incentive or performance award.

Several methods of performance appraisal are popular, and the relevance of each depends upon the philosophy of exchange management adopted by the corporate. For example, if the corporate habitually only covers the booked exposure of, say, 90 days' sales net of purchases, then the three-month forward cover rate is an acceptable measure of the effectiveness of the treasury operation. An all-in sterling conversion of better than the three-month forward position would provide a positive measure of effectiveness on this particular parameter.

Should the corporate be anxious to achieve the best possible rates—clearly an impossible goal, but a probable objective—then appraisal opposite the best rates achieved during the period under consideration would provide a measure of the effectiveness of the treasury operation. In order to avoid too great a pejorative result, it might be best to relate the achievement to a given percentage of the optimal cash receivable rather than to the actual amount of 'opportunity loss' that would undoubtedly be registered.

An important measure adopted by many corporates is the 'budget' or 'plan rate'. If this is to be a realistic method of appraisal it must be possible to cover the relevant exposure at the relevant exchange rate, otherwise the alibi for the unfortunate treasurer on the non-achievement of plan is either that the forecast exchange rates did not materialize or that the terms of reference did not permit the treasurer to sell (purchase) enough currency to protect the budget. Both of these may be reasonable excuses for underperformance, and are indicative of an appraisal system that is not in tune with the active management of the function. In these circumstances it is not the treasurer who is at fault—though he or she is in a prime position to realize the problem and make recommendations for a solution—but senior management or the board in the delegation of the relevant authority for action. Therefore, there must be symmetry between the appraisal measure and the authority to act, and the authority to act must relate to the acknowledged exposures of the corporate.

One single measure of effectiveness of the treasury operation in providing good cover for the corporate is in all probability not enough to avoid the eventual skewing of activity or distortion of approach to the possible detriment of the corporate as a whole. For example, the faithful achievement of reasonable short-term cover, while useful, will not be proof against the dramatic decline in a major currency, and brokers might well downgrade the corporate if—no matter how reactive its pricing policy in the marketplace to exchange movements—it fails to cover against very important 'sea-changes'. Conversely, the concept of covering plan at all costs might be thought prudent if, for example, a prospectus has been declared that requires underpinning. But significant or extreme action to cover plan might well result in depriving the corporate of exchange gains from much better rates that might be obtainable in the marketplace at a later date or when the cash actually flows.

Therefore, a final touchstone of the effectiveness of the treasury operation—and arguably the real arbiter of its rationale in the long run—is appraisal against the most difficult criterion of all: would the position have been better had there been no treasury management at all? Arguments against this criterion are mainly based on the view that, at the time the action is undertaken, the treasurer (and anyone else) does not really know what the future holds, and therefore it is very unfair to hold the treasurer accountable for shortfalls against this measure—or even to bedeck him or her with garlands should success be achieved.

However, the company must be viewed over a long time horizon, and should the treasury produce net losses, these will be reflected in the achieved and published results; conversely, gains will be part of the ongoing progression of figures on which analysts and pundits base their critique and forecasts. Therefore, there is a real value in the beneficial effect of successful treasury activity which is felt not on a price/earnings (p/e) ratio of 1, as some commentators allege when looking at the impact of this activity on the results of companies, but in the ongoing progression of earnings per share, and hence the share price.

If one believes that the responsibility of the treasurer does not cease simply when he has put into operation a given 'deal' to cover an exposure, then it can be accepted that, should the underlying rates improve, the treasurer may at some point change his view on the advisability of the original deal. Provided that the treasurer is sufficiently reactive, both mentally and physically (to both appreciate the problem and be able to do something about it), it may be possible to reverse the deal at some acceptable trading loss, or to dilute it by perhaps buying out half and leaving the short-term cover in place, but not mortgaging the longer term, which might become even more favourable. One can therefore enter the era of the actively managed treasury position. This is either fascinating or a nightmare, depending on one's outlook.

Two combinations of measures of the effectiveness of the treasury's foreign exchange operation that have been perceived to work are:

1 three-month forward rate together with optimal position;
2 one-year plan together with comparison with spot rates.

Combination 1 is appropriate for a large company where the function of treasury is to be efficient in its short-term activities, and where long-term actions by treasury might prejudice the ongoing operations of the corporate, where these are substantial. In this situation, the volumes are often vast, and the activities of treasury, even if concentrated at the short end, are quite considerable. In the short term, treasury can have a marked effect on the smoothing of underlying changes in exchange rates as they affect the underlying business. Longer term, the business might be expected to be too large to be affected by the activities of foreign exchange trading. The long term is in this environment taken as a 'macro' picture, in which the corporate in its own right has a large role in its influence, say, on the government and exchange-management authorities. The short term is the right environment for treasury activity, which can be very reactive to political and economic events, almost independently from the underlying business. In a sense, such a treasury is a small bank, with functions incorporating cash management, funding, lending and depositing, and dealing foreign exchange, mostly to underpin known flows, risks or exposures, but often taking a punt on the direction of the market in the short term.

Combination 2 is more appropriate to the corporate that is sensitive to the effects of foreign exchange on its underlying business, and where it is important to manage the longer term effects of exchange well. Important parameters for the corporate are the effect of smoothing between time periods so that the ongoing earnings growth is maintained, along with the long-term profitability of the treasury function. For the treasury organization, the safeguarding of plan rates becomes the major factor, with an eye to the improvement in rates over those locked in or budgeted. A very reactive stance is also needed, but here the treasurer is making preparations for the longer term instead of taking short-term views, or taking advantage of perceived short-term aberrations or opporunities. It is probable that this approach is more appropriate for the medium-sized corporate, and is amenable to a variety of cover instruments. Strategic rather than tactical might be the description of this combination.

The shorter term tactical treasury actions, which focus on the correction of overbought situations and intra-day movements, are appropriate either to the restricted tactical authorities given to corporate dealers as incentives by some larger companies, or to treasury organizations that do not view themselves as capable of appraisal against the strategic measures outlined above. These treasuries tend to be service functions in large and decentralized companies. They have no budget except as a cost centre. They are neither expected nor encouraged to take positions in a strategic sense. All positions are closely monitored and fully hedged. The scope for activity is limited to small intra-day forays. A profit of 30 pips is closed down quickly. No brave new world here; just an administrative function that puts its head over the parapet periodically for a quick pot-shot profit.

CHAPTER 4

Instruments used

At its simplest, one can divide the treasury function of the management of foreign exchange into three operations:

1 the delivery of foreign currency receipts and creation of payments, which might be termed the physical side of the business;
2 the transacting of forward deals to protect future underlying flows of the corporate, to which might be added—if the company's philosophy extends this far—the protection of the translation exposure of overseas subsidiaries;
3 the use of sophisticated hedging devices, such as options and 'third generation' instruments, to achieve a variety of objectives.

It is sometimes felt that these operations fit into a hierarchy, with the delivery of currency being the simplest and the use of, say, options being the most difficult and avant-garde. Though many corporates evolve through these as grades 1 to 3, in fact the most difficult to cope with both philosophically and managerially is 2, the management of a programme of forward deals. It is in this area that the mega-corporates have their greatest expertise, since a good organization of this area has hitherto required a considerable investment in personnel, systems and professional support, requiring both resources and commitment beyond the reach of many smaller and medium-sized companies.

This, then, is often seen as the real block on the development of treasury operations within companies: they imagine that to manage foreign exchange properly, one requires a very sophisticated system—which apparently requires a specialist to run and an expensive team to provide any hope of value added. Furthermore, knowing a little about the large-scale financial transactions of the larger multinational, they do not see the relevance of such a complex operation for themselves. There is therefore a gulf between (a) their real needs for professional treasury management to control and protect their situation and (b) their concept of a proper treasury that is not clearly addressing their real problems. Furthermore, not knowing how to move from—as they believe—grade 1 to grade 2, they regard grade 3 as completely beyond their comprehension and reach.

In fact the question is sometimes wrongly asked. It is not 'How do I create a treasury system for my own needs without emulating ICI?', but 'What are my treasury needs and how can I meet them most efficiently?' By resolving the rationale for a treasury department within the physical and cost constraints of the company, one is also addressing the issues of the extent to which 'interactive dealing' might be acceptable.

It is common ground that since every international company needs the ability to transact foreign exchange in respect of receipts and payments, then this is the simplest and most essential function. The spot deal—whether the competitive quotation from a portfolio of banks, or a conventional sale of casual receipts by one's in-house clearer, or the payment of foreign-based suppliers by SWIFT, telegraphic transfer or bankers' drafts—will have to be accommodated within the management of the treasury systems.

In moving from the spot deal forward in time to protect or cover the future flows of the company—which is where the real treasury function starts—most if not all companies begin with forward deals. The underlying philosophy dictates that there must be some protection for these future flows and that the forward contract is the simplest method. In concept, of course, it is simple. There is a forward rate published daily, and changing by the moment in the real market, which can be used to 'lock in' the conversion of a future flow, and as soon as a contract is transacted there is a commitment, both on the part of the corporate and the bank, to transact the relevant flows at maturity of the contract. Without, at this stage, becoming involved in the intricacies of 'forward points' and interest differentials, it is clear that there are significant judgement factors and philosophical aspects that weigh on this decision to fix rates, and in the early stages the corporate might not be well equipped to respond to them. Why is the rate acceptable? What if the underlying rates become more favourable and the company starts to produce opportunity (and so far as the deal is concerned, cash) losses? Who has the responsibility for managing this risk? Is certainty of itself worth the associated potential opportunity loss?

A clumsy attempt to move direct from stage 1 to stage 2—which might seem logical to many—is the surest way to reassure the sceptical and uninvolved that one touches treasury and foreign exchange management at one's peril, and that if the company's role is knitting and widgets, then, as the expression goes, we would be better sticking to our knitting and what we understand. This sentiment—understandable though it may be—is a pity if it becomes the accepted wisdom of the corporate, since a good treasury operation is by no means incompatible with decent widgets, and indeed is very complementary. At the end of the day a good treasury can help the widgets to remain competitive in certain overseas markets when the competition is needing to raise prices because of foreign exchange problems. Good forward buying of foreign exchange—which is a commodity like the product of the underlying business—can help reduce the cost of raw materials and give the company an edge in its pricing in the home market.

Seen in this light, it can be demonstrated that the rationale for a corporate treasury is by no means the creation of a structure for the satisfaction of the vanity of the finance director, but the requirement of the corporate to address certain external risks and problems, mostly connected with the fact that, over time, exchange rates change, and the company needs to be responsive to those changes if it is to profit from favourable moves and protect itself against unfavourable moves.

These purposes are clearly not met directly either by merely establishing a sophisticated dealing operation or by putting significant (and dangerous) forward deals—commitments—into the market. One set of unknowns and worries is simply being exchanged for another. While the spot rate is an enemy when rates are going against one's position, it is also paradoxically an enemy if the underlying rates are going in one's favour, once the forward contract is put in place and rates are thereby 'frozen'. If in acknowledgement of this problem one begins to 'manage' the position by a little astute trading, and if this is in advance of the creation of good systems to underpin the dealing operation and the evolution of a philosophy of approach, then an engine for untold grief will have been created as contract builds upon contract and the system grows uncontrollably in a nightmare of complexity . . .

The key to the understanding of the role of the treasury function is the humility of understanding that one does not get something for nothing, and one gets what one pays for. Though ostensibly the forward contract is free of charge, the cost is clearly not simply in the interest differential (the difference between spot and forward rate) but in the opportunity losses potentially opened up should the underlying rates become more favourable. The uninformed view that, with a little luck and judgement, one should be able to outperform the market is too simple to be acceptable, otherwise everyone would be beating the market, and there would be no losers—clearly an impossibility. Arrogance and vanity are possibly the easiest sins to fall prey to in forex management.

The modest and realistic treasurer should encourage peers and superiors that the process of cover of risks for the corporate is not in fact a cost-free exercise, and talk by some treasurers of treating their operation as a 'cost centre'—while helpful in the light of the success of the creation of a new function—actually obscures its real rationale, and makes the achievement of its minimum aims more difficult. Therefore, the job of covering foreign exchange risk needs to be considered as an exercise involving the corporate in a certain amount of expenditure, not simply in the creation of a departmental framework including certain ongoing costs of staff, equipment and software.

What is needed for the corporate is an insurance policy whereby certain risks are covered by the payment of a given premium of up to, say, 5 per cent of the value of the exposure covered—this figure being generally well within the rate of profitability achieved on overseas sales or purchases. It so happens that instruments have been developed to deal with this risk—these are 'options' and their derivatives.

Have we not jumped two levels of sophistication? Are we not trying to run before we can walk? Do you not need already to be quite sophisticated to use these instruments?

No. The option is a very simple concept, easy to operate. No computer systems are needed, and the flexibility is left to the corporate to lock-in given acceptable rates in the future or to achieve better rates in the marketplace if the underlying rates become more favourable. The rigidities of the forward contract are avoided, and there is no requirement to actively manage the instrument. Using options the corporate can put cover in place at an affordable cost without worrying about the management of the position.

Once the principles of options are accepted, the corporate can begin to add its own sophistications, including:

1 reducing the cost of options cover by varying the value covered at the agreed rate by going further 'out-of-the-money';
2 writing options on the upside in order to partially defray the cost of options bought—this secures forward cover at rates better than those obtainable in the forward market, since the rate given away on the downside is added on the upside;
3 contracting forward cover either to lock-in better rates already allowed by the operation of options, to open up exposures effectively closed down by options written on one's position, or to manage the ongoing position after the exercise of options bought;
4 eliminating options entirely by forward dealing when certain 'trigger' rates are passed.

In this scenario it is seen that forward deals are only employed in the more sophisticated areas of risk management when one has begun effectively to graduate beyond options towards a more responsive and proactive approach. At this stage it does become appropriate for the corporate to employ complex dealing systems designed to fulfil a variety of functions for the control of one's position, from accounting and monitoring to the production of confirmations and audit checks. Forward contracts, i.e., grade 2, are therefore seen as an essential part of the armoury of the treasurer, and in some respects more important than options. However, they are judged to be the most difficult instrument to manage, and therefore at the apex of the complexity of instruments that treasurers use. In this book, therefore, the use and control of forwards are investigated after the chapter dealing with options, which are regarded as the most appropriate tool for the corporate embarking on the long and tricky road through financial adolescence to adulthood.

Forward rates can be readily quoted from the Reuters screen or newspaper. In the precision of real live quotations, where rates are moving by the second, it is convenient (particularly for large deals) to split the less volatile 'forward points' element of the deal from the spot rate. It can be profitable, even at the expense of some costs of administration, to transact the forward deal with one bank and the spot deal with another if one bank is not giving the best rate for both sections of the deal. In this situation, the relevant currencies would be routed on a spot basis between the banks.

For example if one is buying US$ 10m for sterling in 30 days' time, and Barclays gives a better spot price but Lloyds gives a better forward points quote, then the spot routeing would be as shown in Figure 4.1.

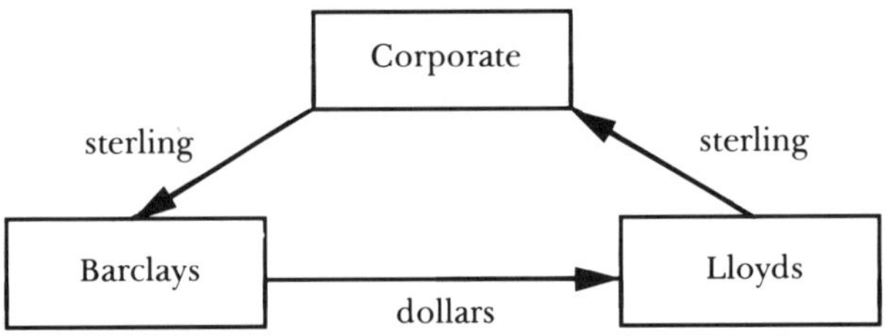

Figure 4.1

The purchase of spot dollars from Barclays (at the better rate) will result in their routeing to Lloyds in exchange for sterling. A forward swap will be put in place with Lloyds, a spot sales of dollars to them (coming from Barclays) being offset by a forward purchase, since their forward rate was the best. Given that Lloyds will not have been put in an exposed position from their total risk perspective, the purchased dollars will be on the same side of the quote as the sale to them and there will be no 'banker's spread', only the relevant forward points.

The forward points will be obtained from the market and for large transactions should be requested separately from the spot rate. In the absence of electronic screens, or for calculation of split dates (and future dates not readily quoted), one can check such quotes using the following formula for forward points against, say, the US dollar:

Number of forward points = [Spot rate × (Interest differential × Proportion of year)] ÷ [1 + (US Interest rate × Proportion of year)] × 10 000.

For example:

Spot rate = DM 2/US$
US Interest rate = 10%
DM Interest rate = 9%
9 months forward deal required (270 days)

Calculation:

Forward points = [(2 × (1% × 0.75)) ÷ (1 + (10% × 0.75))] × 10 000
= [(0.015) ÷ (1.075)] × 10 000
= 140 points

Assume Barclays bid DM 1.998 for the spot deal but 137 points for the forward, and Lloyds bid DM 2.000 for the spot deal and 142 points for the forward. The composite Barclays' price would be 1.9843 and the composite Lloyds' price would be 1.9858. For US$10m to be purchased, Barclays' total price would be DM 15 000 cheaper.

However, if one transacted the spot deal through Barclays and, using a forward swap, the forward deal through Lloyds, then the composite rate that would be achieved would be 1.998−0.0142 = 1.9838, totalling an improvement of an additional DM 5000. Clearly this saving is worth a little extra administration.

It is not the intention of this chapter to confuse the reader with technicalities, nor indeed to oversimplify (note that sterling calculations use a 365-day year, and points in yen are not 1/10 000 but 1/100). It should be noted that if one is entering the sophistication of forward dealing with all it entails, then one should pause before rejecting options lightly, in concept a much simpler instrument.

CHAPTER 5

Foreign exchange management

The establishment of a corporate treasury function requires a response to a series of questions fundamental to its ongoing existence and its relationship to the rest of the organization. These issues are often evaded or not addressed fully, leaving the issues to simmer below the surface and become accepted as significant only after the growth of the organization; consequently, the magnitude of the problem and difficulty of resolution become very much greater. Therefore, it is better that these areas should be aired fully at the outset so that the company can appreciate the parameters within which the treasury is operating, and also that the treasury can (free of impediments real or imagined) address the real issues of the management of the ongoing function.

What then are these fundamental questions?

1 Assuming the object of the function is to safeguard the underlying business, what are the parameters for action? Magnitude, time period, risk-taking v risk-aversion . . . ?
2 Given that not all banks are good at everything, are there any limitations to the scope of treasury decision-taking on who should receive what business? Does treasury have full delegated authority on relationships?
3 A number of instruments is now available in the market for the management of foreign exchange risk. Treasurers are familiar with most, but they include spots, forwards, swaps, options bought and written, a variety of options strategies as well as banks' customized products. To what extent does the treasurer have discretion over which instrument to use for which exposure?

4 Assuming that the role of the treasury is determined by the underlying business, are there any limitations on the number of deals, the value of transactions, and the activity of the function?
5 Is the treasury regarded as a profit centre in its own right, and if so should the relevant staff be remunerated by an appropriate formula related to their success in achieving given goals or, over time, 'beating the market'?

The corporate treasury discipline is still young, and some corporates with established treasury operations are only just beginning to grapple with the issues. The lead is, of course, taken by the largest companies, where with BP an in-house bank has been established and with ICI a sophisticated treasury is established within a framework of interrelated finance companies. But medium-sized corporates can still ensure that these issues are faced without the necessity of creating separate legal entities.

Freedom of action

The response to the series of questions hangs on the basic outlook of the company with respect to its treasury operation summed up in one word: autonomy. The greater the degree of trust by the board in their treasury officers, the more likely the function can operate efficiently within agreed and delegated parameters. Just one obdurate director can prevent freedom of action to protect vital positions and exposures, and without freedom to act the treasurer could resignedly shrug off responsibility for any resultant débâcle. The treasurer should also recognize the statutory responsibilities of directors, and as a *quid pro quo* for the freedom to act should be utterly forthcoming on his positions, turnover, relationships and performance (both realized and unrealized). Instead of the more or less creative tension generated by attempts by the treasurer to secure freedom to sell (say) yet more dollars at steadily worsening rates, one might secure a relationship based on trust and confidence, with disclosure being the pleasurable ability to show tangible gains for the company from the delegated freedoms.

Let us look at the five questions in turn.

Definition of the exposure to be managed

The most limited definition of an exposure which is correct is the 'accounting exposure'—effectively the difference between the valuation of net debt *less* net credit on the books. A somewhat wider definition relates to foreseen cash flows, whether or not the subject of binding contracts. Broader still is economic exposure, which relates to the commercial environment of the company.

Economic exposures indicate the vulnerability of the company to the adverse impact of exchange (either direct or indirect) on its ability to compete. This indicates that, for example, a chemical company will need to be alert to the effect of the value of the deutschemark on its German competitors' ability to compete in its own domestic market, as well as on its own ability to compete in Germany. At the time of writing, satisfactory ways of dealing with accounting and risk management aspects of economic exposures have yet to be devised and agreed.

Most corporate treasuries have already moved away from the concept of management only of the accounting exposure, though some companies use this as a proxy for local accountability, which is ostensibly a 'no risk' position for, say, the operating divisions. ICI's 'booking rates' are an example of such a system. ICI's operating divisions are put in a position of being fully covered on their accounting exposures by reference to forward rates or 'booking rates'. These rates are then used by the finance subsidiary as its own start point for foreign exchange cover action or appraisal.

Simply to decide whether or not to sell the limited exposures actually booked is hardly a creative pastime—the net benefits to the organization of success will be small and arguably a concentration on the short term could imply that more significant long-term issues, such as the decline of the dollar in 1985–87, are completely missed. Most treasurers now address the cash flow exposures of the company or group, which generally increase by several times the magnitude of the exposures needing protection. Providing the treasury department calculates with the agreement of the company the agreed exposures, there should be little room for conflict over the level of exposures to be managed and hence also the main parameters for treasury activity: volume, sensitivity, important rates (e.g., budget exchange rates or forward rates used in contract tenders).

Banking relations

There is often close contact, in some cases going back several generations, between the corporate and one or more main banks. Relationships thus generated are often a firm foundation for a productive dialogue between corporate treasury and the bank's dealing room. However, a bank's product is not particularly differentiated, and competition is very fierce. It could well be that other relationships develop alongside and in competition with older and more established lines. Should these initiatives be encouraged, or should the older relationships be fostered at some quantifiable marginal cost or at some competitive cost to the corporate? The balance between competition and relationship will be closely watched by the treasurer.

It is probably correct to keep the door ajar for some banks whose stance might be described as aggressive or even predatory, since they can provide a spur to competition even at the expense of some cosiness with long-established lines. It could well be that a little frankness behind closed doors could result in the sharpening of the service provided by one old bank that would be good long term for themselves as well as for the relationship. The board needs to be aware that quite diverse relationships might grow, and that the tactics of which bank to use for which service might appropriately reside with the treasurer. It is the responsibility of the board to set overall parameters for bank appraisal, which for large companies can result in significant costs to external advisers. This might result in a list of banks with whom dealing is not permitted for historical reasons. The treasurer could then have the freedom to decide which of the remaining banks to use, and in which circumstances.

Which instruments to use

A reliable watchword is 'no prejudices', since virtually all instruments have a use beyond the novelty of providing particular income for the bank before the competitors catch up. By taking action before the actual realization of the cash flow one is 'interfering' with the market, and in some way 'taking a view'. No pejorative is intended by this, but simply an indicative statement. Activity implies an end result that will be different from passivity. It is undoubtedly this difference that will, in part, show how successful the treasury operation has been over time. One is altering cash flows in either time of maturity and/or rate achieved, and therefore magnitude. Where options are used there is the complication of the premium payable, which also needs to be accounted for, with the additional possibility, for some of the hybrids or options written, of opportunity losses on the exercise of options. The board will not wish to write a blank cheque for options premia, but after experience of the instrument may be content with a tangible cash budget for the treasurer.

The concept of 'options written' is similar to forward cover—and has the effect, if the option is exercised, of fixing a rate for the future conversion of an underlying exposure. Just as some corporates have, through experience, realized that one should not simply leave forward contracts 'on the table', so there is also the duty to manage the treasury exposure on options written. Activity in this area should not be shirked, even if the resultant dealing requires authority from the most senior executives in the company.

Number of deals

There are those in any company who might believe that the value of deals transacted by the treasury department should be a fraction—although perhaps a large fraction—of the turnover of the company. There are those in treasury departments who are concerned that uninformed people might accuse them of overtrading or 'churning' their position should the truth be made apparent. The turnover of a normal healthy corporate treasury is a multiple and not a fraction of the foreign currency denominated turnover of the company. This does not result from the potential inability to net purchases paid for in foreign currency against sales denominated in currencies—even though this could be a contributory factor given the likely failure of the outward and inward flows of cash to occur contemporaneously—but rather it is a natural result of the most effective way to manage currency protection in a dynamic situation. Forward deals need not be structured—as was once considered essential—to coincide with the date of expected flow being protected. The conscious act of taking covering action that will then need to be rolled forward on maturity to a further date (when perhaps knowledge of the underlying flow is more certain) doubles

Table 5.1 The dealing multiplier: example

Transaction	Month	Citibank Sale	Citibank Purchase	Midland Sale	Midland Purchase
1. Sale forward	6	10			
2. Delivery and swap	5		5	5	
3. Swap forward	6		5		
	7	5			
4. Deliver and swap	7		3	3	
	7		2		
	8	2			
5. Delivery	8		2	2	
		17	17	10	0
			44		

the amount dealt. A good dealing system should allow the corporate to test the efficiency of the banking system by putting this new deal out to tender, potentially moving the gross cash twice; this swap forward is not just a paper exercise. It is therefore quite respectable for an active cover policy to multiply the underlying flow by six, approximately. A policy constraining the treasury to a lower pre-determined level of acitivity could well militate against the optimal treasury practice.

An example will illustrate how the dealing multiplier can work. Assume that the company has a long DM position of 10 million, which it decides to cover forward using Citibank. Its normal bank is Midland, through whom conventional cash flows are transacted. Its original forward deal is for month 6, but in reality the cash flows as follows: DM 5 million in month 5, 3 million in month 7, 2 million in month 8.

The transactions are shown in Table 5.1 The multiplier here is × 4.4, without the company having changed its mind on whether to cover or not.

Remuneration policy linked to treasury as a profit centre

At least in the early days of the establishment of a treasury department, and possibly even later, there may be a degree of mistrust of both the motives and the rationale for action on foreign exchange. After all, these dealers are mostly barrow-boys, aren't they? And we all know about the problems of Volkswagen, when the treasury controls were apparently found wanting. What if there were a serious mistake, and the company were deemed to have speculative positions which put its very survival in jeopardy? There is some substance to these misgivings, at least to the extent that it is the proper concern of the board that they both know and approve of the stances—if not the detailed rationale—being taken by treasury on their behalf. On the other hand, given that the treasurer is first in line when markets move to respond to the *post factum* query by the chief executive, is it not good for the company or the individual if some part of remuneration is determined by the individual's success or failure at the sharp end? After all, few today dispute the wisdom or desirability for salespeople to have, in some cases, a large part of their pay determined by results. Although, with the evident overcapacity in the banking industry, the heady days of the expansion in financial services seem to be over, is it wise for a corporate to run the risk of under-remunerating its top treasury officers by comparison, when at the end of the day it is, arguably, in industry, that the underlying wealth is created?

The profit-centre concept causes boards more difficulty than any other aspect of the principles and practice of the establishment of a viable corporate treasury department. Perhaps a worry is that commitments might be open-ended, and that high rewards in the treasury area might unbalance the remuneration policy of the rest of the company. Perhaps it is feared that treasurers might be tempted into ill-advised actions, particularly if it is felt that they have the skill to disguise or hide their actions for a time. Should the worries be about control and accountability rather than about the principle of remuneration related to results, then the answer lies in good systems.

CHAPTER 6

Foreign currency options

Introduction

From the advent of floating exchange rates in the early 1970s, corporates sought to control foreign exchange risk by a variety of expedients. For ten years the main tool was the forward markets, where fixed rates could be locked in place for given future flows of currency, and corporates tried to beat the market by judiciously covering forward (especially if there was a juicy interest differential to be pocketed), which acted as a buffer against the movement of underlying rates.

In the early 1980s this began to change with the advent of traded options on Philadelphia and the Chicago exchanges, and their corporate equivalents, the OTC (over-the-counter) products. Corporate treasuries became more sophisticated and impatient with the rigidities of forward contracts, and the advent of high-speed and large-memory desktop micro-computers enabled better control and appraisal to match the new mood. Therefore options hit the market at the right time, or conversely, the market was now ready for the product. Since options have developed so well and are a customer-driven product, it is surprising that they have not yet become the main strategic tool for more than a handful of corporates. Perhaps, despite the wide publicity given to options by banks and conferences, there are still a lot of sleepy corporate treasury departments, particularly—and surprisingly—in some of the larger companies.

Imagine a normal exporter with a range of net foreign currency receivables and payables probably concentrated in the US dollar. The old method of operating was to look at the booked exposure (where invoices had passed) and take some action to underpin rates for the eventual flows. There could be some aim to 'beat the market', but the extent of this was limited by the purview chosen. If a long view was taken of the 'economic' exposure of the company to those markets, the covering by forward contract of flows one year or more ahead was a venture into the unknown and, with the exception of very few companies, was not entertained for more than a small minority of exposures. Effectively, forex management was a lottery with every risk of producing sizeable losses as well as gains.

There had to be a better mousetrap. The time for options had arrived.

Exercising options

While forward contracts provide obligations, options confer rights. There is a right to purchase or sell the currency at a particular rate on (or before) a particular date. But if prevailing conditions at the time are more favourable than the rate chosen, then there is no obligation to use the instrument. This is a significant step forward in the flexibility and ability to manage exposures, and provides an entire range of possibilities that are known in the market as 'strategies'.

Also, in theory, the day of the infamous foreign currency 'opportunity loss' is numbered. In practice it is simply replaced by the cost of dealing, which includes the option premium—but at least this is more honest than the traditional cover methods, which imply that cover actions are in some way 'cost free'.

The premium is in place as a quantification of the cost or benefit from the buying or selling (writing) of the risk inherent in such option positions. It is also to pay for the transfer mechanisms from one party to another, either from the trading floor to the corporate (or proverbial Belgian dentist), or from one corporate to another via a bank, for the more liquid OTC options. Writers are receiving an option premium for underwriting someone else's risk, and the buyer is paying a premium for someone else to take his risk away. The middle person has to pay for the costs of brokerage and margin payments when exchanges are involved, together with advice, dealing room facilities and tactical daily exposures resulting from mismatches of counterparties for OTC products.

The main variables in determining the price of an option are clearly related to the likelihood of the option being exercised. The greater the possibility of exercise, the more expensive the option; and when the option is certain of being exercised, the intrinsic value of the position is the main item in the measurement of the cost. The option price is related to a range of variables connected to its likelihood of exercise, and to its size and currency. These variables can be listed as follows:

- spot price compared to exercise (strike) price
- time to expiry
- volatility of currencies
- magnitude of the deal
- interest differentials.

The corporate user of options fortunately does not need to be versed in the intricacies of the Black–Scholes formula and its Garman–Kohlhagen variant to be able to use options. There are programs available from banks, relating the cost of options to the volatilities quoted in the markets for particular strike rates and time periods, which enable the corporate at least to ascertain whether the price that has been quoted is reasonable. Beyond that, the calculation of the price of the option is a matter for mathematicians, black boxes and back offices. The corporate need not buy if the price is too steep. Conversely, if the price looks too expensive, the corporate could always move to the other side of the market and write options instead!

A further twist adding to the choice of options and impacting on price is the concept of American options (exercisable at any time) and European options (exercisable only on a particular day). American options are clearly more flexible, and therefore slightly more expensive. The exercisability of options is not a main determinant of price, however, and European options with the same strike price and other characteristics do not significantly affect the efficiency of the covering by the corporate of its positions. One point is worth making: when writing options (notably those on a cylinder basis—see below) it is advisable not to write American ones, since the timing of exercise is not in the hands of the corporate, and the hedge might be withdrawn by the bank at an inconvenient time.

Assuming the premium is not inconsequential either in amount or as a proportion of the exposure, how should it be minimized? Three standard methods are available:

- go out-of-the-money
- reduce the time horizon
- write options on the upside.

Out-of-the-money

Assuming one does not wish to purchase intrinsic value, the most expensive options are those 'at-the-money'—essentially those underpinning identical rates to those that conventional forward cover would create. Acknowledging that forex markets fall and rise, the forward rate may have no particular significance for the corporate, but a rate, say, 3 per cent lower than current spot might. If such a downside is an acceptable minimum, then cover of that rate, while clearly giving away both the spot and forward points should the option eventually be exercised, would reduce the cash cost of protection.

Reduce time horizon

Most corporate currency flows are not known with precision in advance of the immediate event, and many exposures for annual or monthly periods are best guesses. Therefore, the spurious accuracy of protecting a precise flow for a specific forward date is not intrinsically useful to the corporate. Many corporates, while accepting this argument, have not taken the implications for options management that the duration of the cover does not need to match the tenor of the exposure. Conversely, exchange cover can be time and event-related rather than flow-related. If the risk is perceived to be during, say, the next two months rather than the residual four months of a six-month exposure, then a two-month option, with action on maturity in the spot or forward market, may well be appropriate and would certainly be cheaper than a six-month option.

Write options

This is the most controversial of the approaches, but one that should not cause difficulty to the risk taker or the corporate that considers it necessary to cover its exposures at given rates, even though these may not be optimal when the contracts mature. The writing of an option puts the corporate in a similar position to the bank from which it is buying the OTC option on the downside—the corporate is taking on unlimited risk in exchange for the receipt of a premium up front with which, in this example, it buys the protection it is seeking.

This is referred to as 'uncovered call writing', where the corporate has been placed in a vulnerable situation in exchange for premium income. A slightly more respectable variant is 'covered call writing', whereby the option written is matched by an underlying flow in currency to the corporate. The result of the exercise of the option written by the corporate is to fix the forward rate at the strike price that has been agreed. This is not very different from conventional forward dealing, which also fixes the conversion rate, except that, with the option, there would be premium income to assuage the pain of the opportunity loss from the spot rate when the cash flow was worse than the forward rate effectively booked. Furthermore, it can be argued that the effective forward rate that would have resulted from the booking of conventional forwards at the time the exposure is recognized would have been at a worse all-in rate. The risk that has been assumed in exchange for the premium is the lack of cover should the exchange rate go against the company.

A mechanism that combines the protection sought for the purchase of an option on the 'downside', but minimizes the up-front cost of acquisition by writing options on the 'upside' is the 'cylinder' option.

This is a most interesting strategy, and can result in the elimination of the premium entirely. As a simultaneous put and call, it is similar to a synthetic forward though with out-of-the-money strike prices instead of at-the-money. Attempts to link this with some of the strategies used in options markets for those without basic positions have confused terminology, but an acceptable generic term is a *fence*. The controversy for corporates is that while mainly risk-averse animals, they could be increasing risk under this strategy in some circumstances. While prima facie valid, it is not always understood that the risk under a fence is no greater than a forward, but the underlying rate underwritten is tangibly better than the forward rate that would have been applicable. Therefore, while to be exercised under a fence is not as good as a conventional option would have been, subject to the magnitude of the premium saved, this condition should be entirely acceptable to the corporate, otherwise the treasurer would not have consented to write the option in the first place.

This and other strategies are examined later, after a brief review of the role of individuals without underlying 'positions'.

The role of individuals

An individual operating in the options market is termed generically a speculator, and his situation is differentiated from the corporate in that he has no natural position, but is simply looking to profit from moves on his contracts. The speculator needs to look at the traded exchanges, of which there are two quoting currency contracts in London, plus bank-style variants like Barclays' bero options. The biggest plays are clearly in the cable and dollar/deutschemark axis, and these contracts are quoted on both Philadelphia and the Chicago International Money Market (IMM). A broker is a prerequisite for use of these exchanges, and the minimum size of contract quoted is sterling 31,250 and DM125,000. Other currencies are available elsewhere, and a synthetic sterling–deutschemark option can be constructed via a mixture of cable and dollar–deutschemark options. For example, a dollar call against the deutschemark could be paid for by a sterling put written opposite the dollar. What has been bought is effectively a sterling call opposite the deutschemark, which will be profitable if sterling appreciates against the deutschemark during the life of the contract.

Other approaches can concentrate on the direction of the currency being managed. For example a 'bull call spread' (Figure 6.1) is a technique for managing options in the environment of a strengthening currency, which limits the cost of the option should the currency not appreciate, but allows the full benefit of such appreciation up to a given upside rate, and is a combination of a long call bought and a short call out-of-the-money which is written. Converse strategies are appropriate where the currency is weakening.

A straddle option (Figure 6.2) is a simultaneous put and call, either bought or sold, giving a guaranteed premium earned or paid in which the individual is effectively betting on the volatility of the currency. For straddles bought, the cost is the joint premia

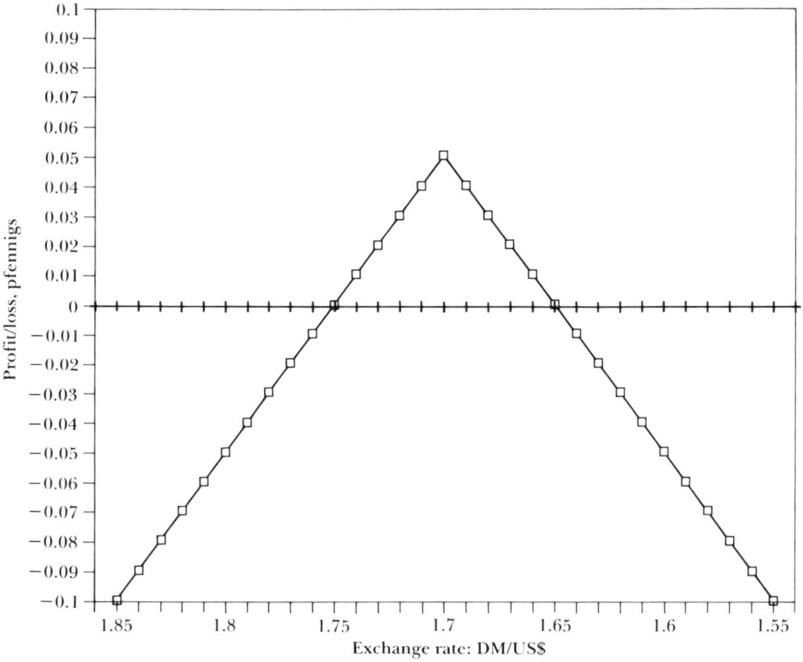

Figure 6.1 **Bull call option (individual)**

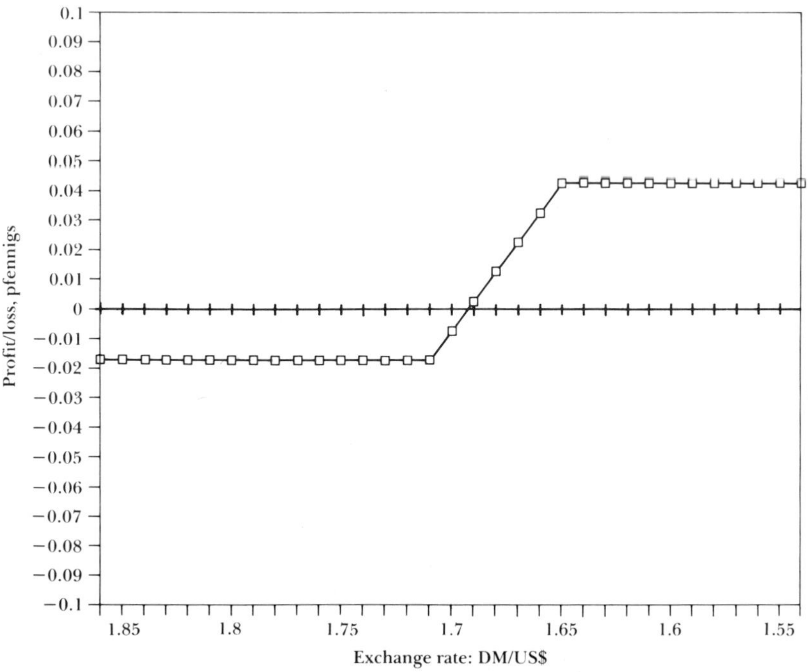

Figure 6.2 **Straddle option (individual)**

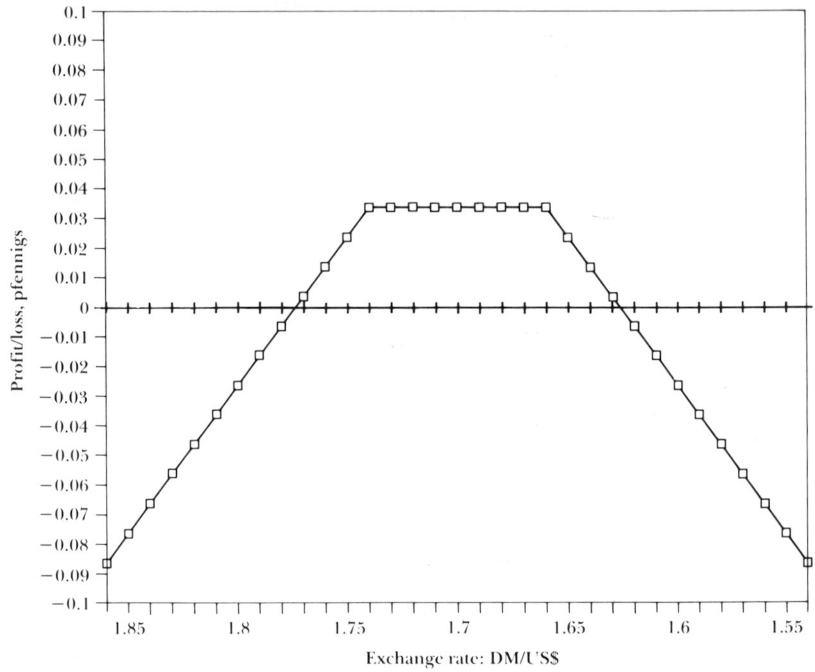

Figure 6.3 **Strangle option (individual)**

paid, and the benefit is the total movement of the currency away from the relevant strike rates. The converse applies for straddles sold, where the individual is writing options for a given premium against an unlimited risk. Other structures include the strangle (Figure 6.3), which is similar to the straddle except that the strike rates are further out-of-the-money, and that therefore the point at which the maximum premium is earned lies between the two strike rates.

One word of caution. The forex markets are the most perfect in the world but, like all markets, the price of the commodity (currency in this case) is the result of marginal transactions. This is why, despite some $190 billion of daily forex turnover in London alone, the central banks, especially acting in concert, can cause significant day-to-day shifts in rates for the expenditure (when timed correctly) of only a few hundred million dollars. Ratcheting rates are a fact of life and a firm constitution is a prerequisite. On the credit side, if, with all the facts openly available, the market thinks one thing, then there is every likelihood that something unknown, such as an earthquake in Japan or US intervention in Central America, could throw it into a different track, giving genuine opportunities for significant gain to those brave enough to take the risk.

Corporate management of options

Let us assume that the company has become convinced that an option is a reasonable investment. It has mastered the learning process connected with obtaining quotations, and understands the inevitable jargon. Probably it has ventured as far as writing some options, perhaps to defray part of the cost of options bought to protect the downside, or possibly plan rates. How does the company proceed from here in the period when, perhaps, the option is to be exercised?

The conventional sterling call

The illustration (Figure 6.4) uses rates deemed as typical at the time of writing, and which could look slightly dated over time. The option was contracted when the spot rate was \$1.65, and the forward rate for the period covered \$1.60. In the example there is a premium of £15 000 per million dollars, a premium of 2.5 per cent at the strike price of \$1.70. The break-even rate for the option is between \$1.74 and 1.75, but at that rate there is a clear opportunity loss of 15 cents over the potential forward rate, comprising 5 cents of interest differential forgone, 5 cents of out-of-the-money loss and about 4 cents of premium paid in cash.

If the dollar appreciates in value above \$1.56 then the rate achieved, even after the payment of option premium, would have been better than the forward rate that could have been achieved when the spot rate was \$1.65. The corporate would have walked away from the option, which would not have been exercised, and in one sense the premium would have been paid for nothing: here the insurance analogy is reasonable, and the rate achieved in the spot market might be much better than that expected earlier had forward cover been instituted.

If the dollar moves downwards towards \$1.80, then the option would have been exercised at a rate of \$1.70. The corporate at the point of exercise would have the choice of either simply maturing

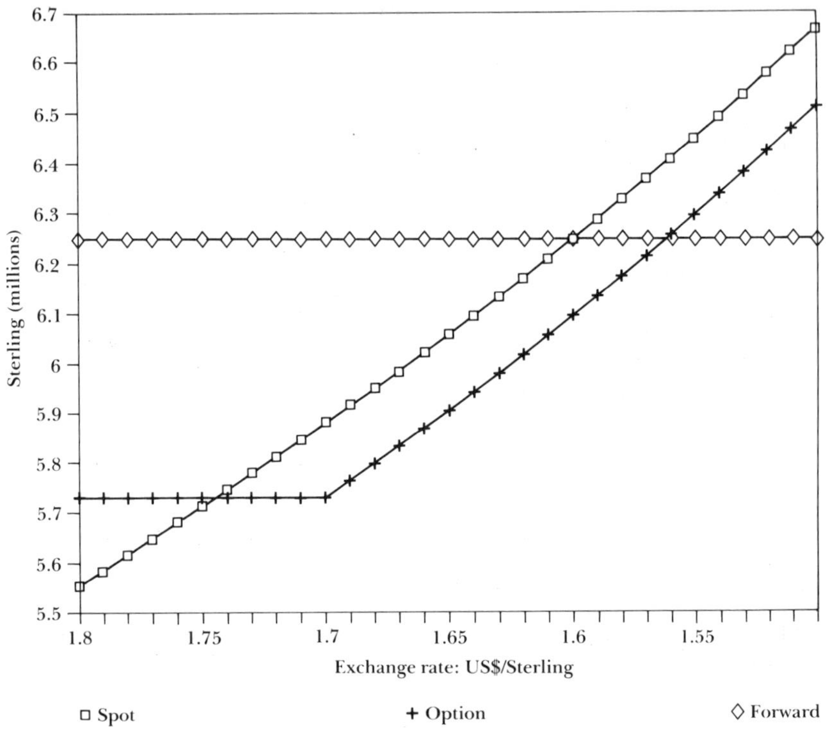

Figure 6.4 **Sterling call option (US dollars, 10m income)**

the option and transacting dollars at a rate better than that which could be achieved in the market at that time, or, conversely, the corporate could 'roll' its cover into a (series of) forward contract(s) to enable the ongoing benefits of forward cover to be obtained. Using the insurance analogy again, the policy will have matured, and one has a degree of grim satisfaction that the cover was in place, even though of necessity the rates achieved were worse than if the option had not been exercised, or the fire insurance had not been claimed.

This example shows that when ordinary options are employed, it is best for the corporate to be able to leave them unexercised. Although it is advantageous for the maturity of the deal to be above the strike rate—unless the option premium plus forward interest differential are covered in a much better spot rate at maturity—the options route may be the worst of the cover alternatives. The option can therefore be seen as a play on the volatility of the exchange rate and its potential to move from the initial spot

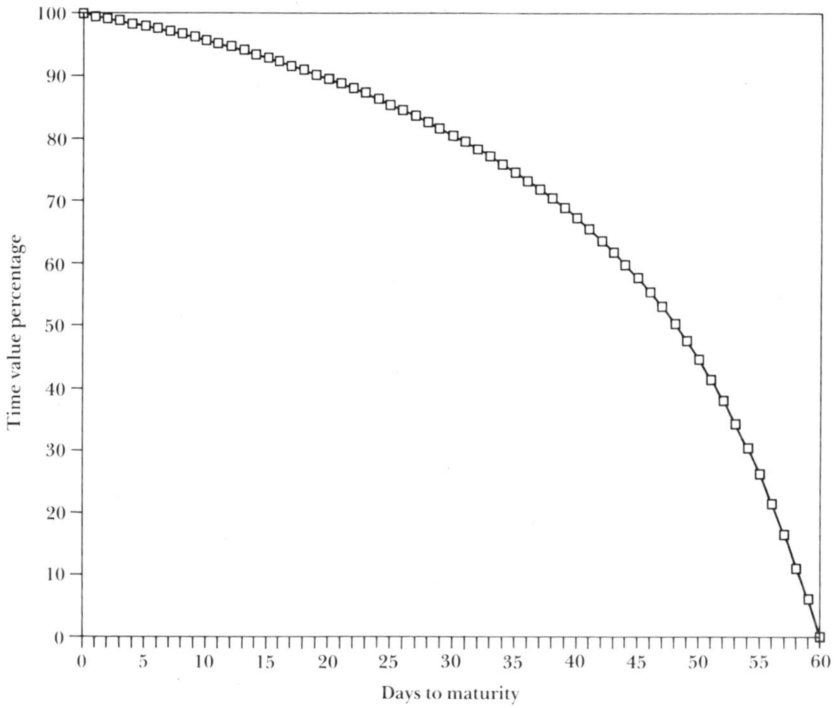

Figure 6.5 Time value erosion

rate by the time of maturity. Options premia are an investment whose paradoxical worth is when good value is not provided, since the underlying rates are better for the company.

Time value and trading options

Even if an option is out-of-the-money, it still has some value, related to the time left before expiry. The time value of an option wastes away at an accelerating rate (Figure 6.5). Therefore in theory it should be possible to trade an option some time before expiry by selling it back to the (OTC) bank from which it was originally purchased. The time value is highest when the option is close to the strike rate, which in the sterling call example (Figure 6.4) is $1.70. However, when the option is at around this rate the corporate is not likely to wish to trade that position, since the option is about to become really useful. Time value is therefore similar to volatility in that, although it cannot be seen or touched, it has a value when it is bought. When one might wish to sell it, however, that value is much less, partly as a result of the out-of-the-money context of the potential sale and partly, to some degree, because the only buyers would be either the selling bank (OTC options being non-negotiable), who will already have covered any risk in the cash market, or other options bought either OTC or on traded exchanges. Therefore the likelihood of a good price is not high, although traders in the market would say this depends on the avenues used. An approach that has been recommended is to purchase more expensive long-dated call options, and sell them back again when they are no longer required. This recoups some of the time value in the period before the dramatic erosion of this variable.

The concept of tradability of options begs the question of the value of the components of an option, and how these vary over time and rate. In principle, the time value of the option erodes at an increasing rate. Therefore, if a four-month option is sold back to the bank with one month still to run, the time value element might be as much as one-half of the original time value, rather than one-quarter—time value does not erode uniformly. Also, however, the time value of an option varies with the chances of the option being exercised. It reaches its greatest value close to at-the-money, and recedes in value each side of the strike rate. Therefore, when trading options back to the bank, it can be quite a disappointment to discover that the time value refunded is a much smaller figure than anticipated, if one has not taken into account the drift in the rate away from the strike rate. Clearly, when the option is at or around the strike rate, even if the option for cover purposes was no longer required, one might be disinclined to dispose of it with such a good chance of the option yielding intrinsic value (Figure 6.6) much in excess of the time value returned.

There is no intention in this book to downgrade the importance and role of traded exchanges, which have been partly responsible for the remarkable flowering of options as a tool for managing foreign exchange since the early 1980s. For certain types of exposures and operations, they can provide a niche that banks find difficult to address—notably for smaller exposures or for private positions. They also enable banks to offset part of their corporate risk, and of course provide a valuable measure of the reasonableness of pricing. For corporates, however, they are not ideal. Their business dealing

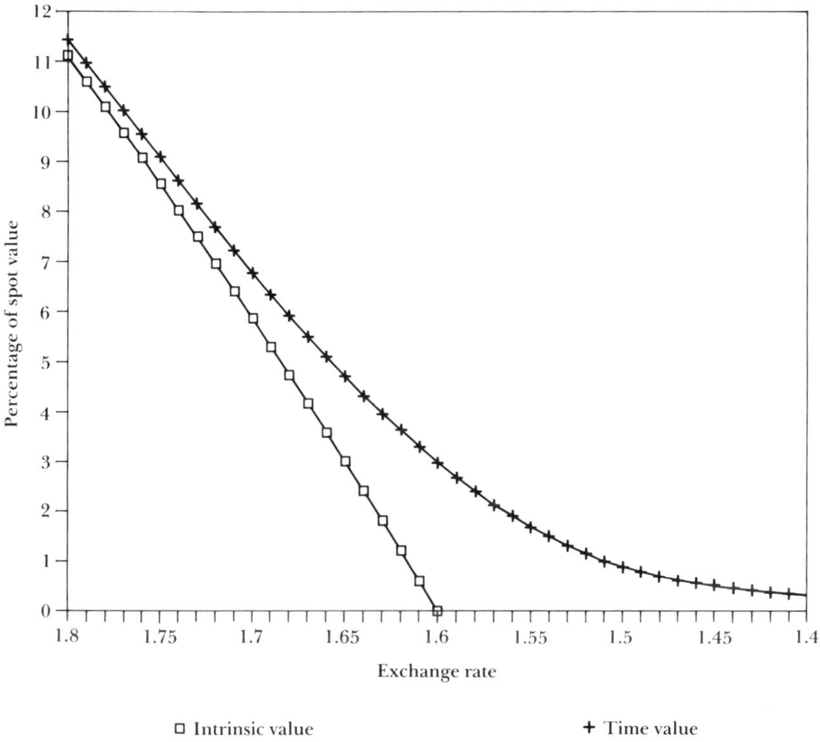

Figure 0.0 Option valuation model (intrinsic and time values)

days may not be convenient. It is necessary to employ brokers for transactions, potentially adding to the expense (though practitioners would deny this compares with the rates added on by banks for their 'tailor-made' OTC service). And where options are being written rather than bought, margin requirements are levied in order to finance ongoing losses to the position. Furthermore, the number of different options dealt, though growing, is still limited, cross-currencies being a particular weakness. Therefore, it would seem that over-the-counter options bought (or sold) opposite banks, in the same way as forward foreign exchange deals, are the best methods available to corporates who wish to utilize this market and its growing list of variants.

Strategies

It is a tribute to the growth of the options market that so-called option strategies have blossomed before common terminology has been established, so that terms that should in some way be generic are perceived to be proprietorial. This is the case with the cylinder option, which is a corporate adaptation of a simultaneous put and call—the put sold and the call bought—where the corporate clearly has an underlying position receiving the currency. The first time the author did a series of these (against sterling), the options written with one bank were at 97 cents and those bought on the downside were at $1.15, and the closest the market could describe the option strategy was a straddle, which, as remarked above, is an entirely different approach. This strategy has now developed considerably over the last few years under the description of *fence*, *cylinder* or *collar*, with variant to deal with the major perceived risk, which is the possibility that one might be exercised on one's option written.

The cylinder option

The cylinder is the corporate variant of the bull call spread or put spread, depending on the underlying position of receiving or paying currency. Figure 6.7 shows the cylinder for similar parameters as the sterling call. The spot and forward rates are as for the simple option ($1.65 and $1.60 respectively), and the parameters for the cylinder are a downside of $1.63 and an upside of $1.57. The psychology of the deal differs markedly from the sterling call. Between the two chosen rates, the spot rate on maturity applies just as if no option had been put in place. Since, arguably, the premium for the option written at a rate of $1.57 will have paid for the option bought at the downside of $1.63, there is no problem in maturity of the option occurring in the $1.57–1.63 range. Indeed, since the rate of $1.57 is underwritten, the optimal end position for this option is $1.57. Should $1.55 apply, then 2 cents of opportunity loss would occur as the upside option written would be exercised at this rate.

If the downside results, then the option bought is exercised, and since in the example the premium is paid for by the option written, there is no cash cost of the option. However, in the opposite

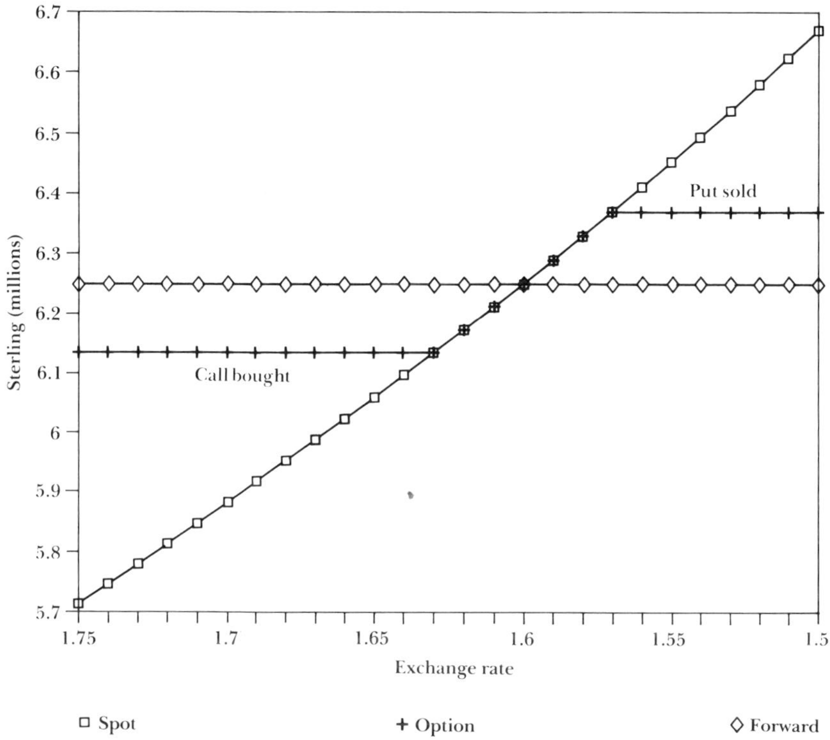

Figure 6.7 Cylinder option (US dollars, 10m income)

direction the simple option really benefits where the currency trades more strongly, while the cylinder cuts off the benefit early.

The most notable feature in the comparison of the downside is that the risk from an unmanaged position is heightened by the additional risk taken on board.

Therefore, the management of such a downside position becomes even more important than the ordinary exposure of the company, since below a particular point, the cost of the option strategy becomes more expensive than the underlying exposure if it were unmanaged. At this point, the corporate would be tempted to intervene, at least to neutralize the effect of the options, for example, by purchasing the currency. At such a point, the company will lock in a dealing loss connected with the option, such a loss matching the gain that would have been obtained had the underlying strategy of writing the option gone in their favour.

Examples of some option strategies

Forward deal

This enables a fixed rate to be achieved for a given delivery date. In options terms, consider the forward deal to be a simultaneous put and call, both at-the-money forward.

Conventional cylinder (zero cost)

This adds an infinitesimal space between the simultaneous put and call of the forward deal, and broadens. This becomes the cylinder, whereby the upper and lower limits are set, and variation takes place between, depending on the spot rate at delivery. The mechanics of the cylinder are, for the following example:

Call purchased at yen 130/US$,
Put sold at yen 140, each for 1 billion yen.

> *Call exercised.* Spot rate at maturity is more expensive than the option purchased. Purchaser of the option (oneself) exercises, gaining the (downside) rate, which had been guaranteed; for example,
>
> Spot yen: 127
> Gain to purchaser: (1 bn/127)–(1 bn/130) = US$ 182K.
>
> *Put exercised.* Spot rate at maturity is cheaper than the option sold. Purchaser of the option (the bank) exercises against ourselves. The upside benefit beyond the (upside) rate that had been guaranteed by the option is gained by the bank; for example,
>
> Spot yen: 143
> Loss to writer: (1 bn/140)–(1 bn/143) = US$ 150K.
>
> But (assuming symmetry in upside and downside from forward rate), the implicit gain to the writer at yen 140 is
>
> (1 bn/135)–(1bn/140) = US$ 265K.
>
> Once the put has been exercised against the writer, the forward requirements should immediately be purchased at the (cheap)

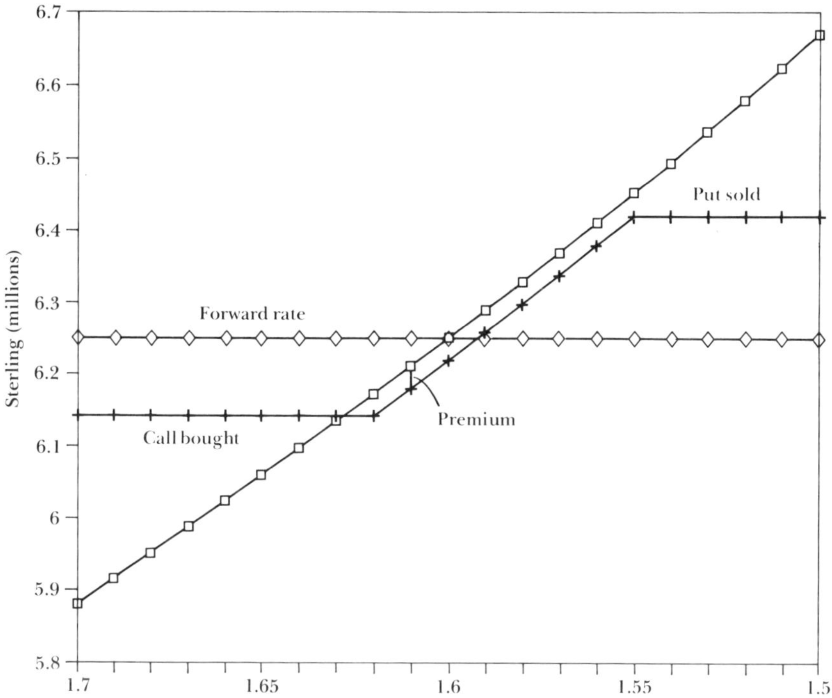

Figure 6.8 Cylinder option—skewed (US dollars, 10m income)

rate prevailing in order to safeguard the effective forward rate that the option written has provided. Technically, this can require the purchase of *double* the amount of currency required for oneself, if the option purchaser requires delivery on the relevant date.

Neither option exercised. Spot rate is between the purchase and sale rates. Both options expire worthless and transactions can take place in the spot market if necessary.

The skewed cylinder

While sharing the main characteristics of the cylinder as to principal amount, exercise dates and maturity dates, there is no broad symmetry between the option rates bought and sold and the forward rate (Figure 6.8). Thus a settlement for the net cost of the option is required to be paid (or received if the options are being written for revenue).

The partial ceiling/floor

This variant allows a complete floor or ceiling to be purchased for the period under consideration, but subsidizes the payment for this by the writing of the equivalent of a cylinder option, but for a shorter period of time—hence the partial ceiling or floor.

For the yen positions under review (Figure 6.9), the option bought (yen call) fixed the ceiling price to be paid. This is subsidized by partial floors written during the life of the option.

Should the yen fall during the life of one of the floors written, and it is exercised, then the corporate purchases the yen requirements at that time. By definition, the relevant exchange rate is better than the forward rate when the option was bought. The option purchased would still have some time value at that point, and could be sold to reduce further the net cost of the strategy.

Should the yen remain within the band safeguarded, then after expiry of the partial floor a further option can be written out-of-the-money, to achieve revenue to reduce the net cost.

Should the yen rise beyond the strike price of the yen call, then the next yen put can be written at the same strike price, thus creating an implicit forward deal but also providing revenue.

Figure 6.9 illustrates the potential evolution of the partial floor/complete ceiling over a seven-month period. It has been assumed that the average monthly premium is just under 0.5 per cent, thus eliminating the total premium for a seven-month yen call after seven months. Provided the yen puts have not been exercised, and assuming a modest depreciation of the yen of 2 yen per month, total benefits over the forward rate of up to 10 per cent could be achieved. In the opposite direction, the downside rate of yen 130 could be safeguarded free of cost.

Hedging

At this point, a word is appropriate on the concept of hedging one's option position. Some might have difficulty with this concept, declaring that the vagaries of delta hedging, for example, are the province of bankers and not corporates. However, when the corporate has become involved in the writing of options, both in cylinder situations and even more so in straddle, strangle or naked call writing, there is implicit in this the need to look at one's position if circumstances change. The changed environment will normally

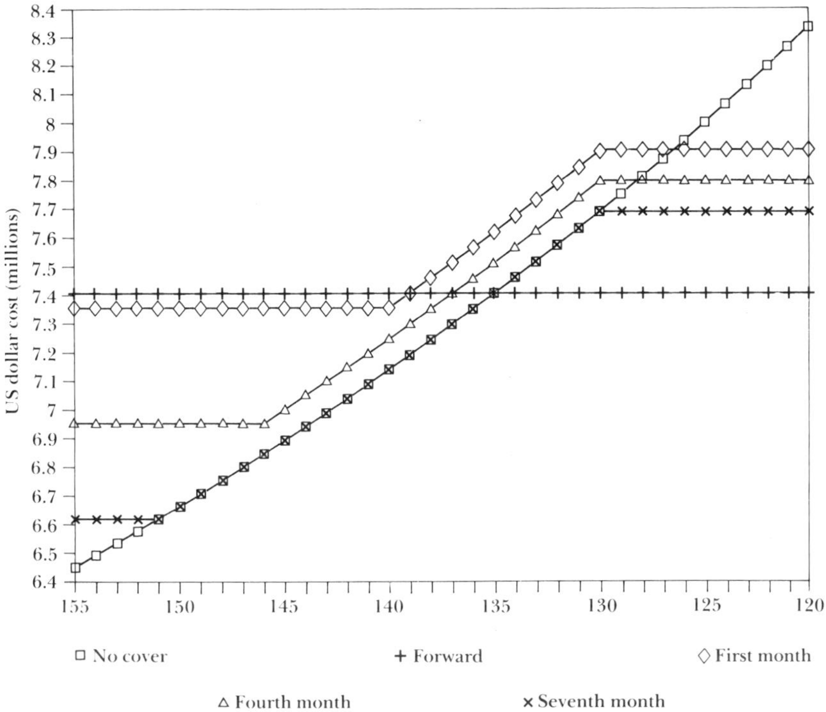

Figure 6.9 Partial floor/complete ceiling (yen purchase (1 bn) – monthly evolution)

be that the option that had been written—which had been earning revenue for corporate treasury's profit and loss account or to pay for options for protective purposes—was beginning to possess intrinsic value. Exchange rates will have moved, and the corporate is required to do something about the position.

The corporate adaptation of the straddle and strangle options (Figures 6.10 and 6.11) illustrates that the income received purchases both an upside protection at a favourable rate and a downside insurance of several 'cents' before the position starts to lose cash. However, owing to the gearing effect such losses are at a faster rate than a naked position, hence the need to manage or hedge the position.

The principle of delta hedging is that, for each minute move in the underlying exchange rate, there is an appropriate hedge.

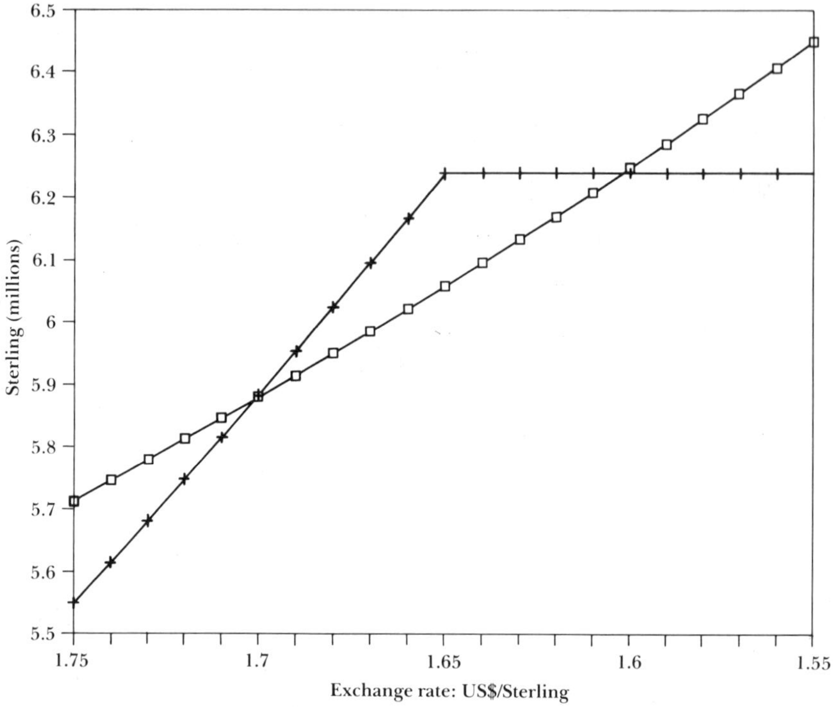

Figure 6.10 **Straddle option (US dollars, 10m income)**

When the option is well 'out-of-the-money', such a hedge is very small; when it is well 'in-the-money', the hedge is virtually 100 per cent. When the option is 'at-the-money', the hedge is 50 per cent. The problem is that markets do not move smoothly, and therefore for this hedging concept to be operational one would be constantly changing position by miniscule amounts, which is clearly impractical (though somewhat easier for banks than corporates). Therefore, a policy decision can be taken to hedge or unhedge on, say, a daily basis, using for reference the rates of exchange at a given hour of the day (which assumes that there is no need to worry about the total exchange rate fluctuations during the day). Alternatively, knowing that the particular strike rate is the vulnerable point at which losses on the position begin to accumulate, a policy decision can be made for cover when that point is reached. The former tactic has a logistics problem, while the difficulty in the latter is that exchange rates do not continue to move downwards, but move up again, and one has then created a dealing loss by interfering with the structural hedge of the option.

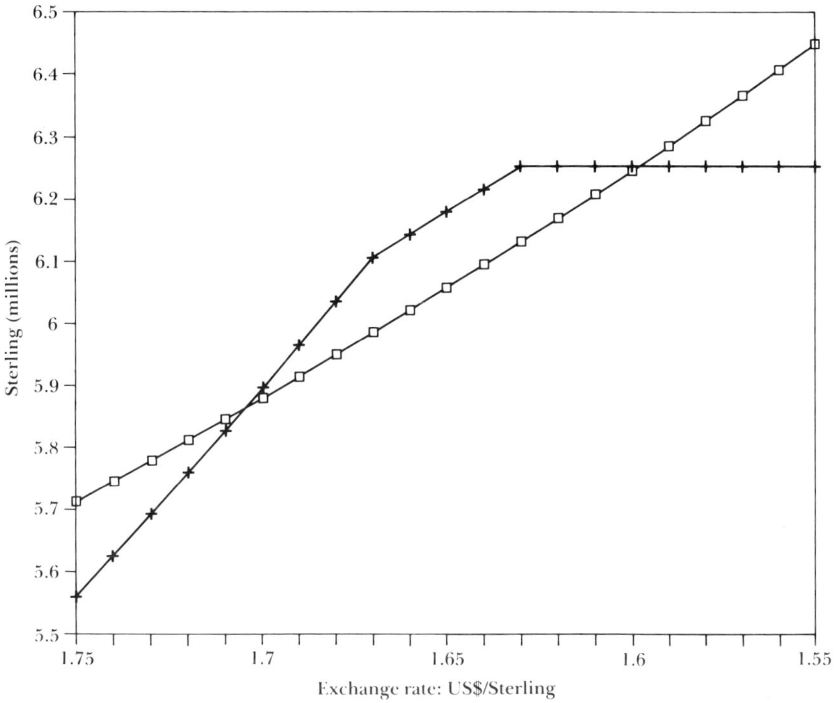

Figure 6.11 Strangle option (US dollars, 10m income)

A compromise alternative, which can work when exchange rates are not moving too violently, is to decide which is the sensitive rate to be protected, and then put actions in place in tranches. This can be less profitable than the swift though draconian step of cutting one's entire position when the relevant rate is reached or breached, but it allows the company gradually to change its posture from being protective to being aggressive. The average rate at which the position is opened up might be worse since, in the process of changing one's position, the markets are in all probability moving against the hedge that is being unwound (providing the impetus for such action). However, senior management can be involved, enabling them to appreciate the motivation for the decisions, and to 'own' the actions in the event of a board presentation or future post mortem. The compromise at least allows the company to avoid the full impact of the undoing of the hedge should rates hit the sensitive rate and bounce back swiftly. The total losses on the options strategy will be contained within an acceptable band (the 'threshold of pain'), and the underlying position of the company

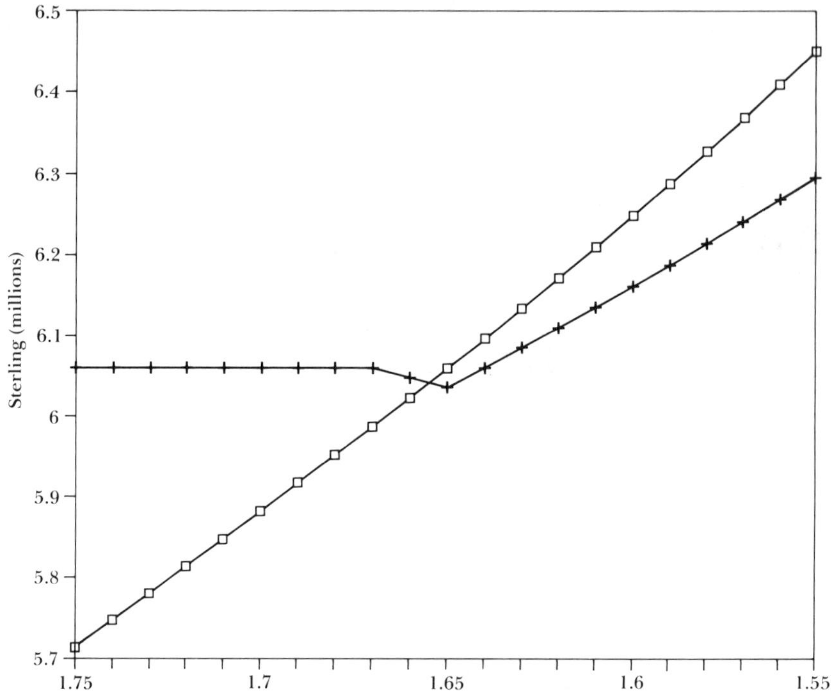

Figure 6.12 Participation (US dollars, 10m income)

will have been improved by this management action.

A further strategy that can be applicable to the risk-averse corporate, and is also an alternative to the cylinder option, is the participating forward (Figure 6.12). Technically (for a currency receiver), this strategy comprises an out-of-the-money call on one's base currency, paid for by an in-the-money put that is sold for a proportion of the exposure's value. The extent to which the two premia offset each other is the measure of the cost of the option. The net result is to put an acceptable floor beneath the conversion rate of the flow, while leaving a proportion of the upside potential for the corporate to achieve; the remainder of the upside goes to the purchaser of the put.

Speciality variants of options have been created and marketed by banks as proprietorial products—although in principle they can be readily created or copied. A particular example is the break forward contract, marketed by the Bank of Boston as the 'Boston

Option' and by Hambros as the 'FOX' (forward with optional exit). This is a combination of a forward contract and an option, whereby a forward rate is booked (at not a brilliant rate, since the rate includes the costing for the option, which allows upside potential). When the option is exercised, the forward contract is reversed, and a better rate for conversion of the cash flow is achieved than would have been operational under the forward contract. The premium can also be hidden in the price.

Several methods have been devised to enable contractors in particular to benefit from options although the certainty of the award of contracts is of course not absolute. One such is Barclays' 'tender to contract' option, whereby the success of the achievement of the contract is tied to the premium payable to the option. Another is the concept of an option on an option, whereby the option to purchase a given currency in, say, six months' time at a given rate can itself be the subject of an option for the duration of, say, six months. The cost of the option on an option might then be only a fraction of the option itself; and while partially duplicating the cost involved, this mechanism at least ensures that the full premium does not need to be paid, particularly if the contract is not won (and/or the rate underpinned by the option seems in the event not to be very attractive).

In order to tackle the problem of the hedging of trading profits (as compared with transactions and cash flows), the average rate option has been created, marketed by Midland Bank as the 'Asian' option. This enables the hedging of the relatively modern concept of average rates of exchange, which are often used for the translation of trading profits of overseas subsidiaries.

A composite example of the main option strategies is shown in Figure 6.13. This looks complex, but in reality, simply illustrates that there is a variety of methods of securing an acceptable result for the company. The common characteristic is that the cost of this is not zero. Even no action at all has a cost, the opportunity cost of doing nothing. A forward cover strategy locks in certainty at the cost of flexibility and potential upside gain. On a conventional call option the premium cost, together with the addition of the loss of forward points and the out-of-the-money costs, can be expensive unless currencies move a long way. A cylinder option provides a nice answer to the conundrum of the minimization of premium cost, while safeguarding forward points (as well as being

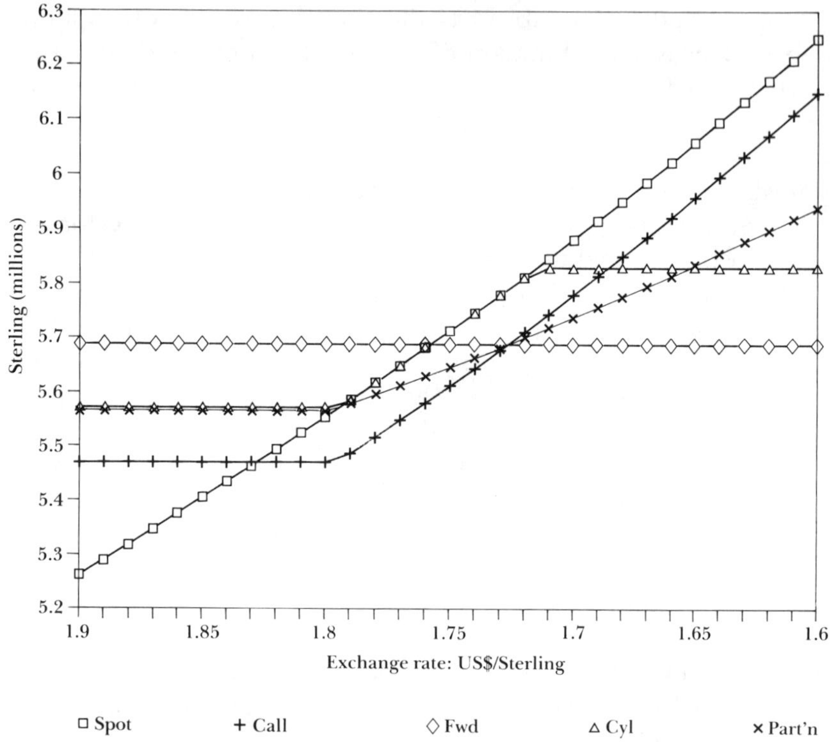

Figure 6.13 Composite example ($10m, 5 mths, spot $1.775)

neutral on volatility costs since one is dealing on both sides of the market at the same time, thus cancelling out this effect). However, when the option written is exercised, this can still look expensive. The participating forward gives extra cash to the bank at the outset, and can be expensive if the upside that has to be shared is a large amount.

Options in decision-making

Below, two examples are given of live situations in which companies have put in place options as part of a strategic cover policy.

Amersham International plc, 1984–87

The main exposure that was causing difficulty was the US dollar, in which over 20 per cent of their exports were denominated. A significant opportunity and cash loss had been caused in 1982–83, when some $12m had been covered forward at $1.75, and the spot rate at maturity 'improved' towards $1.50.

The option strategy was followed in order to:

(i) quantify the extent of opportunity loss by the payment of the premium;
(ii) allow the achievement of annual budget rates, set in the autumn for the following fiscal year.

Three main deals were transacted for each of the four years involved:

1984: Purchase of a sterling call at $1.45, cost US$ 93 000, covering 50 per cent of following year's exposure.

Result: Dollar appreciated.
Option expired worthless.
Gains on budget rate averaged 20 cents.

1985: Structuring of a cylinder by sale of sterling puts at US$ 0.97/GBP coupled with purchase of sterling calls at US$ 1.15/GBP, covering the whole of the year's exposure.

Net option cost: US$ 20 000.

Result: Dollar depreciated.
Options for each of 12 months gained an average of 20+ cents.
Budget rate safeguarded.

1986: Structuring of tight cylinders, zero cost.

Downside rate protected: $1.40.

Upside rate conceded: $1.34.

Result: Dollar depreciated slowly.
Options gained an average of 7 cents.
Budget rate safeguarded.

1987: Purchase of conventional sterling calls, short term.

Downside rate protected: $1.48.

Net option cost: US$ 250 000.

Result: Dollar depreciated.
Options rolled into forward contracts, gaining an average of 15 cents. less
Budget rate safeguarded.

During the whole period, in which the dollar swung from $1.50 down virtually to parity then back up to $1.70, the company was able to produce average dollar conversions of $1.25, $1.20, $1.40 and $1.50. This had the effect of:

- minimizing the annual variability of this key exchange rate
- subsidizing the profits of the group by net financial income (exercise benefit of options *less* total net cost) over the four years averaging 8 per cent of the value of the net dollar exposures.

Zung Fu Company Limited, 1989–90

This business imports Mercedes Benz motor vehicles into Hong Kong for sale into the local market, in which it has a dominant market share. The market conditions, after the 'events in China', were depressed and there was a perceived danger from new up-market cars from Japan in 1990. The dollar was weakening and the deutschemark was strengthening.

The structure that was put in place was the skewed cylinder (see Figure 6.8), whereby a number of tight out-of-the-money DM calls was financed partly by more out-of-the-money DM puts. This allowed an upside potential to be secured of about 10 pfennigs, to enable the company to benefit from a strengthening of the dollar, with downside protection 2 pfennigs out-of-the-money, at the cost of 2 pfennigs.

The deals were done at DM 1.86. In the event, the deutschemark strengthened to DM 1.7 and beyond, realizing gains of about 10 per cent on the spot rate for the purchase price of the cars. The options written, which earned revenue equivalent to 1.5 pfennigs, expired worthless.

It was decided to give away the benefit provided by the options to the market in a once-and-for-all promotion of a sports model, which could provide in one month half of the sales for the whole year. The promotion was a tremendous success, with over 1100

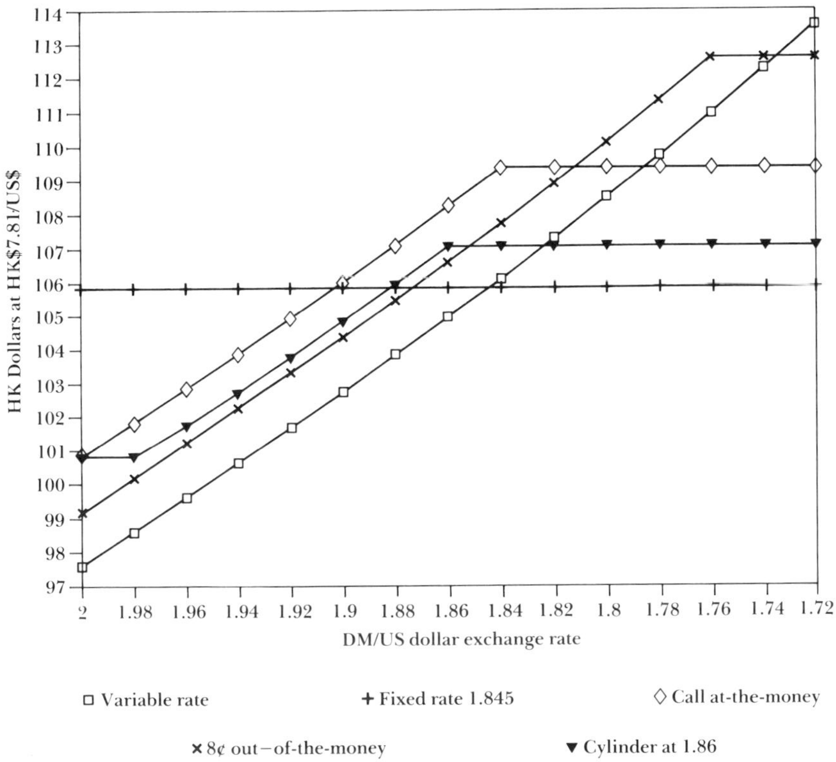

Figure 6.14 **Zung Fu deutschemark model (DM calls v skewed cylinder)**

cars being sold in only three weeks, albeit at the cost of a significant deterioration in profit margins. In this case the primary benefit of the option went straight to the customer, though the secondary effect in the safeguarding of the marketing position for the company was considered a more long-term benefit.

Figure 6.14 shows the parameters in the thinking for the structuring of the options. A number of conventional deutschemark calls were considered at DM 1.84, before a rally in the dollar provided the opportunity to put in place the cheaper skewed cylinder at a good rate.

The sales promotion advertisements (Figures 6.15 and 6.16) are provided by courtesy of Zung Fu Company Limited.

Mercedes-Benz

Zung Fu Company Ltd.
A Jardine Pacific business
General Distributors of
Mercedes-Benz AG
for Hong Kong & Macau

Mercedes-Benz Passenger Cars
Cross-Country Vehicles Vans
Pick-ups Trucks Buses Unimogs
and Industrial Engines

Enquiry Hotline : 895 7228

1990 Manufacture
Mercedes-Benz 230E Sedan
Sport Chassis Version
Unique Price Offer

As the world enters a new decade, we have brought something unique to you - the achievers of the 90's.

Commencing early January 1990 we will offer a limited number of Mercedes-Benz 230E Sport Chassis cars at an advantageous price of HK$395,000 (ordinary price HK$439,800). This offer will be valid until the German factory allocation is taken up but not later than 6th March 1990. A special 36-month finance package is available with a down payment of only 10% and an interest factor of 8%. The cars will be manufactured in Germany early in the New Year.

The 230E Sport Chassis is the latest addition to the highly successful Mercedes-Benz mid size range. With its sleek lines, tuned suspension, alloy wheels and wide base tyres, the new car will certainly give a more sporty drive and yet retain all that is great in the inherent design of the model series. The re-styled exterior protection panels also ensure that this new addition to the family is instantly recognisable as a model manufactured in and commensurate with the new decade.

If you would like to learn more about this exciting Mercedes-Benz model, please visit our showrooms or telephone contact our sales representative today. Please do remember that this special offer remains valid only until 6th March 1990 and is subject to factory availability.

Yours faithfully,
ZUNG FU COMPANY LTD

Robert Au
Sales Manager

Head Office and Showrooms
Bonaventure House, Leighton Road, Hong Kong Tel 8957288
G.P.O. Box 209 Hongkong Cables: Zungfu, Telex: 73226, 73662
Fax 852 8907017
Kowloon Showrooms
023-024 Marine Deck, Ocean Terminal, Tel 7358227, 7351199
Zung Fu Car Park Bldg. Po Loi Street, Hung Hom, Tel 7646919-20
Please address all correspondence to the Head Office

Service Hongkong:
Zung Fu Building, King's Road at Shipyard Lane, Tel 5612241
Zung Fu Building, 36 Wong Chuk Hang Road, Tel 5528298

Service Kowloon:
Zung Fu Car Park Bldg., Po Loi Street, Hung Hom, Kln., Tel 3639396

Service Kwai Chung:
26-30 Wo Yi Hop Road, Kwai Chung, Tel 4273355

Mercedes-Benz — Registered Trademarks of Mercedes-Benz AG, Stuttgart, Federal Republic of Germany

Figure 6.15 Zung Fu Co. Ltd sales promotion letter

Figure 6.16 Zung Fu Co. Ltd sales promotion pamphlet

Conclusion

Clearly if one could make decisions with perfect hindsight, it would not be necessary to play with compromise solutions, which options really are. One is reminded of the aphorism that the only person who has perfect foresight in the company is the chairman, and even that person only tells you afterwards!

CHAPTER 7

Administration, control and accounting

Whether a foreign exchange dealing system is manual or computerized, simple or sophisticated, there are certain ingredients that are essential for proper control of the function. The growth of a rudimentary system towards a more established one requires the codification of procedures. Further growth towards a computerized 'all-singing, all-dancing' system is predicated on sound procedures and controls. These form the bedrock of good management and provide an essential foundation for confidence and integrity on which the whole edifice of a dealing structure and relationship depend.

Separation of duties

This is a fundamental concept of accounting control, though one does not need to be an accountant to appreciate its significance. If an individual has practical control of a variety of related functions—including the raising of a deal, its recording, accounting and bank reconciliation—then there is clearly not just the possibility of error, but, probably more important, the suspicion that some kind of uncontrolled activity might take place. This might be as trivial as the misallocation of a deal to the wrong account, but could rise in significance through the creation of hidden reserves and distortion of profit to actual fraud on the company. The main areas that should be separated are:

- dealing from confirmation receipt and checking
- accounting and administration of deals from control of bank statements.

Checking of confirmations

This might be considered a tedious and sterile activity, being after the event and having no apparent effect on the ongoing dealing activity. However, the importance of this process to the organization should not be underestimated. Since most deals are performed verbally, the written confirmation—whether in letter, telex or facsimile form—is the first opportunity the organization has of checking the accuracy of the agreement. Errors that can be noticed at this stage vary from the wrong transcription of the amounts or rates dealt to premia treated as discounts and vice versa, to the deal being stated in reverse, e.g., a currency sale being treated as a purchase.

The latter is the most critical mistake, for if the corporate thinks the currency has been bought, and the bank is also of this opinion, with neither picking up the error at this early stage, then the misdeal would not be located until maturity, by which time exchange rates might well be quite different. Both bank and corporate will have operated their position-keeping on the understanding that they were long-currency, and since this would not be the case the total loss (or, more unusually, gain) would be double the original figure dealt. Since dealers know what they expect to see on the confirmation from the bank, it is best for this activity to be carried out by another area, either a back office or an internal audit function. This activity also needs to be carried out within the first day of receipt of confirmations, so that any error can be rectified immediately.

All deals should be recorded. While this may seem elementary, it is quite possible in a manual system to mislay deals so that they are late for entry into the books, or to lose deals during typing, or to have deals done by an assistant and not recorded properly or, even worse, to have them carried in the head of the dealer! Only the independent checking of tape recordings of telephone conversations between corporate dealers and the bank would ensure that all deals in the system had actually been recorded, and only a few large corporates (though most banks) have such recordings, the purpose of which is mainly to check for misdeals rather than deals that are not recorded. Procedures to reassure auditors and controllers that no gaps exist in the information system on deals done can include a variety of expedients.

Numbered dealing slips is considered to be a reasonable check on the completeness of the recording of deals, all deal slips being cross-referenced with complete deals, and gaps in sequence accounted for and reported in an exceptions book. However, the accounting for errors, discards, trial-deals, aborted deals, stop-loss orders, and the variety of different dealing activities, including deliveries, maturities, new deals and modern instruments, makes this approach at best cumbersome and at worst an inefficient intrusion into the operation of the dealing function.

Different deal slips for different purposes can enable the dealer to capture the most important aspects of the transaction before the deal is completed, so that the deals can then be correctly filed for action and follow-up later. It is not essential that this later process be done by a separate party, though that is the usual procedure in larger organizations. The importance of this aspect of the dealing activity at the 'sharp end' is that the dealer keeps an ongoing and methodical record of the deals that he or she has done. When activity in the markets has subsided the dealer, or support staff, can input the detail into internal computer systems, and confirmations can be prepared accordingly.

An approach increasingly favoured by corporates and banks is to record the deal struck directly into the computer system. There was some early resistance to this process by dealers who thought of their job as being downgraded to an input clerk, but 'mouse'-style entry systems onto formatted screens or electronic dealing pads and the increased acceptability of computerized systems generally have reduced the objections to these innovations. The advantage to this approach is not only in the reduction of paperwork associated with dealing, but in the reduction or elimination of the time delay before deals are recognized internally. The chance of deals being missed from the system is also greatly reduced, and intelligent controls can be built in as part of the system.

Accounting control

Accounting entries are made for deals only in respect of the actual flows of cash, and where deals need to be revalued at a period end for profit and loss purposes. Forward deals as such need no accounting entries when the deals are made, though there is an undoubted commitment by both corporate and counterparty (normally bank) to deliver given amounts of currency on a given day—even though the routeing instructions, or the netting of the deal with other related deals, might not be known at the time the deal is made.

Apart from the revaluation at some intervening accounting date of the portfolio of currencies bought and sold for delivery in the future, the accounting for dealing activity takes place on the eventual movement of the funds. Coding of the deals for bank statement reconciliation purposes is therefore an important control in which the dealing activity has a prime role since they are often the initiators of the deals and therefore know the deals' rationale.

Provided that the bank reconciliation ('cash office') function has received a ledger posting for each movement on bank statements, the control of the flows will have been adequately monitored. Where treasury-related cash arrives or leaves without the authorization of the treasury function, there is prima facie evidence of an error either by a remitting bank in flowing funds early or late or to the wrong counterparty, or by the treasury function, in failing to record a transaction or to notify the cash office of the deal maturity and flow. Owing to the controlling and monitoring function of the cash office, accepted wisdom dictates that this function should be separated from the main dealing function itself. This protects the dealing function and also gives support to the company.

Maturity diary

It is important for the corporate to be self-reliant in the maintenance of its dealing records, though the final control rests with the bank who may call to ensure that, for example, a particular forward deal maturing in two days is to be closed out or delivered. Internally, the dealing function should maintain records of all 'live' deals, with dates by which time action should be taken to roll or close. Such records are important for good order and general control, but also as an aid to scheduling the flow of work—for example, ensuring that an unacceptable number of deals do not mature on the same day, which cannot only be inconvenient for internal work scheduling, but also might run the risk of breaking some bank limits on daylight exposures. Again, computerized records enable a maturity ladder to be run off easily, but, in the absence of this, a carefully maintained diary can be adequate. In the latter case, for each deal there is the added routine of ensuring that the diary is kept up to date, including the new deals made each day. The maturity diary can be a help in scheduling cash flow forecasts, though it is clearly only one of the lesser important constituent elements of the forecast, paradoxically because the flows can be amended so readily.

Period-end accounting

This is not so much a dealing function as a control activity, being the preserve of the back-up staff or administration and accounting function. However, in smaller organizations, the individuals concerned may be interchangeable. This is of crucial importance to the organization and to the treasury function, in the formal declaration to the company of the results of the dealing activity, by its quantified 'true and fair' impact on the profit and loss account. Two main areas are involved: firstly, the accounting for movements of cash in the period, which is really a day-to-day activity; and, secondly, the revaluation of deals outstanding at period-end. Along with the latter item is the accruing of gains and losses in the balance sheet, and the carrying forward of some unrealized gains in certain circumstances to future periods.

Though some larger companies have developed their own in-house conventions for ensuring consistency of treatment between one accounting period and another, the rules for treatment of period-end cut-offs are not precise, even when accounting policies and the relevant accounting standards are followed conscientiously. Four underlying accounting concepts are recognized, as enshrined in the UK Statement of Accounting Practice No. 2 (SSAP2): the going concern concept, the accruals concept, the consistency concept, and the prudence concept. The two that are at the heart of controversy in the treatment of accounting gains on exchange cover actions are the accruals concept and the prudence concept. These can be overlaid by the practice recognized in SSAP20, which deals with accounting for foreign exchange, of marking to market—effectively revaluing at period-end outstanding deals to ensure they are brought into account at market rates.

Under the accruals concept, all deals realized would strictly be brought into profit or loss in the relevant accounting period. The only deals left to be carried forward to a future period would be those still unrealized at period-end. Under the prudence concept, one should bring into account unrealized losses insofar as they might otherwise lead to a falsely optimistic view of the company, but not unrealized gains, since the advantage of these is uncertain at the time of closure of the accounts. Here we are talking only of timing, being the period in which accounting gains and losses fall, rather than the real change to the underlying profit and loss, which is the result of decisions and treasury action. There is a fundamental conflict between these two concepts, given the way modern treasury departments operate. Deals are not structured simply to cover the precise time of the underlying flow. They are put in place to cover a particular volume of cover for a certain period of time, and are only related to the underlying transactions by reference to the volume covered. Therefore it is possible that the particular deal covering the exposure for next year will have been rolled forward and the cash received or paid before the year-end. Under the accruals concept these gains or losses would be accelerated since the relevant deals would have matured and the cash flowed; but if this involves bringing forward gains, can this treatment be prudent?

Though there is no evidence that the conventions have been misused, it is at least theoretically possible to examine one's forward deals one day before period-end, and crystallize surplus gains thereby enabling accounting profits to be brought forward into the current year. No doubt the accounting conventions have grown in order to establish a framework to enable the ongoing business to be measured and recorded against well-understood guidelines, and to enable consistency of treatment to operate. Auditors have the task of ensuring that they are happy with the way the company has applied the various rules, but in future will need to exercise quite a degree of judgement in this area, which is growing in importance with the magnitude of foreign exchange deals recorded and their significance for the company.

The factors to be taken into account in the consideration of accounting policy for foreign exchange are summarized in Table 7.1, where a detailed example is provided. The revaluation of the sales ledger is an important element in the determination of the net gains or losses from exchange, since the booked rate for the translation of debts will be different from the period-end rate. Remittances during the period will clearly be converted at the relevant spot rate in the absence of forward cover. If full forward cover is

Table 7.1 Accounting for foreign exchange—detailed example

		Period			
		0	1	2	3
Exposures					
Pieces		Economic	600	Booked	100
Dubloons			1200		200
Crowns (plan)			4200		900
Pieces (ex-rate)		2	2.1	1	1.9
Dubloons (ex-rate)		1	1.05	1.08	1.15
Crowns (ex-rate)		3	2.8	2.75	2.6
Cover actions					
(D=deliver, S=sell, P=purchase)					
Pieces			D 50	D 50	D 50
Dubloons		S 1200	P 100	P 100	P 100
			D 100	D 100	D 100
Crowns		S 4200	P 4200		
			D 300	D 300	D 300
S/L revaluation					
Pieces		50.0	47.6	50.0	52.6
Dubloons		200.0	190.5	185.2	173.9
Crowns		300.0	321.4	327.3	346.2
Delivery					
Pieces		25.0	23.8	25.0	26.3
Dubloons		100.0	95.2	92.6	87.0
Crowns		100.0	107.1	109.1	115.4
Cover					
Dubloons	Currency	1200	1100	1100	900
	Sterling	1200.0	1047.6	925.9	782.6
Crowns	Currency	4200	0		
	Sterling	1400.0	0		
Exchange gains/losses					
Dubloons	Realized v. plan		4.8	7.4	13.0
	Unreal'd—coarse		52.4	74.1	117.4
Crowns	Realized		−100.0		

operational, there will be a significant treasury management job in ascribing the profits or losses on the cover activity to the underlying deal, and to rolling forward to the next accounting period the surplus cover. The delivery of currency against an existing contract requires the relevant accounting to be carefully considered. An active treasury operation presupposes some turnover of deals unrelated to either the delivery of currency or the conventional maturity of the deal. Particularly, where the treasury changes its mind and decides it is appropriate to remove part of the cover put in place, the accounting will need to accommodate this new approach. Should the gain or loss be recognized for accounting purposes immediately, or is there a case for amortizing the variance over the life of the original exposure?

Example

The four currencies considered are chosen to avoid the preconceptions of strength or weakness that might be associated with real names. There are three accounting periods, and three currencies. The first currency (Pieces) weakens and then strengthens, and no treasury action is taken. The second currency (Dubloons) is losing value, and the full exposure of 12 months is sold forward at the outset. The third currency (Crowns) is strengthening, but treasury sold the exposure at the outset and then changed its mind in period 1, realizing a loss.

The accounting for Pieces and Dubloons is relatively straightforward. There are no treasury accruals for Pieces (Table 7.2), and the losses and gains from revaluation of the sales ledger are simply taken in each month.

For Dubloons (Table 7.3), where there is full treasury cover, there is no net accounting effect of exchange since the gains from forward cover offset the net losses from revaluing the sales ledger and delivery of the currency. Nevertheless, the accounting entries are fairly complex.

For Crowns, where the cover of period 0 was removed at a loss in period 1, there is a clear problem. Either the loss can be recognized for accounting purposes in period 1, which is clearly in accordance both with the accruals and prudence concepts, or, since the original cover related to the whole year and not just one month, the loss could be amortized. The effect of amortization would not be simply to take one-twelfth of the loss in period 1, since the booked exposure consisted of two months. Nevertheless, the disincentive from carrying out a treasury action that seems to be justified by future exchange rate movements is significantly reduced if the penalty from crystallization is reduced. In one sense, the creation of a loss provision within the treasury area—for

Table 7.2 Simple case: Pieces—no cover

Month	Sales ledger						P & L account				Cash	
	Curr.	Sterling		Curr.	Sterling		Sterling		Sterling		Sterling	Sterling
		Dr			Cr		Dr		Cr		Dr	Cr
1: Exch 2.1												
B Fwd	100	50.0	Cash	50	23.8	S/L	3.6			Sales rec	23.8	0
Sales	50	25.0	C Fwd	100	47.6							
			P & L		3.6							0
		75.0			75.0		3.6		0.0		23.8	0.0
2: Exch 2.0												
B Fwd	100	47.6	Cash	50	25.0			S/L	2.4	Sales rec	25.0	0
Sales	50	25.0	C Fwd	100	50.0							
P & L		2.4										
		75.0			75.0		0.0		2.4		25.0	0.0
3: Exch 1.9												
B Fwd	100	50.0	Cash	50	26.3			S/L	3.9	Sales rec	26.3	0
Sales	50	25.0	C Fwd	100	52.6							
P & L		3.9										0
		78.9			78.9		0.0		3.9		26.3	0.0

Table 7.3 Complex case: Dubloons—full cover

Month	Sales ledger					P & L account				Cash		
	Curr.	Sterling		Curr.	Sterling		Sterling		Sterling		Sterling	Sterling
		Dr			Cr		Dr		Cr		Dr	Cr
1: Exch 1.05												
B Fwd	200	200.0	Cash	100	95.2	S/L	14.3	Exch.	4.8	Sales rec	95.2	0
Sales	100	100.0	C Fwd	200	190.5			Booked	9.5			
			P & L		14.3							0
		300.0			300.0		14.3		14.3		95.2	0.0
2: Exch 1.08												
B Fwd	200	190.5	Cash	100	92.6	S/L	22.2	Exch.	7.4	Sales rec	92.6	0
Sales	100	100.0	C Fwd	200	185.2			Booked	14.8			
Reversal		9.5	P & L		22.2							0
		300.0			300.0		22.2		22.2		92.6	0.0
3: Exch 1.15												
B Fwd	200	185.2	Cash	100	87.0	S/L	39.1	Exch.	13.0	Sales rec	87.0	0
Sales	100	100.0	C Fwd	200	173.9			Booked	26.1			
Reversal		14.8	P & L		39.1							0
		300.0			300.0		39.1		39.1		87.0	0.0

Month	Forex cover Curr.	Sterling Dr		Curr.	Sterling Cr		Exchange Sterling Dr		Sterling Cr
0: Exch 1.0									
C Fwd	1200	1200.0	B Fwd	1200	1200.0				
		1200.0			1200.0				
1: Exch 1.05						P & L			
Purchase	100	95.2	B Fwd	1200	1200.0	—realized	4.8	Forex	57.2
C Fwd	1100	1047.6				—booked	9.5		
Exchange		57.2				C Fwd	42.9		
		1200.0			1200.0		57.2		57.2
2: Exch 1.08						P & L			
Purchase	100	92.6	B Fwd	1100	1047.6	—realized	7.4	B Fwd	42.9
C Fwd	1000	925.9				—booked	14.8	Reversal	9.5
Exchange		29.1				C Fwd	59.3	Forex	29.1
		1047.6			1047.6		81.5		81.5
3: Exch 1.15						P & L			
Purchase	100	87.0				—realized	13.0	B Fwd	59.3
C Fwd	900	782.6	B Fwd	1000	925.9	—booked	26.1	Reversal	14.8
Exchange		56.3				C Fwd	91.3	Forex	56.3
		925.9			925.9		130.4		130.4

amortization as the underlying cash moves—is in line with the theory of the accruals concept, since one is linking the treasury action with the intended flow.

The net effect on balance sheets and profit and loss accounts is summarized in Table 7.4. It will be seen that the rigorous application of accounting lore results in the production of a considerable loss in period 1 and large gains in subsequent periods. It is a matter of judgement whether that approach is really true and fair. Alternative (b), which spreads the losses over subsequent periods producing a smoother flow of gains to the profit and loss account, might be considered a more credible representation of the real actions of treasury.

The importance of this subject is not in the first order 'creation of wealth', since parochially the statement of gains or losses of itself has no effect on the underlying actions. However, the indirect effect of the presentation of results on the constraints within which treasurers operate can be considerable. If one really thought that the effect of crystallizing a loss (by changing one's position) would result in a significant adverse impact on the current accounting period, then one might well be deterred from doing what might be the 'right thing'. In this instance, the accounting tail would be wagging the treasury dog, and the potentially adverse effect on the freedom of treasury to control its actions would be seriously curtailed. The creation of wealth—as perceived by the company in real money value—then really would be affected.

Table 7.4 Net effect on balance sheets and profit and loss accounts

Accounting for treasury	Period 1		Period 2		Period 3	
	Balance sheet	Profit & loss	Balance sheet	Profit & loss	Balance sheet	Profit & loss
Dubloons						
Realized		4.8		7.4		13.0
unrealized—booked		9.5		14.8		26.1
—unbooked	42.9		51.9		78.3	
Total	42.9	14.3	51.9	22.2	78.3	39.1
Crowns						
Total recognized						
(a) write off		−100.0				
(b) amortize	−75.0	−25.0	−66.7	−8.3	−58.3	−8.3
Treasury						
(a)	42.9	−85.7	51.9	22.2	78.3	39.1
(b)	−32.1	−10.7	−14.8	13.9	19.9	30.8
Total accounting:						
Pieces	−2.4	−3.6	0.0	0.0	2.6	3.9
Dubloons	33.4	.0	37.0	.0	52.2	.0
Crowns (a)	21.4	−71.4	27.3	36.4	46.2	61.5
(b)	−53.6	3.6	−39.4	28.0	12.2	53.2
Total (a)	52.4	−75.0	64.3	36.4	101.0	65.5
(b)	22.6	.0	−2.4	28.0	42.6	57.2

CHAPTER 8

Taxation and foreign exchange

The task of the treasurer in deciding the correct policy to follow for the management of the currencies under his control is complex enough without the overlay of fiscal considerations. However, such is the magnitude of the decisions taken, and the effect on the bottom line for the company, that the full after tax effect of treasury action needs to be thought through.

The function of treasurers in foreign exchange management rests not only on the appropriateness of their actions with regard to the exposures of their companies and the timing of the relevant actions, but also on the correctness of the stance when seen in full perspective of the total effect of those actions on their companies. While many companies are happy to look at profit before tax as the main variable on which attention should be concentrated and for which actions in foreign exchange management should be directed, there is an increasing view that the treatment of taxation as a function or problem quite different from the items that gave rise to the tax charge is misconceived.

UK perspective

The purpose of this chapter is to review some of the thoughts current in UK corporate treasury circles and to offer some thoughts on taxation reform. Surprisingly, UK tax law is unclear on a subject of fundamental importance to the treasurer, namely the performance of the routine and conventional function of the covering of the foreign exchange risk of the company. However, if the treasurer is unsure of the law and its personal applicability (and the concept of a swap is not yet recognized in UK taxation), then this uncertainty also extends to the City of London, to the banking community who are often responsible for promoting hedging products, and to the trading exchanges. Only the very volume of transactions convinces the practitioner that, despite the lack of codification of the tax law, all should be well at the end of the day. However, this sentiment is more often based on trust, hope and expectation than on the hard evidence of Acts of Parliament and case law. Everyone is in the same boat, and it needs to be fairly large; as with the secondary banking crisis of the mid 1970s, everyone is involved.

Optimally, there would be full symmetry in the taxation treatment of both the underlying cash flow and its foreign exchange hedge. This means that if the underlying transaction makes a loss and the hedge a gain, then the one would be tax allowable and the other chargeable to tax, the reverse also holding true. Symmetry implies that if the hedge is effective, then the tax effect of the hedge should be neutral in its profit impact. Unfortunately, as will be illustrated, the existence of such symmetry cannot be taken for granted. Therefore the whole transaction, the underlying exposure and cash flow, plus its hedge—whether a straightforward deal or an option or series of other deals—plus, if necessary, further deals in relation to the management of the position, needs to be looked at in full perspective.

For the purpose of analysis and action, the foreign exchange 'book' can be considered in three divisions. The first is the most important area of *trading exposures*. This is where currency is receivable or payable in respect of transactions related to the company's trade. Here one would expect foreign exchange gains to be taxable and losses to be allowable. The second is the *liquidity* book—effectively those deals related to the financing of the business, the effects of which are felt 'above the line', by being credited or charged against profits. Here, similarly, foreign exchange gains might reasonably be expected to be taxable, and losses allowable, whether from the underlying currency or from its foreign exchange hedge. The third book is the portfolio of *'matching' transactions*, as recognized in SSAP20 and in the fundamental accounting concepts. Here assets are hedged by overlaying liabilities, and generally, with the exception of interest payments, no cash moves between accounting periods. Since no real profits have been made, but only on paper, no tax should be due; likewise, since the hedge exhibits the same characteristics as the underlying position, no tax allowance would also be due.

In January 1985, the UK revenue authorities issued a Provisional Statement of Practice on the treatment of exchange differences, which attempted to bring at least part of the practice of taxation of exchange differences up to date. This referred in particular to balance sheet exposures, where assets were hedged with liabilities denominated in the same currency, and therefore to the third book above. The case that gave rise to this was *Marine Midland* v *Pattison*, where the bank had a matched loan on which the Inland Revenue (IR) had contended tax was due even though (because there was no liquidation of the asset) there was no possibility of offset. While the IR lost the Marine Midland case, they sought to achieve the applicability of the principles to the corporate sector. However, the application of this was not mandatory, and it was left to the corporate to decide whether to avail itself of the potential advantages of this case. Their provisional statement was succeeded by a final statement in February 1987, which ostensibly gave some codification to the treatment of foreign exchange.

It is unfortunate that this potential breakthrough in terms of the flexibility with which intricate tax problems might be dealt with was marred by the requirement for the hedge to be in the same currency—at variance with the pronouncements of the accountancy profession in SSAP20 in which it was argued that a hedge could be general and need not be specific. Further, the implication is that if items are not specifically matched, and therefore taken out of the scope of taxation, then they are necessarily unmatched and within the scope of tax. The very principle of hedging is that one is seeking for an offsetting deal. Should the item to be hedged reside in the capital account—a concept at the heart of many of the arguments of the Revenue—then, of necessity, the hedge has to be a capital item too. For the IR's purposes, options are not considered hedging at all!

While most attention of commentators has been concentrated on the Marine Midland case, with its apparent green light for the matching principle enshrined in SSAP20, scant attention has been devoted to the equally important *Beauchamp* v *Woolworth* case, in which borrowings were contracted under term facilities in Swiss francs and then converted into sterling for normal business purposes. On repayment there was a significant loss, which was not allowed by the High Court for tax purposes. The implication of this goes beyond the particular circumstances of the case: it becomes important not only how the cash was used, but also how the cash was raised.

It would appear that the IR have chosen to argue that losses on term loans are not allowable for tax unless such loans are exactly offset by assets in the same currency.

One might assume that the revaluation of overseas assets over time—often the investments in overseas subsidiaries—should not cause UK multinationals tax problems, since the ventures will be retained over a long period. However, the longer the period retained, arguably the greater scope for tax problems should the company eventually dispose of the assets, since their value might have been affected greatly by currency factors. Therefore, should the hedge (currency borrowings) have losses that are non-tax-allowable owing to its long-term nature, the gains on the asset might none the less be taxable on realization, giving a significant problem caused by lack of symmetry in the taxation treatment of the two items.

These long-term problems can be circumvented if the corporate 'manages' its way into a short-term hedging position. Short-term interactive cover using forward contracts might be an effective expedient in the cover of a particular capital asset or liability. In some circumstances such an approach might not be to the taste or serve the purpose of the corporate. Also of their nature such forward deals are variable and 'trading' items, rather than fixed or capital, and the IR does not allow the validity of this approach. Hence the treasurer could achieve the worst of all worlds: the taxability of gains on the hedge along with the non-allowability for tax purposes of losses on the underlying asset or liability.

Likewise, there has always been a difference in UK tax law between income arising from the trade and extraneous income. The former has been taxed under Case I of Schedule D, where there was provision for losses made in any year to be carried back for up to three years, and to be offset against any income chargeable to tax. Non-trade income that was not interest was taxed under Schedule VI, where losses were only available for carry forward and offset against income from the same schedule. When futures and options exchanges were first established, gains that could not be described as part of the trade of the company were taxable as Schedule D Case VI—a considerable disincentive to the potential user. In 1985 this unfavourable situation was changed to another unfavourable position, by the enshrining of such gains as capital not income, and therefore eligible for capital gains tax, which has its own restrictions on the allowability of losses. Therefore, corporate treasurers can happily use the exchanges for hedging their trading books, but should they decide to use options for non-trading purposes—for example, the hedging of investments or currency-denominated loans—then they could find a different tax regime applying to this hedge from that which applies to conventional foreign exchange business.

The taxation of the second book—the management of active assets and liabilities—is influenced by the classification of loans as 'long term' or 'short term', the latter implying that the loans are repaid within a period of one year, but also by the hedging strategy adopted. Short-term loans are where 'annual interest' is payable, and where the gains or losses on exchange are treated as short term and therefore taxable or tax allowable respectively. Where loans are on the balance sheet for over a year there is an argument for treating them as long term, with consequential treatment as hedging assets on the balance sheet by 'matching'. In this case the movements of these loans, as the underlying assets, would be tax free, but any cash hedge overlaying them would be taxable since it would be shown in the profit and loss account 'above the line'.

While this chapter is not looking at interest flows so much as exchange rate effects, one problem that is not understood by fiscal authorities and the law (and probably also the accounting profession at large) is the classification of the interest differential. For example, a deutschemark loan can be hedged by the purchase of marks and sale of pounds for a future date, the hedge being rolled forward on maturity. The true cost of the transaction should be zero, but for tax purposes (assuming that UK interest rates are higher than German) there will be an exchange loss on the deutschemark purchases, even though exchange rates may not have moved over the accounting period. This is because tax law, along with accounting practice, does not recognize as interest the differential between the underlying currency loan and the effective sterling borrowing that is created by the deposit.

This confusion in tax law of the real nature of interest extends even to where interest equalization payments are made, as in currency swaps. These transactions, where there is an effective exchange of principle of different currencies between two parties so that, until maturity, they assume the interest flows of the opposite number, may be regarded as long-term foreign exchange contracts. The exception is that instead of the interest differential being included in the forward rate, the rates for maturity are left the same as at the outset, and the interest differential is 'unbundled' and made subject to (mostly) semi-annual payment. Even these payments are not regarded as interest for tax purposes, but are deemed 'annual payments' on which tax needs to be deducted at source, and which are accounted for on a cash flow basis rather than under the accounting accruals concept.

This misunderstanding of the nature of the interest differential regrettably extends to the accounting profession, where it is common to find confusion on the nature of the forward market and the status of the 'forward points', some in the profession still looking at forward rates as some kind of forecast, and at the interest differential as a measure of the comparative supply and demand for currencies at future dates. Small wonder then that no attempt has been made properly to apportion the interest differential to different accounting periods by making accruals in respect of deals outstanding. Therefore, through its neglect of fundamental treasury concepts, the accounting profession is regrettably acquiescing in the temptation for period-end window-dressing and distortion resulting purely from the timing of relevant foreign exchange deals, which clearly can have an effect both on the profits for the period and also—generally in the opposite direction—on the taxation charge.

The first book—the conventional hedging of trading transactions—is clearly the simplest to comprehend, with neither difficulties of the applicability of capital gains tax, nor problems of annual interest. However, this area is not devoid of accounting and taxation gremlins, not least being the period-end accrual, and the possibility of affecting the profit for the period by a few well-chosen deals or maturities on the final day. Currency options should be an area reasonably at one with the maturities of the underlying exposures, but here too there is scope for taking cover action for the following year using options, but writing off the option premium in the earlier period since it is paid 'up front'.

Taxation is a factor in a sense extraneous to the major decisions of what action to take to cover foreign exchange risk, and has in the past been considered as the preserve of the specialist, dredging for nuggets of information after the event and powerless to affect the ongoing business at the time active decisions are being taken. Tax was the consequence of historic actions, amenable to discussion and even dispute, but not active consideration before the event. This view has come under challenge in the light of both the IR's acknowledged ability after the series of Rossminster cases (notably *WT Ramsay Ltd* v *IRC*) and the celebrated *Furniss* v *Dawson* case to probe circularity and look at a series of transactions as one effective deal, and the increasing profile of taxation as an important variable in the total results of the enterprise. It is now a commonplace that there is little point in safeguarding an accounting or economic exposure if one thereby opens a fiscal exposure.

If, as a treasurer, one were simply to acknowledge that taxation law is in a mess on its applicability to foreign exchange, one could take the view that gains would be likely to be taxable whether or not losses were allowable, whatever the rationale. Provided that one had confidence in one's strategy and approach, the level of foreign exchange cover taken could be factored to allow for the tax payable, so that the net after tax position provided the full after tax hedge that was being sought originally. The problem with this approach is that, prima facie, one would have cover at an inflated level compared with the underlying transactions, and therefore, strictly defined, a degree of speculation would have crept into an essentially hedging strategy. Provided that the hedge worked satisfactorily and the underlying trading loss was protected by offsetting treasury gains, then no one would complain. However, the position would be open to scorn and ridicule as soon as treasury losses were recorded, which would be inflated by the needless taxation excess. The answer is not to trade oneself out of the tax problem, but to use legislation to clarify the position and to make the taxation of exchange gains (net) comprehensible and rational.

While in some respects the UK revenue authorities have tried to extend their level of competence by looking at the transactions either in full or dissected into constituent parts at their discretion, they, in common with other tax authorities, have been fighting a steadily losing battle with multinationals—especially those who have set their face against the payment of any tax they could avoid. Even the country of location of the hedging vehicle can be outside the purview and control of the taxing authority, so that the more advanced of multinationals can structure their hedging strategy to enable a profit-centred treasury operation to escape tax at all but a marginal rate on the net profit made on its hedges, while the parent company achieves tax relief on the losses made (whether quantified or not in a treasury-related way) on its 'unmanaged' book.

Effectively the tax authorities are trying to catch up with the thinking and terminology of the accounting world in addressing issues raised by interactive and sophisticated treasury operations, which are inventing new and clever ways of solving today's and tomorrow's problems. For example, in the late 1980s treasuries were tackling the thinking behind swaptions (options on swaps), while the accounting authorities had not yet compiled any standard for the treatment of foreign currency options. The IR meantime are just beginning to realize the existence of such a thing as an option that can be bought on exchanges, and have yet to address the question of the treatment of options sold—since, as they are not an asset (they are a liability), they are not amenable to treatment as capital with all that this implies in the possibilities for capital gains tax.

The problem with the taxation of exchange differences is really that the IR have inherited nineteenth-century terminology and thinking, when the problems that are being addressed are those of the environment of global trading in the twenty-first. For example, the expression 'circulating capital' (which is used in the 1985 Inland Revenue Provisional Statement of Practice SP3/85) was meant to imply capital of use in the working of the business, but not tied up in fixed assets or available for distribution as dividends, is a quaint example of the Victorian jargon that is still applicable in law today, even though no accounting textbook recognizes the validity of the term. Indeed, the whole capital/revenue distinction is misleading and arguably biases attention towards the fixed and static and away from the wealth-generative and useful. 'If you can see it, tax it' was at one time a socialist maxim, whereas, arguably, if you can see it, it is no longer being useful and to tax it makes it even less valuable.

The requirement for the IR to cope with advances in corporate treasury techniques had led to a series of expedients linked to open-ended statements, like the Statement of Practice, which might seem to resolve positions, but in fact leave the edifice of capital taxation reasonably intact. For example, swaps are ostensibly taken out of conventional Case I corporation tax by the offsetting provisions of assets and liabilities. However, the menace of capital gains taxation is neither countered not denied, where on the unwinding of the swap, gains on the asset would be a taxable item, but liabilities are not assets, and by definition losses on them would not be capital losses to be offset against the gains.

The very principle of the taxation of capital *per se* is questionable. Firstly, the economic utility and commercial sense (from the country's point of view) of the tax is dubious. Secondly, there is the injustice of taxing inflation (or of differential inflation when the worst iniquities of capital gains tax are assuaged by the acceptance of indexation). Thirdly are the demonstrable inefficiencies of the heavy-handed collection mechanism and the comparably poor net tax take. Fourthly, the complexities and inconsistencies of the particular animal that has evolved over a generation have created a structure in which the resultant liability bears scant resemblance to the rationale for the relevant underlying gain. The acceptance of taxes on capital has been at the root of the myopia of the legislature and revenue bodies, and has been at the core of problems that have confronted treasurers and still encumber the traded exchanges. An abolition of capital gains tax would lift the dead hand from the new traded instruments, simplify administration, cheapen taxation advisory services, make the taxation system more efficient and also, probably, improve the inflow to the treasury. The law would also be shortened by several chapters. How nice also to consign the expression 'circulating capital' to the archives along with compulsory archery practice on Sundays.

Unfortunately—though the demise of such old taxes as the Selective Employment Tax (SET), the Development Land Tax (DLT) and Capital Transfer Tax (CTT) might illustrate that it is not impossible to dispense with defunct taxes—it is probably fair to remark that the chances of removing a tax are inversely related to the longevity of the tax itself. After all, income tax was originally a temporary expedient to help raise revenue to fight the French in the Revolutionary War, and then revived by Sir Robert Peel in the 1840s to help abolish the Corn Laws. Although he attacked the new tax to good effect, Gladstone, when he became Chancellor of the Exchequer in 1852, found income tax to be a very useful source of revenue for the Crimean War, and once established the tax simply grew.

Given the inventiveness of the bureaucracy, it is perhaps surprising that the taxation of capital *per se* waited more than a hundred years until 1965 before being enshrined in law. The concept of capital is seen as something tangible which quite happily can be regarded as a source of revenue to the authorities (although, to an accountant, capital and revenue are contradictory terms). Capital is also in the Marxist sense a kind of bogey symbol of gain (and also probably ill-begotten). The concept easily predated mid-nineteenth-century socialists, even the younger Disraeli attacking it as something foreign ('Dutch capital'—although the predominance of the Dutch financial markets had been dealt a mortal blow by the Napoleonic invasion over a generation earlier). The concept of capital as disreputable and antisocial is probably too ingrained into the folklore of England—perhaps going back to Blake's 'satanic mills'—for the beautiful simplicity of the debunking and abolition of taxes on it to be politically acceptable, let alone electorally popular.

However, the reforming UK government of the 1980s has moved some way in the standardization for companies of capital and income tax rates in their 1987 Finance (No. 2) Act. Profit has been redefined for tax purposes to incorporate capital gains, so that advance corporation tax can now be offset against capital gains tax payable, as well as income of the current period, which is a small but significant concession. This only leaves the small anomaly of the ability to carry losses on income back to previous periods, but not losses on capital, which would be clearly a somewhat more significant gain for the taxpayer. Thus, some standardization of the taxes has removed some inconvenience (but not all), but unfortunately has not lifted the requirement to examine each transaction to ascertain whether or not it can be categorized as 'trading'. Options in particular are subject to capital gains treatment if they are not strictly within the Schedule D Case I category of arising from standard hedging as part of the company's trade. So, unfortunately, a move designed to help the corporate has probably reinforced the outdated concept of the separate taxation of capital gains, by implying that the taxes have been rationalized when in fact the whole structure of capital gains tax was ripe for demolition. That such a process would make fiscal and industrial sense is a consideration that weighs too lightly for the hope of its acceptance now to be anything but a dream. The taxation of short-term 'speculative gains' had been enshrined for many years before the advent of capital gains tax in 1965, so it is not surprising that the hope of the removal of this outdated shackle seems to have receded from the possible to the improbable.

In the absence of an imaginatively and unambiguously iconoclastic approach, it is probable that the future of taxation of exchange differences will continue to be a series of skirmishes, compromises and case-law, building nice intellectual edifices for those who delight in games of mental chess. The IR will continue to search diligently for the magical taxable gain coupled with the non-allowable loss (unconcerned about the possibility of killing the golden goose). In fear of taxation problems, treasurers will continue to have their best ideas rejected in favour of a safety-first policy which in fact does not address the real needs of the corporate. New instruments will continue to be hobbled by the difficulty of operating without volumes of case-law, and at worst the London financial markets will lose ground to offshore centres that are not prone to the national (and anti-multinational) sentiments of local legislatures. And the taxation industry, despite all the simplifications that have taken place over the last few years, will continue to make hay.

A note on taxation in the USA

To compare the chaotic situation of the United Kingdom with the codified and logical tax law of the United States is to experience a culture shock rather than simply jet lag. Instead of doubt there is certainty. The Tax Reform Act of 1986 (TRA) has regularized a previously rather arcane system, and introduced precision of definitions along with a close relationship to accounting standards, in marked contrast to the UK.

Before the TRA, the US tax law with reference to foreign exchange was not too different from the UK position. There was a layer of voluminous and occasionally inconsistent Internal Revenue Service (IRS) rulings, Internal Revenue Code provisions and Treasury Regulations, together with various court decisions. This sounds familiar to a UK practitioner. The tax treatment of relatively new instruments like swaps was unclear, and doubt pervaded the treatment of branch operations, dividend remittances, foreign tax credits, and exchange differences on foreign currency loans.

While the concept of foreign currency being 'property' is

retained by the TRA, and exchange gains and losses are required to be computed separately from those of the underlying business, the TRA has codified the law and introduced clear definitions to enable to tax liability on forex gains and losses to be calculated with a degree of certainty. Consistency and clarity have been produced where there was doubt and uncertainty before.

Among the terms defined precisely are 'functional currency', 'qualifying business unit' and 'nonfunctional currency transactions' (ref. Code sec. 988). Seemingly innocuous but potentially perilous routine terms such as foreign currency gains and losses are defined by relation to applicable paragraphs so that timing and quantification are not in doubt, the definitions including 'booking rate', 'acquisition date' and 'disposition'. A hedge is dealt with in its economic sense by being linked to the underlying transaction. The perils of UK tax fragmentation have been avoided in this sensible piece of legislation.

Since part of the object of the legislation taken as a whole was to correct the distortions that existed when businesses were technically based offshore while their actual business was on the ground, the law has defined residence in terms of where the principal place of business is located, thus widening the tax net usefully. Some US companies who, in the old confusing days, had attempted to evade taxes in this way are now wishing they had been slightly less clever.

There are special provisions dealing with forwards, futures and options that are 'marked to market' (Code sec. 1256). Regulated futures contracts traded on exchanges fall within this provision, but, with only two minor exceptions, all foreign exchanges are outside the scope of this provision. These trades, together with foreign currency denominated contracts, are dealt with under the catch-all section 988. Similarly, swaps are caught within this latter provision, since they are not traded on an exchange and marked to market.

Other provisions deal with the tax treatment of profits from branches and from controlled foreign corporations, while the treatment of foreign tax credits is also addressed. Capital taxes are part of the total mix, but their application has been narrowed virtually to a voluntary levy, most taxpayers opting for income definition. The FASB52 provisions, particularly on the separate calculation of profits in 'nonfunctional currency transactions' notably for subsidiaries, are recognized in the legislation, although the accounting standard *per se* is not given statutory force. Thus the need for the corporate to conduct hedges for the whole group's translation exposure (which had been the result of the old FASB8) has been killed by FASB52 and buried by the TRA.

The long-term effect of the legislation is, as yet, a little difficult to assess, but clearly the tax avoidance industry from Grand Cayman to Bermuda has been dealt a crippling blow. The consensus that has built behind the reforms has been for 'fair' corporate taxes and low personal tax, a further factor leading both to simplification and to greater propriety. There is a clear link between good law and good civic conduct. It is to be hoped that just as the common sense of FASB52 was shared by SSAP20, so the tax reforming zeal of our US cousins will be taken to heart by the UK in more than simply the reduction of marginal rates—nice though this might be.

CHAPTER 9

Decision-making

To manage foreign exchange properly, there can be no avoidance of the need to make decisions. It is best for this fact to be understood by all connected with the problem, so that the right attitude and response can be generated when a changed situation demands a different approach and set of decisions. Decisions can be active or passive, structured or reactive, made by relation to external advice or internally generated data, information or ideas. The common aspect is that they impact on the business to a significant extent, and that they can be right or wrong. However, they are also vital for the business, since *not* to decide is to decide by default, and that might be much worse than an active decision.

Active and passive

Passive decisions hardly need comment, but are highlighted here so that their existence can be recognized. It is easy to convince oneself that they do not really exist in one's own environment and workplace, and that one's own area is characterized only by well thought through attitudes and policies where inertia, habit and prejudice have no place. Unfortunately, though some treasurers might not like to admit it, such an environment is not the real world. If we are honest, we can all acknowledge that these human characteristics are to be found in our own department as well as those of our competitors, and if they are prone to bouts of indecision and weakness, then, from time to time, so are we.

A passive decision might not be wrong for all that. A decision is a decision, and depending on the criterion for its appraisal—of which there could be a variety—the answer can be right or wrong, almost like the toss of a coin. However, if it were that easy there would be no committees, no boards and no economists. All decisions would be a matter of chance, and treasury meetings would take place around the ouija board. How much more comforting than to have the inconvenience of putting oneself on a limb, simply to take refuge, say, in one's underlying exposure. If we are regarded as a dollar-related company, are we not cheating the shareholders from their risk in owning us by selling the dollar forward? If everyone thinks the dollar is going down, surely at some point the majority is wrong. 'Look how far the currency has moved already—it must surely be the wrong time to do something now!' The number of excuses for passive decisions are legion, but the motivation is very often to keep a low profile, and avoid the vulnerability of personal responsibility.

Active decisions are characterized as those that are made deliberately. They involve a carefully weighed appraisal of the risk to which the corporate is exposed, both its definition and volume, plus time period. The factors impacting on the changing parameters (e.g., exchange rates) are discussed, and the possibilities of change from the currently evolving situation are debated. At the end of an active decision-making process in foreign exchange management, there emerges:

- firstly, a positive decision either to sell or buy a currency, or to do nothing;
- secondly, a view on what would need to change from the view taken in order to change the perspective and possibly also the decision itself;
- thirdly, an action, being either the relevant deal, and/or perhaps a record of the discussion so that the relevant parameters can be logged for future reference.

Just as passive decisions can be right, so active decisions can be wrong. What separates the two is the ability to react to changed circumstances should the original decision be shown in the light of evolving circumstances to be wrong or questionable. Passive decisions can rarely be changed or modified, because they do not include in the decision-making process the requirement and discipline for a timely review. A passive decision-making environment does not encourage the debate, questioning and cut-and-thrust of the interrogative reappraisal of the previous position. As such it is not only less reactive, but also less accommodative of different approaches, and mistrustful of novelty and innovation. It is probably also less successful, though only after a significant débâcle might well-entrenched passive decision-makers be unmasked and defrocked. This does not happen very often, since their strength is the way they merge into the background and avoid the high profile that might be dangerous should snipers be hidden in the undergrowth. They will not be killed in battle, unless the entire war is virtually lost and there is no place left to hide after the decimation of their defensive squares.

However, if active decisions can be wrong, they can also have their error limited in extent, by policy, by review, by internal criticism, and by another active decision. At some point one may find, unusually, that two active decisions are wrong consecutively, and this can be used by passive decision-makers as critique against the whole active approach, which may be characterized as reactionary, or fundamentally flawed since the concept of managing detracts in the ultimate from the business one is really in.

An example is where a position is being managed by reference to stop-losses: where the currencies are volatile but directionless, an active approach may yield losses, while a passive one would quietly avoid danger. It is wrong to generalize from the particular, and in this case to imagine that because active decisions might not be ideal for certain market conditions, then they are not correct for all—when in fact the whole of experience over a range of different market environments needs to be taken before such prejudices can be graced with a semblance of respectability.

Short term v long term

The tenor of a decision that is taken is related to the reactiveness of the decision itself. The longer the term covered by the decision, the less easy it is in general to reverse that decision. The reason for this is that such a decision is generally taken for strategic purposes—and strategies are not proved to be mistakes unless the battle is almost lost, which requires a significant change in underlying parameters. Similarly, the longer term the decision, the greater the potential magnitude and effect on the total business. Therefore, there is no pejorative in the terms short and long term, and there is a need for an array of policies and parameters addressing both short-term and long-term currency positions and structures.

Clearly, however, there is more potential for reactive decision-making with short-term items—for example, the cover of foreign exchange liabilities, where the view to cover or not to cover depends significantly on the day-to-day view of the comparative currencies rather than longer term perspectives, even though there is also a place for these. Should treasurers allow themselves to be influenced significantly by these short-term items? The danger of too active an approach is not that a treasurer will make too much profit and distort the perspective of the business, but that he or she will be accused of sacrificing the long term for the short.

It is true that there is some profit and cash to be made from an active dealing stance. One can react against an oversold position for a currency by buying it, only to sell again perhaps two cents later. But this is not the function of the treasurer, it is a by-product of the treasurer's skills and expertise. It should not become an all-consuming goal, to the detriment of wider and more important objectives.

The long term is the area where the treasurer's reputation is made or lost. While not needing specifically to predict significant currency moves, the treasurer can structure a position in which advantage can be taken of changes in the forex markets. For example, the decline in the dollar, which commenced in March 1985, had been predicted for several years before it happened: the judicious use of options to cover the downside would have yielded significant benefits to the treasury position. Similarly, following the 25 per cent devaluation of sterling against the deutschemark in 1986, it was conceivable that sterling would recover at least 10 per cent of its value against major continentals. Those treasurers who had structured their long-term positions to take advantage of such a move would have been significantly rewarded in subsequent periods. And the further ahead they had sold, say, the guilder or the franc, the greater the reward opposite spot at maturity.

Organization for decisions

Given that the high profile of treasurers is the result of the perception in industry and in the financial world of the importance of the stances adopted in the management of funding and currencies, the profile of currencies needs to be organized in such a way that the main items for decision can be highlighted immediately. For example, if one is managing a multicurrency portfolio of borrowing, then the main factors requiring decision are the proportions borrowed in the various currencies (mix) plus the switches from one currency to another (timing of deals). A simple schedule would be yesterday's closing volume of currency loans, plus the optimal or agreed weightings of currencies, together with proposed change for today.

Transaction exposures are often the subject of currency management meetings on a regular (monthly) basis. Documentation is covered later, but given the structure of the data on exposures, the meeting needs to be organized so that relevant actions can be elicited clearly and expeditiously. This implies a correct weighting of responsibility and expertise so that authority to act is clearly established and that decisions can be taken in the light of all relevant factors—sometimes after considered and weighty debate. An argued decision may still not be right, but might just stand a slightly better chance of not being wrong!

Similarly, if the chief vulnerabilities are, say, the dollar and the deutschemark, then it is appropriate to keep a close watch on the daily movements of these currencies, with the production of daily charts and even intra-day fluctuations. An intimate appreciation of the relevant currencies for the particular exposures should enable a swift and appropriate response to be taken to unexpected moves in exchange rates.

It is quite acceptable to let one or two favoured bank dealers know what is influencing a treasurer's thoughts, so that they can build into their thinking some of the reactions that he or she might wish to make. For example, if a treasurer has sold yen and would prefer to repurchase them at a modest loss rather than risk an open-ended treasury loss, then this could be looked at by a bank dealer, which could prompt a given response should a preselected rate be triggered.

Program dealing

In the light of the increased stock market volatility culminating in the market crash of October 1987, the concept of computerized 'program trading' received some approbrium. However, for foreign exchange dealing such techniques can be a valuable mechanism to enable the dealer or treasurer to be extricated from a potentially difficult position by reference to pre-agreed rates, rather than wait for the rates to be triggered, and then open an internal debate on whether to act at the time the rates are becoming inexorably worse.

Two orders may be placed with banks. The most common is the *stop-loss*. Here the corporate has an underlying position that must be covered at a rate 'no worse than' a given downside, or the corporate has already covered the downside but does not wish to lose too much of the profit on the contract should the underlying position improve. Often the large moves can take place outside one's own time zone, and such orders enable at least the worst acceptable position to be dealt if the rates are seen. The danger is that though the rate might be seen and the deal done, the market might bounce off those levels leaving a deal that one would have preferred not to have. Alternatively, the market might move so far and so quickly that the particular level selected might not be seen, resulting in a worse rate dealt than one had hoped.

The second order placed can be a *take-profit* order, where perhaps one has an exposure that is gaining value as the currency appreciates in value, but the treasurer perceives that there is a realistic limit to further advances. A take-profit order would allow the bank to deal if a given rate better than the spot rate is seen, thus giving the corporate an extra level of profit and providing possibly a buffer should the decision later be seen to be tactically incorrect.

The advantage of these structures is that they allow corporates to feel in control of their positions round the clock, as the order can be sent around the world while they are asleep, and be executed, say, in Melbourne. The structures also bring the corporates back to basics: they have to decide what they are managing, what motivates them, what they can afford to lose, and what they want to safeguard. As such the structures place a significant discipline on the individual and can be a particular help to a corporate—notably where the treasury team is small and resources are limited—and they enable the banks to establish a closeness with the concerns and motivations of the corporate, which can be of mutual benefit.

Timing and environment

It is a truism that the correct timing of decisions can be as important as the principle of the decision itself. It can be considered a bold action to sell forward, say, one year's dollar receivables. Provided the timing of the deal is chosen carefully, then both the value of the deal itself might be maximized and the potential damage minimized should the decision appear dubious later. If, on the other hand, no structure was in place to enable actions to be decided calmly and rationally, then a decision might be delayed until the rates had already moved to a level that was uncomfortable. Without sales contracts in place, one might either stand back, appalled and shell-shocked like a rabbit transfixed in the headlights of an oncoming juggernaut, or chase after the rate to try to get some cover in place no matter what, and then find that one has achieved a poor rate and is exposed to the potential whiplash as dollar buyers perceive a bargain.

Timing is therefore of the essence in a good decision. But often senior officers cannot be convinced that action is needed until rates have actually moved, and the company is beginning to hurt. Attention therefore needs to be concentrated on the problem of heightening the awareness of the board and currency committee to the magnitudes and sensitivities of the exchange picture. There are various ways in which charts can illustrate occasions when one should be structured long term, short or long of the currencies. This section deals with the environment for discussing such concepts, so that with plenty of forewarning the board (say) can be given to expect that, on a move of (say) the yen below a specific rate, authorization would be sought to buy with a view to profiting from later yen strength. The quality of the total decision-making process is improved if the environment is nurtured carefully so that the responsibility of managing is not limited to essential fire-fighting operations once the forex markets have become uncontrollable.

Timing is particularly important for foreign currency options, where volatility of exchange rates is a prime determinant of the up-front cost. Options are cheapest when volatility is low. It is at such a time that boards and senior management are most somnolent, believing in some way that sleeping dogs are best left undisturbed. The treasurer should be aware of the opportunities provided by judicious timing of option purchases, where not only can options be bought cheaply in a quiet period, but also the downside rates protected might be reasonably acceptable for the corporate. The treasurer needs to agitate strongly for an active protection policy well ahead of the market, and to be allowed a reasonably generous budget for options, so that the non-availability of funding is not used as an excuse for delay when the moment comes to press the plunger.

It should be recognized that, say, the sale of next year's French francs is a decision required in principle, with the timing of the action decided by the treasurer. If the currency has already moved before permission for protective action is either sought or granted, the best that might be said of the result is that the timing was not optimal.

Authorities

There are two main models for the provision of authority by the corporate. The first is the hierarchical model, where no action is permitted until or unless it has been agreed by a higher body. At best this ensures that the situation is tightly controlled, that scandals like the infamous Volkswagen affair are not allowed to occur, and that the function carries on in as low key a manner as possible. At worst, it denies the relevant officers the ability to protect the company from the vagaries of the market until the market has already moved, or the board has already met (whichever is the later!), thereby crippling the possibilities of any kind of reasonable exchange cover achievement. The lack of positive results might then be used by the board to convince themselves of the wisdom of denying the delegation of authority to act beyond some very elementary deals. The second is the functional model, which is by definition much more attuned to the requirements of the treasury function to be professional and reactive. It is acceptable for the personal authority of the treasurer to be constrained by a committee or steering group, which might discuss on a daily or more occasional basis the desirability of given actions and the appraisal of past or current strategy. It would not be part of this approach to deny authority to proceed simply because the chairman was out of the country or two or three directors could not be gathered together.

The dangers of rigidity in attitude point the way towards a reactive, delegated and professional structure. Reward should match the risk taken, and there is a clear trade-off between security of employment and the success of the function.

It is well known that the propensity of committees—especially at senior level—to expend energy in detailed matters increases in proportion to their triviality. This is the 'bicycle-shed' syndrome, coined in ICI planning circles where GBP 500 million crackers apparently went through on the nod, while of course everyone could relate to GBP 500 on bicycle sheds, and everyone had a point of view. The same is true for foreign exchange, which touches most boards almost as an afterthought, and generally is passed without much discussion. The rubber-stamping nature of such important decisions is a powerful argument for removing them—along with signing authorities for cheques and money transfers—from the board, whose attention really should be devoted to important long-term and strategic considerations.

In an atmosphere of delegation and responsibility for decisions and reactions, it is important to establish a viable team to look after the positions along jointly understood lines. This is the 'under-the-bus' syndrome—namely, making provision for that dreadful unexpected contingency that would throw the company into disarray without adequate forethought. No forex position is proof against the requirement to make adjustments not only for ongoing changes like currency deliveries, but also for the level of cover and the limit to the amount of unrealized loss that can be carried comfortably. Such provision is a mixture of the right level and competence of supporting staff, and also a matter for systems of dealing and accounting. The parameters for action are matters that the company will have developed over time, and to some degree the absence of senior officers will deprive the company of their specific contribution to the debate. Nevertheless, if those officers have done their jobs properly, their presence should not be needed all the time since the structure and system will take care of most contingencies, over the short term at least.

CHAPTER 10

Reporting back

Internal reports

The treasury meeting

Information is the treasurer's stock-in-trade, and therefore he or she should not be shy of creating, sharing and using this valuable commodity.

Information is the essential prerequisite to good (informed) decision-making. Data form the mechanism that enables information to be created, or, to maintain the analogy, are the raw materials which, when worked on, produce the stock. The stock is then marketed and sold: and so it is with information—it does not just lie there, it is to be used.

Information is the friend of the treasurer who should therefore be adept at creating it by analysis of relevant data. Furthermore, the treasurer should have the confidence to promote information to bring about the correct and relevant decisions for the business's particular circumstances. Micro-computers are as essential to the modern treasurer as the hand-held Hewlett-Packard was to predecessors in the 1970s. They provide the mechanism for the rapid assimilation of data to produce meaningful information in a variety of formats: written text, spreadsheets and charts.

It is important for the company that the treasurer does not work in a vacuum—in particular he or she must have the confidence of the finance director and the board. Authorities are generally delegated within particular limits for various levels within the organization—budget authorities to sign for items of expenditure, but, more importantly, the authority to act for the company. It is right for the company to keep a watching brief on the results of the exercise of this delegated authority. By holding regular reviews, and by believing in the correctness of these meetings, the treasurer should play an active role in the design and production of the relevant reports.

Reports

Clearly the reports produced depend upon the constitution of the meeting, the number of participants, and the amount of time allowed. A monthly meeting may be regarded as a reasonable compromise between the day-to-day pressures of short-term management and the more strategic view taken, say, by quarterly board meetings or high-powered executive reviews. The reports will also be affected by what they are to achieve—for example, reports on delegated actions requiring a different style from reports designed to elicit decisions on actions themselves.

Exposure report

Since this provides the data on the exposures to be covered by forthcoming action in forex management, it is perhaps the most important of the reports produced. It should enable clear decisions to be taken on action for a range of exposures by currency, by type (e.g., transaction or liquidity) and by time period. This can be a list of the total exposures by currency by month, or can provide detail of the actual flows in each period (e.g., interest payments alongside suppliers' payments and receipts from sales and royalties), or can be a detailed picture of the flows expected for each individual currency.

Liquidity report

When a multicurrency programme of loans and deposits needs to be managed, the format of the liquidity report might need to take account of the foreign exchange effect of currency loans, alongside the normal interest effects. A highly organized and reactive stance can be developed, in which such reports provide perhaps a snapshot of the varied borrowing structure (which might change daily). The value of reports on a monthly basis is that they can enable the profile of the evolution of the cost of borrowing over time to be followed. The main elements in this report will be the underlying loans categorized by type and currency, including intra-group funding, plus counterbalancing deposits by currency, and overlaying this structure the forward deals to hedge the liquidity exposure where necessary. The costs are clearly the relevant interest charges, and the revenues are monies from deposits, plus or minus the exchange effect from hedging. The net of these costs (if the company is net borrowed) divided by the average borrowing provides the all-in cost of funding. Because of the exchange effect (which will also include the interest differential between currencies) and the use of true average figures in the denominator, the net cost will probably be quite different from the coarse figures resulting from examination of the formal accounts alone. Arguably this net all-in cost of borrowing is a much more realistic measure of the effectiveness of the treasury operation in liquidity management.

Exchange management report

Certain companies can be quite shy of producing reports that, periodically, could be construed as being critical of the operation of the treasury function. Such reticence is misplaced, since only if the operation is consistently unsuccessful need there be any embarrassment at disclosure. Therefore, should information be difficult to extract from the treasury then this might be because there are some skeletons in the cupboard—disclosure, investigation and even interrogation might be the order of the day in order to expose the problem (and people) and eradicate the difficulties. Should the treasurer be, say, the 'wrong wide' of the yen, then this should be highlighted clearly so that remedial action can be authorized if necessary. At the least this report should be able to illustrate variances from plan rates and also from a 'zero action' position, enabling a perspective view to be taken of the cover operation. Detail should include an individual currency perspective, with perhaps variances from last time, so that a picture of the whole year to date can be built up. Periodically it will be appropriate to summarize the evolution of the series of such reports, to provide a much more accurate appraisal of treasury performance than might be available for, say, salespeople or production engineers in their quite different environments.

Supportive charts

It is not unusual for a summary of the advice of pundits, together with supportive charts and tables, to be provided to a meeting where decisions are to be taken on specific action to cover forex exposures. Some of the formats that help highlight areas for decision-making are shown later. Also used periodically are charts showing the effects of interest differentials on the resultant exchange rates locked in by forward cover, the three- and six-month forward rates being, firstly, coterminous with the time period and, secondly, displaced to illustrate the effect of selling forward. These can be important for larger multinationals, where the magnitude of the flows is large enough for the interest differential to form a significant part of the decision-making process. Smaller companies might be only too glad to have some kind of procedure to enable themselves to feel confident they are on the right side of the currencies individually rather than try to second-guess future rates in comparison to the forward rate that can be locked in today.

Financing tables

While not necessarily connected closely with the decisions on foreign exchange, it is often appropriate for intra-group financing, including subsidiary balance sheet structures, to form part of the input to the treasury meeting. The content of these will clearly vary with the structure of the group, but a view of corporate liquidity together with intra-group loans and deposits may be appropriate. This may be supplemented by a schedule of central loans and deposits, split between the various categories, e.g., local authorities, trade bills, certificates of deposit (CDs), gilts and treasury instruments. If the currency figures are considerable, one report in local currency might be produced, and another converting all the values to the base currency of the group. In the latter, of course, the intra-group financing numbers will resolve to zero for the group as a whole. The purpose of these schedules is to keep a watchful eye not only on the total group liquidity numbers and ratios, but also on individual subsidiaries, where, for example, there might be the occasional requirement to inject more equity into a local selling company whose sales and working capital are expanding too rapidly for financial comfort.

Group cash flow statements

In order to put into context the decisions on comparative financing—including the views on foreign exchange—it is appropriate for a summary to be provided of the month's historic and expected cash flows of the group. A popular start point is the parent company, with the major cash flows of receivables and payables (which should reconcile with cash flows on the currency exposure schedules), tax and other periodic payments, and group requirements. Although theoretically correct, it is often not practicable to produce this schedule in the conventional historic fashion, by starting with profit, adding back depreciation, and taking differences between balance sheets (working capital and fixed) in order to build the forecast. Provided that the monthly cash flows are reasonably predictable, the treasurer might prefer to build estimates from the cash movements that are seen, rather than rely on the often wayward and undependable estimates and forecasts of peers in the finance area or operating divisions. Like the steeplejack, the treasurer will be responsible for his or her own supports.

Summary of banking relationships

This varies with the profile of the company, but the two main areas where banking relationships are capable of quantified comparison are, firstly, the level of lending to the corporate, together with the relevant rates (say margin over the eligible bill rate (EBR) for sterling acceptances), and, secondly, the number and value of foreign exchange deals transacted. It is probable that the latter will include several times as many banks as the former, since both the scope for competition is wider, and paradoxically there is more possibility for niche openings for less well-known names. The discipline of opening to scrutiny the breadth of relationships keeps some of the more important banks in the minds of directors and senior executives, and also acts as a useful restraint on the all-too-easy temptation of corporates to be modestly 'overbanked'.

Record of decisions

These often take the form of formal minutes, the objects of which are:

- to record faithfully the actions agreed

- to enable the relevant action to take place in a timely fashion
- to record something of the thinking process behind the decision for later reference, or to brief colleagues or senior staff who were not at the meeting.

For small sections it is important not to allow a tendency of over-bureaucratization to become established—if the format of the minutes, and the niceties of who said what begins to be the priority of the chairman of the cash management committee, then it is probable that the real business of the meeting is taking place elsewhere, and the meeting itself is simply for form's sake. Good decisions are snappy, are capable of précis, and should take up no more than say two sheets of A4 paper. Nor should the minutes attempt to list onerous actions that are incapable of achievement before the next meeting, or are of too general a nature to be accomplished without a special task force. The treasury meeting is about specific items and controls, not the creation of matter.

However, depending on the topics to be discussed and the potential for controversy or dispute, the meeting itself, particularly if it is a more occasional one (say monthly), might take fully half a day. It is important, particularly for senior management, to ensure they have devoted sufficient time to the meeting, since this may be the one structured opportunity to examine in detail the actions proposed and appraise the performance achieved in this extremely sensitive area. Morale of the often quite small treasury team is very sensitive to the moods and tremors emanating from the Board, and demotivation is much easier to engender than to assuage.

Additional items

The treasury meeting is the ideal venue to promote ideas in senior financial circles on new concepts or the revision of old. For example, leasing has ebbed and flowed in its usefulness for corporates, and electronic banking might yet have its day. Exploratory papers on financing or new instruments can be a fruitful mechanism for both clearing the mind of the writer and enabling the potential usefulness of the concept to be debated and appraised in a reasonably low profile way, prior to perhaps a more formal presentation to the executive committee.

Actions

Monthly meetings, whether of the cash management committee, the treasury meeting, the continental exposures meeting, or the executive of the board (or even the board itself) are not good times to authorize actions for tactical (as opposed to strategic) purposes. Should these meetings (often, with due respect, including those perhaps more senior but also less informed about the detail and the immediate motivations of the dealing and treasury areas) be referred to as the sole arbiters of the necessity to take action, then it is highly likely that the timing of the action will follow the meeting very closely. As such, the actions may in all probability be mistimed, if not ill-conceived. Optimization—always an elusive goal—will be impossible even to aim at. Demoralization might easily set in, with debilitating effects on the self-esteem of the whole dealing team.

Therefore, while the timing of the executive meeting, for example, might coincide with the best opportunity to, say, cover the dollar, the proposal, should it be made, is best couched in phraseology enabling a decision in principle to be taken by the relevant committee, but delegating the timing to the treasurer and his or her staff. Then short-term factors can also be taken into account in the decision-making process, enabling at least the theoretical possibility of propitious timing to complement a correct decision in principle.

Training

Since it is a forum for the development of ideas and policies for the management of the financing and risk management of the corporate, the treasury meeting, in whatever guise, is the ideal training ground for the young and aspiring financial executives of the future. They can perceive the drift of debate and sense the driving forces and motivations for decisions. They can see senior finance personnel in action, and begin to cut their teeth on the discussions and corporate decision-making processes. Their contribution may not actually change opinions, but they can build their own influence and self-confidence. Often it is in the interests of the senior management to encourage the participation of young blood both to keep the atmosphere alive and vital, and, on a more mundane level, to help in the preparation of the relevant papers and collation of the minutes.

External reports

Foreign exchange and the company results

The impact of treasury management on the results of the company is most apparent in the efficiency of the foreign exchange cover policy of the treasury function. Given a significant foreign exchange receivable exposure of the company, the treasury can in times of currency strength enable benefits to the company to accrue from a light or near zero cover policy. Conversely, provided that the company has a reasonably reactive cover policy, it can provide significant protection for the company from the adverse effects of currency weakness. If the currency exposure is a net payable position, the contrary scenario will apply.

While the cover policy adopted by the company is a matter of strategy and tactics, seen in isolation, the impact of foreign exchange management on the results can be considerable. The profit and loss effect of treasury actions is pound for pound equivalent to the action taken, unlike sales of product, the profit effect of which is diluted by production and other costs. Therefore, the treasury function has an impact on profits out of all proportion to the personnel involved and resources committed.

The composite examples (Tables 10.1 and 10.2) show the identical result for the company from different treasury action, but depending on the exchange rates, entirely different mixes of apportionment of gain and loss.

How is the company to respond to this? Does it celebrate the successes and lament the failures of its treasury team? Does it look with embarrassment on the situation, and try to minimize the perceived impact of the treasury management? Does it simply ignore the impact except when the results are poor and then send for the axeman?

Most companies adopt a mixture of these reactions, preferring to think of themselves as in the widget business instead of banking, even though the turnover of the latter (possibly unexpectedly) might be much larger than the former. Accounting standards do not recognize foreign exchange dealing turnover and, as will be shown later, SSAP20 is open to interpretation as far as the reporting of profits is concerned. Therefore, although the effects of treasury—either directly through actions taken or indirectly through actions

Table 10.1 Treasury action: composite example (i)

Economic exposure:	Currency 300K
Current exchange rate:	Currency 1.5/pound
Exchange rate at time of invoicing:	1.8
Product costs:	Stg 180K
Exchange rate on settlement:	2.0

Calculations

Trading loss:	300/2−180	=(30)	Currency gain:	300/1.5−300/2=50
avoidable:	300/1.8−180	=(13)	accounting hedge	17
hedged:	300/1.8−300/2	=(17)	treasury gain:	33

	Trading loss	*Currency gain*		
Profit	(13)	33	=	20
Hedge	(17)	17	=	0
Total	(30)	50	=	20

Table 10.2 Treasury action: composite example (ii)

Economic exposure:	Currency 300K
Current exchange rate:	Currency 1.5/pound
Exchange rate at time of invoicing:	1.4
Product costs:	Stg 180K
Exchange rate on settlement:	1.3

Calculations

Trading profit:	300/1.3−180	=51	Currency loss:	300/1.5−300/1.3=31
underlying:	300/1.14−180	=34	accounting : hedge	17
hedgeable:	300/1.14−300/1.13	=17	treasury: loss	14

	Trading gain	*Currency loss*		
Profit	34	(14)	=	20
Hedge	17	(17)	=	0
Total	51	(31)	=	20

avoided—might be very significant year on year, the real effect is frequently disguised.

It is questionable whether this policy or approach is wise. It is thought sometimes that if the treasury function's effect on the results is ignored, then their effect might be credited by the market with a greater reward than a price/earnings (p/e) ratio of unity. By disguising the effects of treasury the hope might be that the underlying p/e ratio of the business will be the only profit effect recognized by the market, with consequential benefits to the share price. However, if the result is to dispense with smoothing—which is the duty and, frequently, effect of an active treasury department in the eyes of analysts—then they may well feel that the business is more vulnerable to the swings in fortune consequent on poor or zero exchange management. In this case they may well exclude the effects of treasury from their calculations, and consider the stock more cyclical or vulnerable to the vagaries of movements in the exchange markets than is really the case. The correct p/e ratio of the company might well be modified from the first figure conceived, to the detriment of the company, cancelling the advantage that the board might have tried to engineer by its selective presentation of the results of the company.

Therefore, it is considered just and appropriate that companies give a fair presentation of the effect of treasury management on the achieved results (inconvenient though this may appear from time to time, either to the board or to the treasury department). The former should consider themselves as the custodians of the facts of the running of the company for the benefit of shareholders. That function includes the full management of the company, both the underlying business and supplementary activities such as treasury management, which can have such an impact, both beneficial and adverse. The latter should consider themselves the custodians of the main area of volatility in declared results of the company, and therefore subject to more than the normal level of scrutiny for the efficacy and direction of their activity.

An aspect of the declaration of results that should not be overlooked is forecasts of the out-turn for the current year or next accounting period. Often, discounting the experience of the period just passed, brokers and analysts concentrate their attention on whatever prognostications they can pick up for the subsequent period. It behoves boards to be extremely careful about the inflection of their comments, and not just the precise truth of the specific words that are uttered. Taking refuge in the precept that, since they have told no lie, it is for others to divine the truth, some boards retreat into phrases that are not necessarily untrue but provide a flavour of performance that is taken as the responsibility of analysts and commentators to deduce. Then, practising the policy of not correcting errors of interpretation of analysts for fear of favouritism or of prejudicing an even-handed approach to City contacts, they observe the market capturing a train of thought that they started through the flavour of their comments rather than the precision of what they had said. And the market might be completely misled.

These games can be extremely distressful to the innocent treasurer, who might have conscientiously done his or her duty in a timely fashion opposite the latest currency crisis, but who is by implication, criticized roundly for a risky policy of only short-term cover, or for 'mistakes' that are really interpretations of sparse facts and future rumours, with little relation to the real picture. The longer term external effect on the company might again be much more harmful than the short-term gains are beneficial, since at some point the utterances of the directors become devalued. When statements cannot be accepted at their face value, but have to be interpreted to discover the real meaning and to winnow away either red herrings or disinformation, then they lose their force as market-directing tools, becoming to some degree counter-productive.

A good statement, on the other hand, contains hard fact about what has been achieved in the past, including the acknowledgement of mistakes or shortfalls where these are significant, and provides a reliable interpretation of where the business is going in the future. Detail *per se* is not as important as the correct flavour of the strengths and weaknesses of the business, but where detail—particularly of the effect of exchange—can help to underpin the story, it should not be eschewed. Comment on the political or economic outlook is not necessarily out of place, but should be strictly rationed and confined to the direct effect of, say, EMS entry on the company's business. It should be noted that it is not the business of the company to score party-political points: the business should be above the smoke of battle of political controversy.

There is some sensitivity about the correct degree of detail to provide for the declaration of results—notably on the question of whether the provision of certain information might provide a precedent effectively tying the hands of directors for the future. Clearly the relevance of given facts will vary over time, depending on external circumstances, but there is no hard evidence that the provision of certain illustrative facts one year leads inexorably to the requirement for the publication of comparable information each accounting period thereafter. In one sense, it should be possible for analytical supportive information to be provided in a standardized format before each announcement of results to the relevant members of the board and to senior executives who might have the task of communicating to the press and to brokers. In this case there need to be no misgivings about the potential for an ever-increasing volume of data to be requested by commentators, since the relevant part of the story will vary over time as the business evolves and is subject to different pressures, and the commentary package caters for the standard information required.

These fears are sometimes voiced where the supportive information is not all that might be desired, where accounting systems are not too robust, and where internal conventions are apt to change abruptly as staff move on or as internal whims alter. The fears are therefore evidence of certain weaknesses, and are clearly well founded to the extent that the weaknesses are real. The answer to this conundrum is not the restriction of information provided (out of fear that the correct information might elicit questions that might be inconvenient either because the answers are difficult to establish or because systems are not efficient enough to provide a dependable response), but the correction of the internal weaknesses which make the provision of supportive detail such an embarrassment and potential hazard.

The optimal situation is where the announcement of results is seen as a positive process, giving the company the occasion to provide an update to shareholders and potential investors in order to promote the company and increase awareness. The announcement is in this case an opportunity rather than a problem. It enables the board to project themselves and further the aims of the company. Shareholders are welcomed into the sharing of information; analysts are encouraged to analyse and commentators to comment. In this situation, a success by the treasury department in foreign exchange management is seen as a company success in which all can share. It is not at the expense of anyone (except, perhaps, the external market in the long run, if the foreign exchanges are seen as a zero-sum game ultimately), and certainly not the underlying business. The directors should be equally as happy for gains on exchange as on the underlying business excluding exchange. A good treasury section is evidence of a good company, and if decent results are attributable to certain individuals, then they are also indirectly a compliment to the directors who put them there and who had a hand in some of the more significant decisions.

As an example, Table 10.3 illustrates the comparative effect of both the actions of treasury on the results of a company with a considerable exchange exposure during a period of four years exchange variability, and the effect on the share price of the attitude adopted by senior management to the net profits resulting from treasury management. The position shown is for three years of currency strength and one of considerable weakness. The underlying position for the company is a constant growth in sales and a constant profit margin. The main annual variability on the results is exchange, and the different approaches to the management and declaration of this imply quite large differences in the share price over this period—assuming for the purposes of this example that the actual results (whether perceived and therefore anticipated, or achieved and therefore historic) are the sole determinant of the share price, given an accepted price/earnings multiple for the company.

A complete hedge would remove any variability of the results and hence share price from the picture, and this is taken as the base case (Case (ii) in Table 10.3). It is acknowledged that in practice the date of creation of the hedge is critical in establishing its efficacy, but for the sake of illustration it is assumed that the perfect hedge—that elusive goal—is achievable. With the removal of the variability of profits due to exchange, the share price is affected only by the growth of the business, and in the example grows in a straight line.

The other extreme from the perfectly hedged position is the zero hedge. This is shown in Table 10.3 as Case (i), where the profits fluctuate widely in an uncontrolled way. The board would be at pains to explain the injustice of market signals being provided from declared profits in entire contrast to the steady progress of the underlying business. This situation cries out for good exchange management, to even the distortions to reported results.

Case (iii) shows a partially hedged situation, where the windfall benefits in Years 1, 2 and 4 from foreign exchange are halved, but where the deficit in Year 3 is also halved. At least the company can be said to be trying to manage the adverse effects of the volatility of exchange on the reported results, and the standard deviation is more than halved from 0.7 to 0.3. Theoretically, a more stable share price should result in a more favourable treatment from analysts, and to a better price/earnings multiple in the long run.

Case (iv) is an optimal situation, where the object of exchange management has not been, crudely, to even the gain and losses from exchange over time, but actually to make decisions whether or not to cover specific exposures. Though in one sense what is illustrated is an optimum that is as unachievable as the perfect hedge, it is feasible that good treasury action could achieve better results than the zero cover situation where the home currency is losing value generally, since there could be some currencies even then against which it is gaining value, and receipts from which could profitably be hedged. However, for the purposes of illustration, this case is treated as optimal, where no cover is appropriate in three years, and full cover in the third. This case provides not only smoothing over time, but a net benefit to profits over the four years considered, and furthermore a reduction in the standard deviation of profits to half the fully covered case. Therefore the value of the profits resulting from exchange management in this example—even though they arose in different years for different reasons (in three years from 'windfall' benefits from forex through zero cover, and in Year 3 from positive treasury action in fully hedging)—is every bit as important as the profit from the underlying business.

The way these actions are portrayed to the market in the company's announcements will have a significant effect on the perception of the company in the marketplace. This statement seems to be a truism, but it is not. Consider the zero hedge. If the directors were to 'pocket' the windfall benefits in the first two years without acknowledging the effect of the 'hands-off' exchange management policy, then the market could easily believe that the company's fortunes were in real decline. Their suspicions would seem well-founded in Year 3 when the company is knocked sideways by an uncovered exchange position. A reasonable reaction would be to

Table 10.3 Effect of actions by treasury in a company with exchange exposure

Share price volatility and the price/earnings multiple (part I)

Example	Year 1	Year 2	Year 3	Year 4	
Sales—Const XR	100	110	120	130	
FX exposures	80	88	96	104	
Profit/sales (%)	20	20	20	20	
Exchange rate (%)	-10	-5	15	-3	
(i) No cover					
(ii) 100% cover					
(iii) Smoothing					
(iv) Optimal					*Cum total*
Profits	20.0	22.0	24.0	26.0	92.0
(i) Exchange Mvt	8.0	4.4	-14.4	3.1	1.1
(ii) 100% cover	-8.0	-4.4	14.4	-3.1	-1.1
(iii) Smoothing	-4.0	-2.2	7.2	-1.6	-0.6
(iv) Optimal	0	0	14.4	0	14.4
Net profits					
(i) No cover	28.0	26.4	9.6	29.1	93.1
(ii) 100% cover	20.0	22.0	24.0	26.0	92.0
(iii) Smoothing	24.0	24.2	16.8	27.6	92.6
(iv) Optimal	28.0	26.4	24.0	29.1	107.1

Calculations		Year 1	Year 2	Year 3	Year 4		
	Deviations as percentages (/100)					*Mean profit*	
(i) No cover		0.20	0.13	−0.59	0.25	23.28	
(ii) 100% cover		−0.13	−0.04	0.04	0.13	23.00	
(iii) Smoothing		0.04	0.05	−0.27	0.19	23.14	
(iv) Optimal		0.04	0.02	−0.11	0.08	26.88	
	Deviations squared					*Sum*	*SD*
(i) No cover		0.04	0.02	0.35	0.06	0.47	0.684
(ii) 100% cover		0.02	0.00	0.00	0.02	0.04	0.194
(iii) Smoothing		0.00	0.00	0.08	0.04	0.12	0.339
(iv) Optimal		0.00	0.00	0.01	0.01	0.02	0.143
Using p/e 15× for standard	(historic) *For 100m issued shares*						
Case (ii)	EPS	0.2	0.22	0.24	0.26		
Share price	(ii)	300	330	360	390		
Exchange effect deviations using p/e 1							
(i) No cover	EPS	0.08	0.04	−0.14	0.03		
Share price	(i)	308	334	346	393		
(iii) Smoothing	EPS	−0.04	−0.02	0.07	−0.02		
Share price	(ii)	296	328	367	388		
(iv) Optimal	EPS	0.00	0.00	0.14	0.00		
Share price	(iv)	300	330	374	390		
Share price at full p/e 15×	(historic)						
(i) No cover		420	396	144	437		
(ii) 100% cover		300	330	360	390		
(iii) Smoothing		360	363	252	413		
(iv) Optimal		420	396	360	437		

change the policy for Year 4 to full cover, and in the example shown in Table 10.3 this would result in significant suboptimization.

However, if the company explained carefully to the market the full effect of exchange on the results, then there is every possibility that even though the 'excess' in the first years might be downgraded by a lower p/e ratio being ascribed to it, the deficit in Year 3 might also be less badly viewed. Should the company accept that some management of exchange was appropriate, then the smoothing pattern of Case (iii) might result, which requires quite sensitive explanation to avoid the charge of treasury incompetence in every year, resulting from the treasury dealing losses in the good years, and the still poor performance against the absolute standard of full cover in the bad year. A misconstruction of the objects of treasury management in senior circles can be demoralizing for the section and debilitating for the individuals concerned, as well as being counterproductive for the company, since, as illustrated, this is a much better situation than the extreme of no management.

Consider finally the possible if not probable outcome of a net benefit from treasury activity over time by judicious decisions to reduce or eliminate cover in years of currency strength, and to increase cover in periods of currency weakness. Should the company adopt the policy of not explaining adequately the effects of exchange compared to the underlying business, then the significant job of protection in Year 3 could be missed entirely by analysts, since they will not have been informed in earlier years of the beneficial windfall effects, and they may not be expecting bad news at least of that degree. The vulnerability of the company to exchange will have been understated, but since that will have coincided with its virtual elimination (on the understanding that this good performance can be repeated in the future), the practical results of this might not be significant. The company might consider it appropriate to regard all the profits made by treasury as really an integral part of the business, and not an unexpected benefit. As such, it might be to the company's benefit to regard the figure gained as 'bankable' and as having no significance as an influence on the company's p/e ratio.

In this rare but theoretically possible situation, one is stating that to some degree the company is correct in arguing that there is a long-term benefit from the activity undertaken by its corporate treasury. Analysts might also have a point in registering the fragility of the 'excess' profits earned above the result of simple hedging. The latter might be downgraded in terms of its durability and repeatability, and therefore give rise to a somewhat lower p/e ratio than a different business. However, such a p/e ratio would also be a reflection of the performance of the business as a whole, so if the effect of treasury action has been to smooth performance and to improve the figures over time, then this effect should be acknowledged in the company's total rating. Therefore, there might be some trade-off in net p/e ratio applicable to the company. The important thing is clearly to provide the relevant data to the analysts so that they can make the relevant deductions.

The vulnerability of the company in this optimal situation is that the treasury management which brought about this happy outcome might be tempted away to greener pastures, particularly if the evidence is that the board (as opposed to the market) do not realize how fragile is the treasury benefit—the difference between a good and bad decision being merely a word on the telephone coupled with the right person being there at the right time. It is for the board to convince themselves of the worth of the treasury activity, which in this case will have improved the total profits of the company as well as providing for smoothing of the effects of exchange and the certainty of given rates. The danger for the company is that a nicely controlled situation could become unstable again because they had become convinced by the success of their treasury operation that their vulnerability was less than was really the case, and then only realize their error when control of foreign exchange risk is lost during a subsequent administration.

CHAPTER 11

Foreign exchange and the role of the treasurer

As the world becomes more interdependent, with trade becoming more important, the complexities of the City and foreign exchange are raised in profile for the ordinary company. Gone are the days when invoicing in sterling to the 'sterling bloc' countries is a reasonable substitute for true international trade. The largest markets today are Europe, North America and Japan, and along with the success of industry in challenging these markets comes the responsibility of managing the resultant foreign currency denominated cash flows.

It is no accident that today the 'bonanza' of the North Sea oil has been replaced for the UK by the pre-eminence of the City of London. We now have the most cosmopolitan and efficient money and foreign exchange market in the world, for many of us only at a distance of a 10p telephone call. There is no excuse for ignoring, to the detriment of our companies, the enormous potential in advice, resources and efficiency of this huge 'invisible' benefit to the UK economy.

Just as the trading and capital flows between the OECD nations in particular have become larger and more complex, so the fluctuations in relative currency values have become more pronounced. Therefore, there is an added reason why all companies with a foreign exchange interface should make at least the minimum investment in the basics of a treasury system—possibly specifically manned by a treasurer rather than the more traditional financial controller or chief accountant, since both the breadth and specialism of the role have grown to create a separate discipline.

Looking at foreign exchange specifically, it is the function of the treasurer to ensure that the underlying cash flows of the company are protected. For example, a contract for delivery in six months' time with a net margin of, say, 10 per cent could become unprofitable if sterling were to rise by 10 per cent over that period. In mid-1987 the dollar-value of the pound was $1.58 and by the end of the year it had risen to over $1.80—a relative appreciation of sterling of 15 per cent. Unless dollar receivables were protected, or covered forward by either forward contracts or options, money would be lost.

What factors impel a company to take action to cover its currency receivables or payables? After all, just as sterling gained between 1985 and 1987 against the dollar, it lost value against the deutschemark and the yen. If the currencies were simply left to be converted on receipt, would a company not be just as well off if it interfered with the workings of the market and sold receivables in advance of their receipt? The answer has two parts: firstly, all companies have different exposure profiles and vulnerabilities; and, secondly, views can be taken on the appropriateness of a given stance opposite currencies and the timing of cover actions.

Direction of currency

There are many pundits, advisers and economists who produce documents—some by subscription—on the direction of currencies. It is one of the purposes of the treasurer to sift through this plethora of often contradictory information to derive views on the best course of action for the company. Then, not least, the treasurer has to secure approval and authority to put any recommendations into practice.

Let us examine some of the types of information produced.

Economic reports

These are mainly the preserve of banks who often have in-house economists whose role is to examine the international tea-leaves and make pronouncements—often in the guise of forecasts. The thinking underlying the numbers is often more important than the numbers themselves, though it can be interesting to compare economists' views with those of their colleagues or with the views those same economists expressed in a previous period. The overall scene painted on this canvas is more important for the long-term perspective than for the short-term decisions, such as which currency should be covered and, equally importantly, when it should be covered.

Trend analysis

Somewhat of a black art, but much loved by dealers, is so-called 'technical analysis' by which certain chart points can be identified for action. At the most extreme this resolves into intra-day activity prompted by the relative movements of exchange rates between certain 'support' levels on the downside and 'resistance' levels on the upside. More long term are daily, weekly and monthly 'point and figure' charts which at least enable the trend of currencies to be seen. Since near-perfect markets resolve in the ultimate to crowd behaviour it is interesting to perceive what is motivating the market, and it can be profitable to anticipate market moves and be positioned to take advantage of them. This game is not for the faint-hearted, and with the best will in the world it is no excuse, when all goes wrong, to claim that it was the guru's fault!

Moving averages

Though not every business can justify the expense of live rates via Reuters or Telerate, the *Financial Times* costs only pence, and graph paper is not expensive. A few moments' thought on a routine basis will enable a reasonable view of the direction of the market to be obtained. One can fairly easily appreciate the effect on one's business of daily movements, and the latest rates are always available from banks or services such as Prestel. As important as the particular rate applicable is the pace of change. This can be established by examination of moving average rates—for example, 10 day, 30 day, 50 day, etc. In this respect the 90-day moving average is a good indicator of the underlying direction of currency, and does not change direction very readily.

Momentum charts

These track the complexities of the variabilities of different moving averages, and purport to show when a currency is 'overbought' or 'oversold'. The assumption is that there will be a natural reaction in the market to correct the position, and therefore the right action is to react countercyclically by selling in an overbought situation and buying in an oversold market. Unfortunately markets may be more or less perfect, but they defy logic—except in retrospect. Therefore, while there is clearly some merit in using such tools to optimize the timing of action which, for a business or 'fx' reason, is already contemplated, momentum charts are to be used with care, and are a tool of more use to the trader than to the hedger.

Recording systems

A quick survey of the methods of divining the direction and timing of actions might convince the layman that the author is a chartist. Most 'ists', 'ites' and 'isms' are terms of disapprobation used by their opponents. Rather than worry about the connotations of the methodology, perhaps it is more profitable to look at the results, though of course these will only be apparent after the event.

For a corporate treasury foreign exchange operation there needs to be a carefully established policy, methodology and system. This provides a framework for action—a coherent set of parameters allowing the operation to be appraised over time, and the practical means of putting the agreed actions into practice.

Given, firstly, that the company has perceived the needs to manage its foreign exchange exposure and, secondly, that the treasurer is aware of the motivations for action, how can this be done practically? There are mysterious computer packages on the market—many from banks, and some from software houses. Should the treasurer invest in one of these?

Clearly the answer to the practical questions of the efficiency of the in-house operations depends on the sophistication of the company and the complexity of its forex business. A small company with, say, a few foreign exchange deals each week should be able to manage quite happily with either a manual or 'spreadsheet' system—logging the deals made, rates and values locked in and the gains or losses on the activity—that will be needed for appraisal purposes. If the volume of deals rises to, say, two or more per day (note volume, not value, since the same amount of work is needed in-house irrespective of the size of the deal), it will then be worth while to see what is available in the marketplace either to underpin or at best replace existing systems.

Conferences on electronic systems are held fairly regularly—indeed the Association of Corporate Treasurers holds one annually—and publicity is available from promoters. This is an area that is evolving rapidly, and opportunities are arising for the marketing of corporate-developed systems, thus obviating the need for an extensive internal commitment and duplication of effort. It is probable that the market will eventually consolidate into three levels:

1 in-house banks, with mainframe or local area network minicomputers, whose software is comparable with—and possibly developed by—banks;
2 medium-sized corporates having small staffs but more or less complex requirements, with stand-alone or local area networked micros, whose software has been developed either in-house by another corporate with similar generic problems, or by a software house who might then have the marketing rights;
3 small corporates, with smaller staffs (even one-man-banks) and reasonably simple requirements who only need a decent micro-computer and the ability to use and develop relevant models—where inspired hacking is more the order of the day.

At present the market is naturally most developed at the top end. There are some packages available at a price in category 2, but extensive customization can be a problem. Category 3 is virtually ignored at present. Consultancy is expensive for a small company, and often the answers would be available from the experience of others, if only they can be contacted.

The role of the treasurer in foreign exchange is therefore fairly plain: to manage the exposures, to follow the markets, and to control his or her actions. Facilities have developed rapidly over the last few years and the City is more dynamic than ever before. The corporate world is also more aware. The average treasurer now has more computing power than the largest company had less than a generation ago. Provided that the corporate will is there, the benefits from a constructive approach to foreign exchange can far outweigh the relatively modest resources needed to tackle the problems meaningfully.

The message is therefore twofold: to the treasurer—do not be daunted by the complexities of computerization from getting your system under control: to the finance director—do not be daunted by the complexities of the treasury operation from authorizing the computerization of treasury.

Some treasurers regard it as their function simply to administer the cash flows of the company, and, with regard to foreign exchange, simply to act as an intermediary between product divisions who are responsible for the company's bottom line and the market. This puts the treasurer in a neutral position regarding the quality of the decisions—at most, together with the normal facilitating function, the treasurer would have an advisory role. It must be said that such a truncated view of the job undervalues the role that the treasurer could and should play in both tactical and strategic currency management, and at least limits the scope for computer-minded decision-making and the need for systems. Nevertheless, it is a position adopted conscientiously by some treasurers and their directors and therefore merits comment.

Firstly, in such a position the measure of the value or cost of the treasury function is not in terms of staff or budgeted overhead cost, but in the benefit or cost of decisions made or forgone in the management of exposures for the business. This is a major lacuna that is often not recognized by the myopic.

Secondly, and related, is the confusion given to the underlying business by not separating the controllable variables of cost and revenue from such exogenous factors as exchange movements. Real management decisions in the business could be obscured.

Finally, and unrecognized by the antediluvian, is the potential for the treasury areas to be a bone fide centre of excellence in the company—with accountability for profit contribution. To be effective this needs the best information and the slickest system that can be introduced. As more companies move in this direction, the demand for good systems will increase inexorably.

Charting country groupings

While traders use charts to ascertain short-term trends, longer term players, among whom can be numbered corporate treasurers, are interested in fundamental moves. Attention is often conveniently concentrated on the US dollar, partly out of consideration of volume and liquidity and partly out of convention, though many treasurers maintain records relating to their own domestic currency. Therefore, the illustrations which follow are related to the US dollar, though similar conclusions to those drawn below could be drawn from comparative data drawn up on other bases.

In the ten years of the 1980s, when the floating regime established in the early 1970s became properly accepted internationally, there has been a most significant change in international parities. The industrialized countries of the post-war world, including western Europe, Japan and some of the NICs of the Far East, have improved their status, notably in the years after spring 1985, when the dollar reached its peak of overvaluation. Other weaker currencies have not profited from the opening up of international markets in the same way, and have lost ground internationally. For example, the yen appreciated against the dollar by 60 per cent, while the South African rand depreciated by almost 70 per cent; the yen is therefore five times more expensive in rand terms than ten years ago.

Some currencies have been managed close to their main trading partners, in order to avoid undue speculation, and in some cases to provide protection for fragile financial structures or relatively favourable exchange rates for export markets. Examples of these are the Saudi riyal (Figure 11.1) and the Hong Kong dollar. It is interesting that while militarily the Saudis did not acknowledge their dependence on the USA until the Gulf crisis of 1990, they had pegged the riyal to the dollar (for which it had been a proxy for many years) as early as 1986. Hong Kong meantime had suffered its normal periodic crisis of confidence in the early 1980s, when the currency depreciated erratically, and chose to peg itself to the UD dollar in 1983 (Figure 11.3). The result of this has been not only to virtually eliminate speculation in the HK dollar *per se*, but also, more importantly, to peg the rate applicable to Chinese re-exports very advantageously, and therefore to build a considerable Chinese trade deficit for the US.

The nascent unification of Europe is illustrated by the EMS chart (Figure 11.2), which illustrates the closeness of the exchange rate movements. The strongest currencies are the deutschemark and Dutch florin, which have been managed virtually as one, followed by the Danish krone, Belgian franc, French franc and finally the Italian lira. The fact that the lira was managed for most of the period within a 6 per cent band rather than a 2.25 per cent band

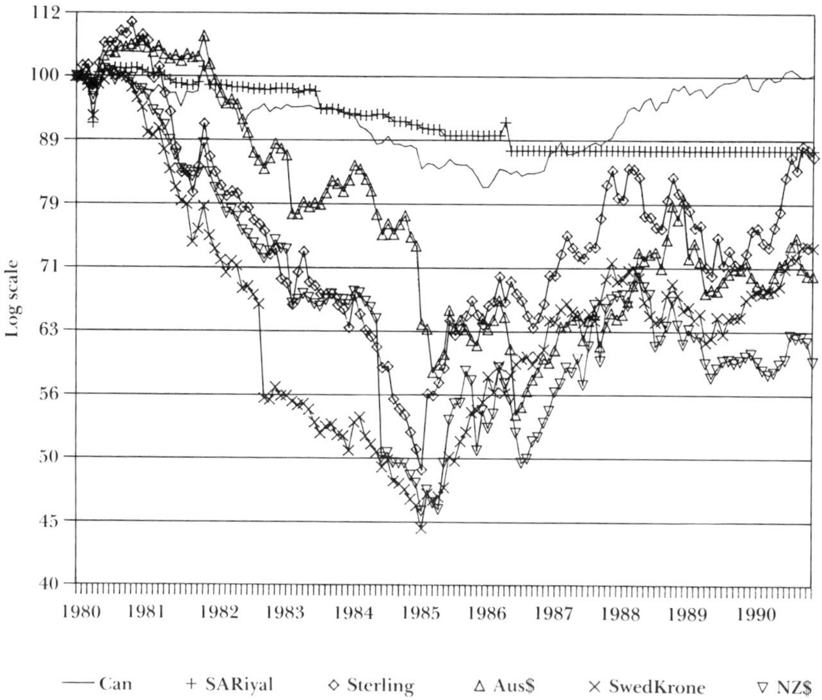

Figure 11.1 US dollar-related currencies

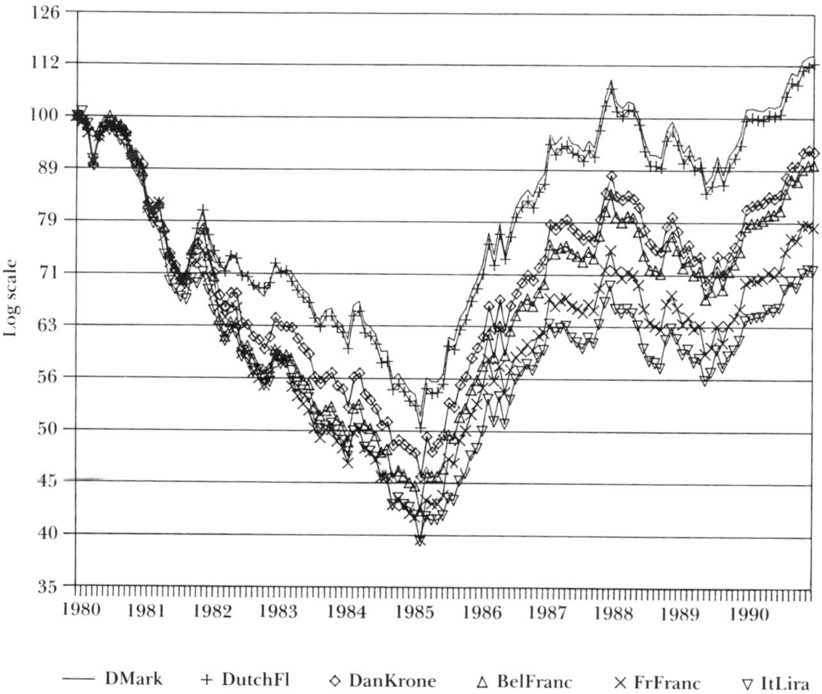

Figure 11.2 Main EMS v US dollar

does not seem with hindsight to have significantly adversely affected the ability of the currency to keep pace with its stronger brethren. Total divergence over the decade charted is only about one-third, and the average annual divergence is well under 5 per cent, which compares most favourably with, for example, the Japanese yen, which has very much led a life of its own (Figure 11.4).

Several currencies trade by reference to their main trading partners, particular examples being sterling and the Swedish krone. For convenience and for illustration, these have been grouped with certain more explicitly dollar-related currencies (see Figure 11.1). Reference has already been made to the Saudi riyal, and the Canadian dollar clearly shares more than simply a common frontier with the US. Given the generally higher interest rates applicable to the Canadian dollar (one of the 'queen currencies' beloved of Japanese swaps specialists), the comparative resilience of the Canadian dollar in the last four to five years of the decade provided good all-in returns on deposits. The other currencies, while managed as separate entities, do show remarkable similarities over time, even allowing for the wide variations in particular years. For example, the Australian dollar was fairly resilient in the early 1980s against the even more powerful greenback, and the Swedish krone (which is managed domestically opposite a currency basket, the largest element of which is the US dollar) was particularly weak. However, by the end of the 1980s, partly as a result of the higher trade flows with the rest of Europe, the krone had recovered, while the Australian dollar had problems of its own in 1986 from which it is only slowly recovering. The New Zealand dollar, not unsurprisingly, matches the Australian dollar quite closely, though at a lower level.

Sterling is a mystery and an enigma, which kept it out of exchange rate mechanism of the EMS during the decade, and therefore off the EMS chart for illustration purposes. Following its petrocurrency status and the high interest rate policy of the government, sterling reached the dizzy heights of US$ 2.4 in August 1980. Against such a measure, any performance during the following years would be bound to appear lack-lustre. Accordingly, as the oil price and interest rates subsided, sterling led the field in depreciating against the dollar in the run up to 1985, when both national and international concerns at the deficits and disparities led to a sharp correction. In the later 1980s, supported by a high

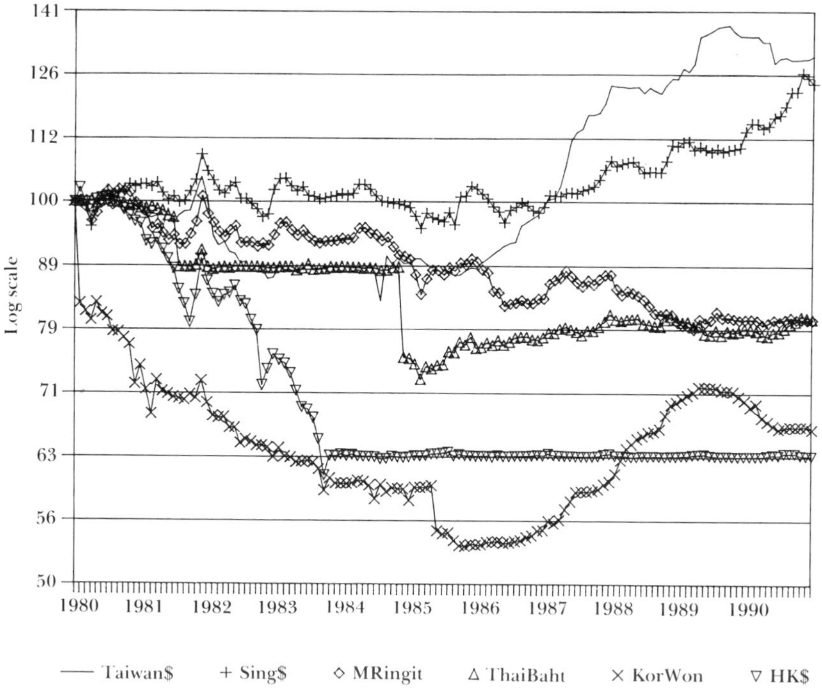

Figure 11.3 Asian 'Tigers' v US dollars

interest rate policy, sterling has been both more resilient and has periodically shadowed closely the EMS (or the deutschemark as proxy), particularly given the UK's increasing trade with Europe in the run-up to 1992. This trend has been emphasized by the Middle East crisis of 1990 which emphasized the particular natural advantages of the UK in being self-sufficient in oil.

Much has been written about the newly industrialized countries (NICs) of Asia, generically also known as the Asian Dragons or Tigers (Figure 11.3). These include Taiwan, Korea, Singapore and Hong Kong. Recently the emerging Asian countries of Thailand and Malaysia (though not the Philippines) have been added to their number. The performance of these currencies has been charted, which illustrates a curious phenomenon. There is a paradox between the desire of the authorities to devalue and the markets generally to revalue the currencies. The trade factors commented on above in relation to Hong Kong are probably a motive for the desire of governments to see a relatively devalued local currency, thus imparting to these currencies similar benevolent conditions which helped Japan so much in its comparable situation a generation earlier. Whether from international demand or monetary pressure, three of the tigers in particular have seen significant revaluation since 1985, notable the Taiwan dollar and the Korean won (whose currency movements in the late 1980s were closely correlated), and the Singapore dollar. Devaluations in the early 1980s seem to have helped both the Taiwanese and Korean economies to develop rapidly, which has spilled over into the valuation of the currency, whereas Singapore managed both industrialization and currency appreciation without ostensibly artificial currency movements. A devaluation of almost 20 per cent in the Thai baht in 1984 has helped create benevolent conditions for the boom in real estate and manufacturing at the end of the 1980s, which has kept the currency in steady demand. However, Malaysia has not yet reached the lift-off stage, and steady currency depreciation is the result.

A variety of currencies are charted agains the yen, to illustrate comparisons with the best performing currency of the decade. The yen broadly kept pace with the US dollar during the latter's appreciation phase in the early Reagan years, a performance matched only by Singapore. However, as the dollar has declined, this linkage was broken by the Plaza accord and other international agreements, so that after virtually doubling in value, the yen was trading at about 60 per cent over the rate applicable at the start of the decade (Figure 11.4). The Swiss franc behaves like a supercharged deutschemark, retaining its close link to the German currency resulting from the predominant trade flows, but also benefiting from the independence, safe haven status and prestige traditionally associated with the Swiss. The Norwegian krone is more like an anaemic sterling, with petro-driven surges dampened by economic problems. Spain illustrates some of the characteristics of Korea, with a European flavour. It has democratized and devalued, and has been industrializing rapidly while retaining a distinct cultural identity. This has given a platform for a significant improvement in the fortunes of the currency, which has been underpinned by entry into the EMS, albeit with wider trading bands (*à-là-Italia*) and supported by high interest rates. Finally the Philippine peso, which as mentioned does not qualify for discus-

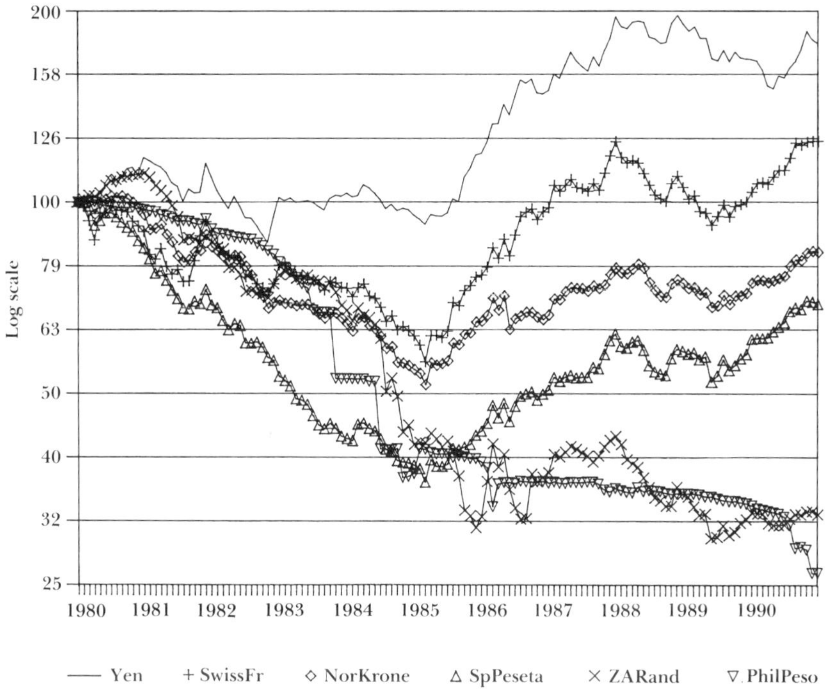

Figure 11.4 Sundry currencies v US dollar

sion along with the Asian currencies, and the South African rand. For two currencies with little trade and no exchange rate agreements, they display a quite remarkable correlation year by year over the decade. Both are worth under one-third their value in US dollar terms since 1980.

The object of this section has not been to provide a pointer to short-term actions. Such advice would rapidly be outdated by events, even if valid at the time of writing. However, it is worth considering how currencies relate to each other, so that actions taken can be consistent and logically thought through. If, for example, the possibility of adverse US tariffs for Korean goods were to pressurize the Koreans to allow the won to revalue, then it is worth considering the effect on the Taiwan dollar, Singapore dollar and possibly Japanese yen. If the opening up of eastern Europe stimulates the deutschemark, would not the peseta also benefit?

It is clear that the floating rate system of exchange will lead to continued changes, reflecting comparative economic and political strengths, as well as the significant capital flows world wide. The Bretton Woods system—which, with the exception of certain (at the time) significant devaluations and revaluations, seemed to provide the model of stability and durability—is now seen to be a historical phenomenon applicable only to the particular circumstances of the post-war generation. Likewise, the non-convertible centrally managed arrangements, which have been breaking up in eastern Europe during 1989 and 1990, can be seen as historical aberrations. These can be related to the particular circumstances of war and reconstruction linked to the ideological dominance of a crudely materialist philosophy which was not sophisticated enough to cater for the requirements of the modern age. The next stage need not necessarily be the continued fragmentation of the socialist east, which will probably see the painful establishment of zones of convertibility akin to the Singapores of the west. However, the emerging and impoverished eastern European countries will want to establish their own convertible currencies, which will trade weakly for a generation until they have learned the lessons of management of a more sophisticated structure.

The 1990s will see the creation of a stronger EMS, both with the accession of sterling and the creation of an inner bloc which will lead to a single currency operable from the Atlantic to the Oder. The central bloc (probably not called the ECU) will comprise the deutschemark, French and Belgian francs, Dutch guilder and Danish krone. The satellite currencies closely aligned will be geographically and culturally more diverse, namely sterling, Irish punt, Spanish peseta, Portuguese escudo, Italian lira and Greek drachma.

Accession to this club will be sought avidly not only by Turkey and Norway, but by some of the more advanced of the eastern European countries, namely Hungary and Czechoslovakia, if not Poland. With the possibility of greater understandings with Moscow, the gravitation of Austria and Finland towards the EMS is not out of the question, though Switzerland and Sweden would be likely to remain aloof from any formal arrangements.

Asia will continue to be a dynamic motor of the world economy. There are no supranational arrangements which seem likely to bring competing and disparate countries closer together in a similar way to Europe. Therefore, currency moves will most likely continue to be relatively uncoordinated, but possibly generally reflecting the transition to a higher standard of production and service economies.

No comment has been made about South America or Africa in general. Neither continent is expected to play a significant role in the development of currency markets over the next ten years. In both areas significant development has to take place in the real economy before this can be reflected meaningfully in measurable elements like exchange rates.

The most exciting possibilities for new arrangements and structures are possibly in the break-up of the Soviet Empire. Provided this can continue to progress relatively peacefully, there is every possibility that new currencies will reflect the emergence of separate independent nations, and that the freedom to trade these will be taken as evidence of growing freedoms and a sign of coming of age.

Where the major currencies will be, comparatively, is an open question. As the largest creditor nation in the world, Japan is clearly in a strong position. From an external investment perspective, the UK, Taiwan, Germany and France are also favourably placed. The biggest debtor nation is clearly the USA, followed apparently (though numbers are not available) by the Soviet Union. This cannot bode well for either great power, and therefore a continuation of the erosion of the comparative positions of both is to be expected. This should be evidenced by further erosion over time in the value of the US dollar, particularly when debt service costs are factored into calculations of the balance of payments. For the Soviet Union, evidence will be provided by more states desiring to secede, feeling they would stand a better chance managing their own affairs; this could eventually lead to the establishment of a looser confederation of states under Russian military protection to replace the monolithic Brezhnev model.

Finally, a move away from the concept of freely floating exchange rates is not envisaged. Even the development of the EMS structures should be seen as a specifically local response to the historical challenges of both reconstruction and competition, rather than as a move back to pseudo-Bretton Woods thinking. The continued development of floating rates is seen as evidence of and a prerequisite for more prosperity and greater freedom world wide.

Sterling and the exchange rate mechanism

Two events which impacted significantly on the currency markets in the latter half of 1990 were the entry of sterling into the exchange rate mechanism and the Iraqi invasion of Kuwait. The combined effect was to strengthen sterling, by underpinning its relationship with the key EMS currencies and to increase economic uncertainty in the world. The latter was evidenced both by the turbulence in the price of oil, which reached $40 per barrel at one point, and by the pervasive weakness of the US dollar, as the US sought to reduce interest rates to lower the impact of the pending recession. In the light of higher German-led interest rates in Europe (caused by the Bundesbank's desire to restrain inflationary pressures following German unification in summer 1990) and in Japan, this led for the first time in over a decade to the dollar trading at a premium to the deutschemark and the yen. Therefore, economic pressures were leading to a lower dollar, despite the military build-up in the Gulf, and the consequent reluctance of traders to be too short of the traditional 'safe haven' currency.

The entry of sterling into the EMS was viewed as the culmination of a five-year campaign, and therfore was seen as a significant event. In reality, sterling had been shadowing the EMS currencies for at least four years, and trading in fairly close proximity to them (with the exception of two periods, 1980–81 and 1985–86) for ten years. This is illustrated in the comparison of the indexed levels of sterling and a mid-range EMS currency, the Belgian franc (Figure 11.5). Much has been written about the problems caused the UK economy by the experiment in shadowing the deutschemark, conducted by Chancellor Lawson in 1987, when in his desire to restrain sterling at a level below DM 3.0, he instituted a series of interest rate reductions which overstimulated the demand for domestic and corporate loans, and resulted in the later extreme squeeze on liquidity and the most sustained period of high interest rates since the early 1980s. In the event, the rise of sterling towards the level of DM 3.3 in 1988–89 did not remove sterling from its close tracking of the EMS. The entry of the currency into the exchange rate mechanism simply formalized a relationship which had been in evidence for several years.

There is also debate about the level at which sterling entered, the mid-point being DM 2.95. At the time, sterling had traded

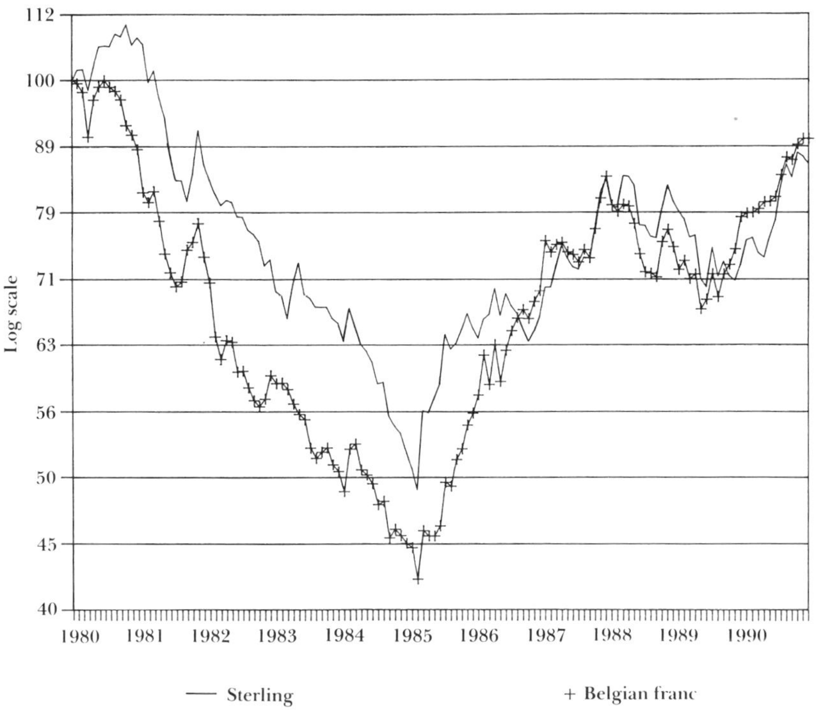

Figure 11.5 Comparison of sterling and Belgian franc

down to DM 2.75, and therefore the rate chosen was deemed to be quite high, particularly since the inflation rate in the UK had annually been over 5 per cent higher than in Germany, implying a 15 pfennig annual devaluation. The behaviour of the deutschemark in the light of German unification and the developing recession perhaps illustrated that sterling's problem was of an undervalued deutschemark rather than an overvalued pound particularly. The problem of the formal linkage to the ERM is seen to be the constraint under which this puts the domestic economy to retain high interest rates for longer than might otherwise be deemed appropriate. Therefore, deflationary policies were obliged to be retained for a painfully long period, since the currency was not permitted to depreciate within the ERM.

Paradoxically, while the UK has been leading the world into a recession (along with Australia and followed by other English-speaking countries), sterling has therefore had one of its recurrent periods of significant outperformance. So long as the dollar remains under pressure because of the low interest rates applicable in the US (in contrast to the rest of the world), sterling is likely to remain well-bid.

Summary

The major developments in currencies in the 1990s are more likely to result from the evolution of the recession and its aftermath than the Gulf War and its consequences. Contrasting developments may be expected from the lags of the German and Japanese economies behind the English-speaking economies. As the latter emerge from recession in the latter half of 1991, the former are likely to be entering recession. With the re-establishment of the dollar discount, the dollar could bottom out, and quickly trim the 30 per cent dollar undervaluation on a purchasing power parity basis which some commentators allege exists. Given the way that currencies tend to trade in wide swings, lasting for about five years, this could be the start of a period of extended dollar strength during the period of peacetime recovery from the recession and the over-borrowed 1980s.

CHAPTER 12

Models

Given that the prime function of the corporate treasurer is to protect the company from risk, it might be considered irrelevant, unnecessary, or even unethical to create models to allow the company to take risks. Treasurers are more often in the business of reacting to threats than forecasting future events. The concept of actually opening up an exposure is anathema to some. Nevertheless, the role of the treasurer is not only to protect the company from risk, but also to enable the benefits from favourable exchange moves to accrue to the company, and not to disappear in opportunity or cash and dealing losses.

There is therefore a grey area where probabilities of future beneficial moves in exchange rates play a part in the decision-making process. Even where the risks and vulnerabilities are not quantified, the treasurer will know if the exposure and cover profile are acceptable. There is clearly a case for constructing models to enable the treasurer to clarify the interrelationships between currencies, and the effect of various moves on the company. With the establishment of relevant parameters for action, the treasurer can be armed with a portfolio of actions contingent on the evolution of currency movements to enable him or her to position the company advantageously. Note, though we are talking here about probabilities, that the actions are the result of certain underlying moves in rates and are not indelible forecasts of future moves.

The ability to construct relevant models—and even large organizations can be replicated satisfactorily for the critical decision points to be established—depends on a series of factors, half within the company, and half outside.

Within the company

The treasurer should be in control of all the cash flows of the company, even where the company is decentralized, or structured on a divisional basis with ostensible authority for movements and decisions delegated to (sometimes) conflicting regional officers. Should there be any doubt on the guidelines for local autonomy, then there should be a steering committee (possibly conducted telephonically by a conference-call) to ensure that the group profile of actions is consistent and rational. For example, if the German subsidiary is selling the dollar it does not make much sense on a group basis for the Dutch subsidiary to be buying it.

The treasurer needs to have a reasonable knowledge of the currency denominations of the cash flows of the company or group, their magnitude and timing. This forms a crucial part of the data on which any decision-making on exposure policy will be founded. For example, the internal view on the vulnerability of the company might well be at variance with reality. Often the dollar is seen by UK corporates as the major vulnerability, but in being the largest market it might also account for a large proportion of payables and, it may well be that the net exposure (receivables *less* payables) is modest compared with Europe as a whole, or even individual markets such as Germany or Japan.

The group structure is an important input into the model of the company's exposure, since it is not only the flow to and from the parent company *vis-à-vis* the outside world that determines the position the treasurer needs to manage, but the overall picture, including the interactions between group companies. Local profitability is another important area for attention, if slightly more controversial. The view once accepted as conventional wisdom was that one only took cover action where real cash flows were involved. It is now becoming accepted that part of the vulnerability of the group is the translation of local profits into the parent currency for consolidation purposes, and therefore forecasts of local profitability need to play a part in the creation of the model of the group's exposure.

Once a reasonable picture of the group has been obtained—which, at its simplest, should be capable of summarization on one sheet of computer paper not a mile long—then the various comparatives from different combinations of exchange rates and actions can be applied. Popular among the comparatives are:

- this year's budget rate
- last year's budget rate
- last year's actual achieved rates
- 'constant exchange rates', notably for long-term planning.

An interesting exercise is to simulate group performance had historic rates been fixed at a particular point in time, which for a given structure of relative inflation can show the often very large first-order effects of exchange on the results of the company.

The purpose of this part of the exercise is clearly to establish the orders of magnitude of the flows and currencies involved and to clarify the parameters for decision-making. For example, if the annual variability due to exchange is 10m, then the expenditure of 1m on currency options suddenly seems not an undue or extravagant commitment. Clearly, in the appraisal of the net effects of treasury action in, say, safeguarding budget or in achieving a performance no worse than the previous year, the full costs of all actions need to be taken into account. These include the cash cost of cover taken—whether premia for options bought or the net payment for 'marking-to-market' of options written—and the gain or loss at maturity (spot rate versus forward rate agreed) for conventional forwards.

Outside the group

It is not the purpose of this section to denigrate the services of consultants, banks, advisory bodies, or forecasters and analysts. All these and more can provide information to enable good and better decisions to be made in the company; but, however good the individual advice offered might be—even where these services are used consistently (and most are only used occasionally on a 'mix and match' basis)—they do not have the virtue of being *dedicated* to the particular corporate. In providing services to the market in general they miss the specificity required by the company—and all companies consider themselves unique.

Therefore, it is becoming more accepted that corporates should build their own databanks of exchange rates, and models derived from these, to enable the corporate to take rational decisions based on a consistent approach. The content of the database might include interest differentials where the rationale for forward cover includes this element of sophistication (note that for larger corporates the value of this in cash terms can be high). Similarly, divergence indicators from EMS norms can provide useful indicators of probable short-term moves within Europe. Of importance to the database are comprehensiveness and consistency. For example, daily records should not have gaps, except perhaps for bank holidays, etc., and such records should be of the rates at a particular time of day. One large corporate insists in ensuring that the rates they quote in their database are 'live' rates at 8.30 am, while others might be happy to use the closing rates of the day as quoted in, say, the *Financial Times*.

Calculations using the database can be simply the evolution of the spot rate of the currency, or the creation of moving averages, say for one month or for 50 days. At its simplest, the intersection of the spot rate with the 50-day moving average could be a trigger-point to buy in a move from weak currency to strong, and to sell in a move from strong to weak. This would at least provide a rationale for action that was not dependent on the whim of the relevant manager, and would be related to the market. However, it is not proof against short-term swings or periods of indecision by the market when strictly one might need to be selling and buying on alternate days, chalking up dealing turnover and losses on the spread quite needlessly.

A somewhat more sophisticated approach is to relate actions to the underlying sentiment in the market, by standing back from the spot rate *per se*, and predicating actions on the comparative movement of different moving averages. If the object of treasury management of foreign exchange is to be 'on the right side' of the currencies, this means in dealing terminology being long of the currencies when they are strong and short when they are weak. The more important decisions are not to stay on the back of a steadily weakening currency, but to change one's mind when the currency has turned. What motivates a treasurer to a change in viewpoint? How does a treasurer decide that a previous ostensible turning point was incorrect, and that the currency should be sold again?

Moving averages might not be considered very profound in themselves, since of course they are determined simply by history. If one knows what has happened on a daily basis, is that knowledge in any way amplified by moving averages of different time-scales? They do, however, provide a sketch in somewhat more depth of the way the currencies have been moving relative to each other. If one believes that currency moves are not entirely random, but are capable of a degree of predication based on recent or previous experiences, then a picture of the different moving averages might be helpful.

Momentum models

Momentum is a phenomenon used by many technical analysts to establish positions where, in the short term, a currency is overbought or oversold. This can best be established by the comparison of the spot rate with a given moving average, or of two different moving averages with each other. This enables a degree of rationality to be applied to decisions where an opportunity is seen to take a position counter to the current market view. For example, if the short-term momentum (spot v 10-day moving average [mav]) sterling–dollar fluctuates between −3 and +2 per cent, then on a short-term basis it might be profitable to buy sterling at −2.5 per cent and sell again at +1.5 per cent. However, the long-term treasury strategist might argue that if momenta are only valid for short-term countercyclical views, then their usefulness might be as transitory as the positions taken.

Momentum, in fact, really proves its use in the establishment of parameters for long-term action. Here, the important point is to be behind the market on the long-term moves that often occur, and continue for many months. But just as one cannot foretell the future, so one is jealous of the gains one has made in the past. Therefore, there is a great temptation to 'bank' the gains from currency cover or, just as importantly, to take cover at good rates where one has profited from a low or zero cover strategy. What are the parameters for such action? Clearly they can be to put away GBP4m benefit, because that is a lot of money and pays for the treasury function for many years to come. But, firstly, this is not very scientific and, secondly, might result in another, say, 2m being sacrificed in opportunity loss.

The longer term momentum parameters that are relevant in enabling the corporate to be comfortably positioned are the 30-, 60- and 90-day moving averages (mavs) (including weekends). Clearly, if one is motivated to action by the shorter term momenta (say spot v 10-day mav or 10-day mav v 30-day mav) then one will be taking action for major turning points nicely ahead of the rest of the pack. However, one might also need to reverse such action more quickly if the signal is 'false' and, say, the dollar continues its (apparently?) inexorable slide into oblivion. The treasurer will not want to inflate a dealing turnover more than necessary, especially since to reverse a position causes a degree of heartsearching and tension, not to say occasional associated losses, and the shorter the term of the deal the more important is the banker's spread. Therefore, it is not inappropriate to look at the longer term parameters (say 1-month mav v 3-month mav) to establish if one is in a strong or weak currency scenario. If strong, buy the currency, and if weak, sell—and change position when the underlying tone alters.

The prescription seems sensible, and the result is to reduce the number of changes required to a reasonably small figure of only three or four per annum.

Is it profitable? The answer depends partly on where the decision points are taken. One might not wish to authorize action merely because the 30-day mav has dipped below the 90-day mav. Perhaps one might prefer to wait until it is −0.5 per cent before triggering action, when one would be somewhat more certain that the zero level had really been broken. The effect of this would be to reduce the profit from deals since the rates dealt would in all probability be worse, but it would also reduce the number of deals transacted, and therefore lower the likelihood of dealing losses when the market is tracking sideways. The eight charts shown in this chapter illustrate the effect of this strategy for the yen, deutschemark, sterling and Australian dollar plotted against US dollar for the six years 1985–90 inclusive.

The parameters that have been chosen are the 'long-term' measuring averages of one month against three months. Each set of charts consists of the momentum, or percentage variation between the two parameters, negative if the short-term average is below the long-term (implying dollar weakness against the yen and deutschemark and sterling weakness against the dollar), and positive if above.

When a definite trend has become established, the momentum moves to a very high positive or negative figure, which also implies a high probability of a favourable trade when the position has to be reversed. In the event of an uncertain trend, the momentum level either does not reach a higher figure, or rapidly reverses

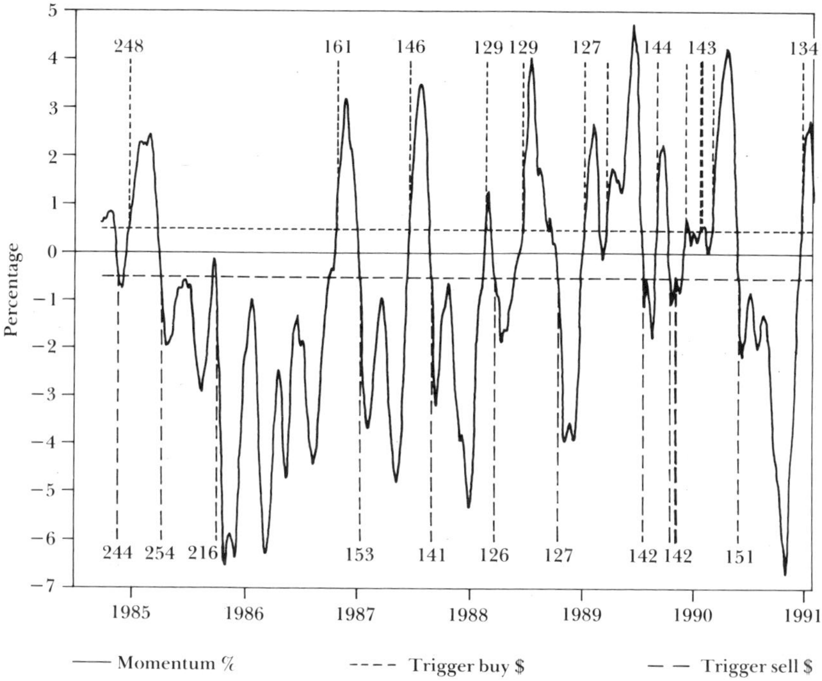

Figure 12.1 Japanese yen v US dollar

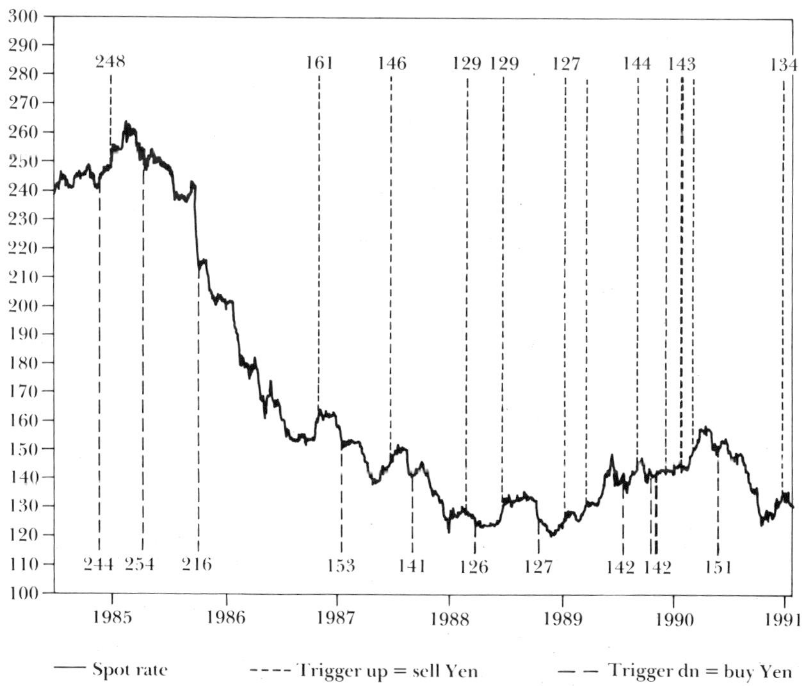

Figure 12.2 Japanese yen v US dollar

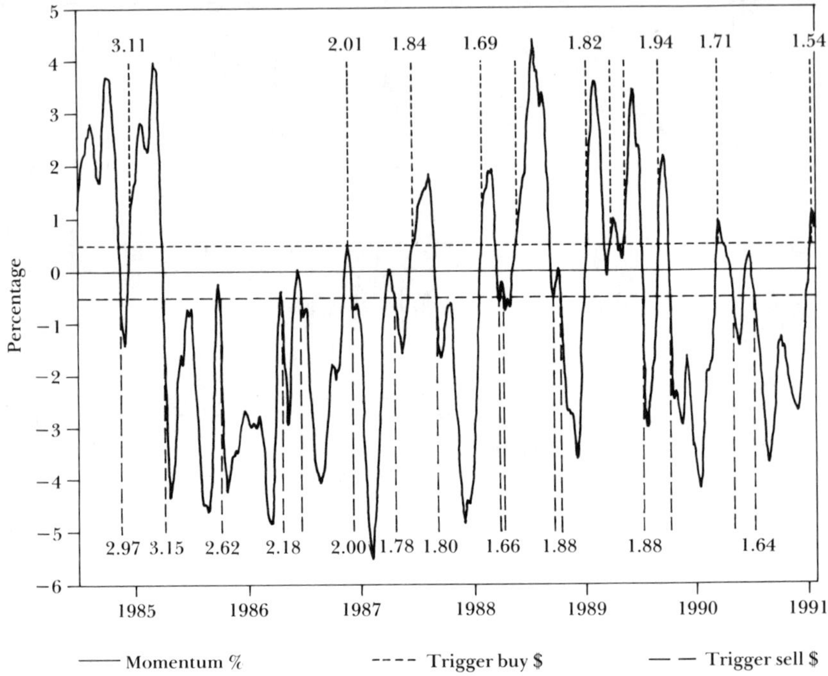

Figure 12.3 Deutschemark v US dollar

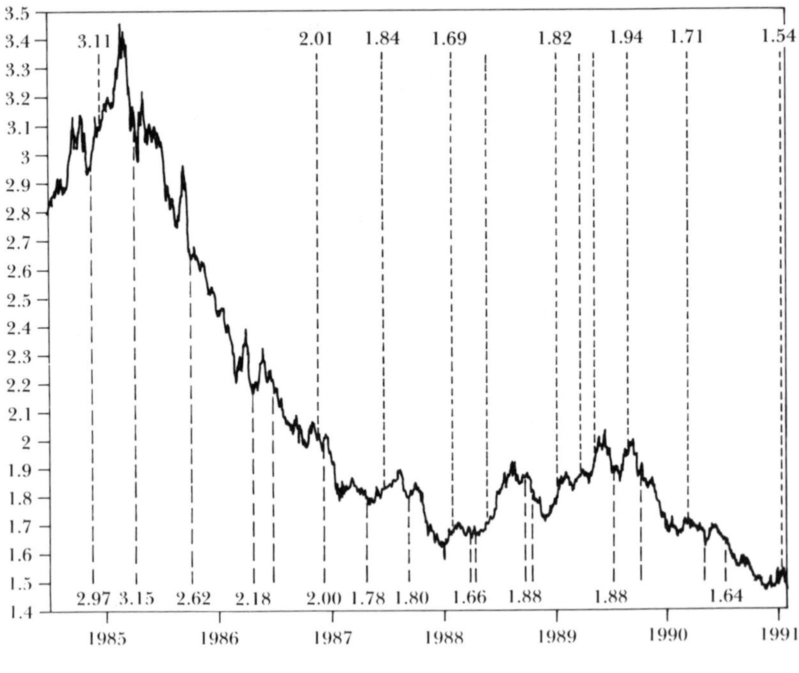

Figure 12.4 Deutschemark v US dollar

once high figures are attained. The reversal of positions in these circumstances can lead to unprofitable trades.

Looking at the yen (Figures 12.1 and 12.2), one can perceive that during the period of significant yen strength, from autumn 1985 until summer 1988, the system provided significant benefit. After being short yen at 248, a long yen signal was provided at 255, which was reinforced at 216. Profits were then taken at 161, and this was then followed by a period of less profitable trading over the next year as the yen topped out. However, for the next two years, a series of unprofitable trades took place, since the yen was fairly trendless. A basically covered or unprotected position would have been more profitable than jobbing in and out of the market.

Looking at the deutschemark (Figures 12.3 and 12.4), a broadly similar picture is provided in 1985–87, but a somewhat clearer trading pattern later. From being short deutschemark at 2.72 and then 3.11 (taking a modest loss of 14 pfennigs between 2.97 and 3.11), the system goes long deutschemark in autumn 1985 at 3.15 which is reinforced by further signals at 2.62 and 2.18, before profits are taken eventually at 1.84 in late 1987. The following three years show the model long marks down to 1.66 with the loss of 7 pfennigs out of 18, and then short marks up to 1.94 with the loss of 11 pfennigs out of 28. The model reversed in 1990 to become long marks again at 1.89 down to 1.50 with the loss of 7 pfennigs out of 39.

Sterling has been a complex currency, measured against the dollar or on a cross-currency basis against the yen or the deutschemark. A much less clear picture emerges than that which applied to the yen and the deutschemark. The model (Figures 12.5 and 12.6) was quite successful in 1984–85, then positive signals for the dollar were provided at 1.41 and 1.20. The rapid reversal in spring 1985 saw a loss of 4 cents at 1.24, and a further loss of 11 cents up to 1.46 a year later out of a total beneficial move of 22 cents. Clearly this latter period provided only a 50 per cent success ratio. An improved performance was shown over the next two years, as sterling strengthened against the dollar. In mid-1987 the positive signal at 1.47 was reinforced twice up to 1.85 with the loss of 11 cents in a total move of 38 cents. The reversal to 1.58 in late 1989 was triggered at 1.82 from a loss of 3 cents, and showed intermediate losses of 7 cents for a total move of 24 cents. Clearly

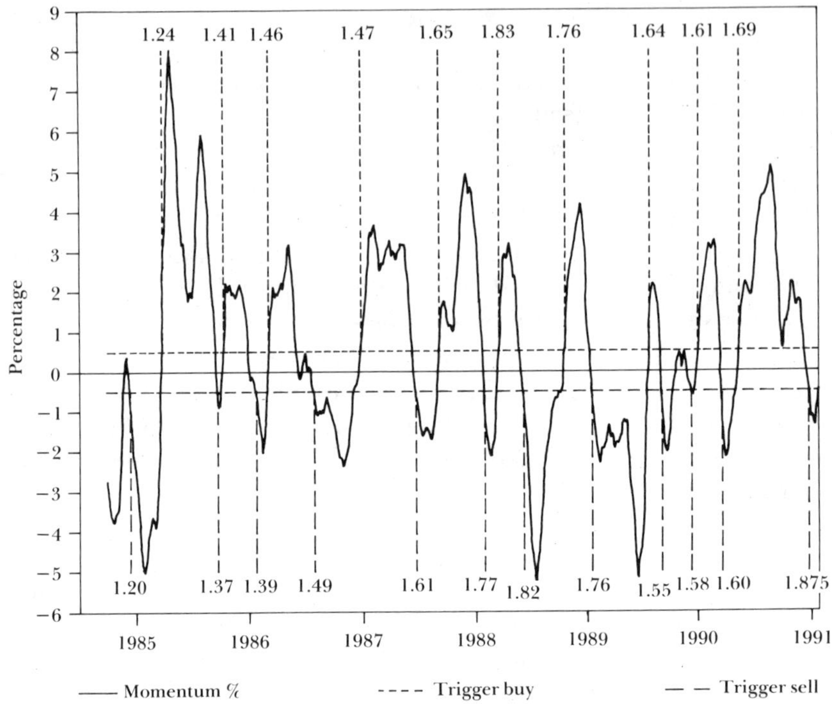

Figure 12.5 **Sterling v US dollar**

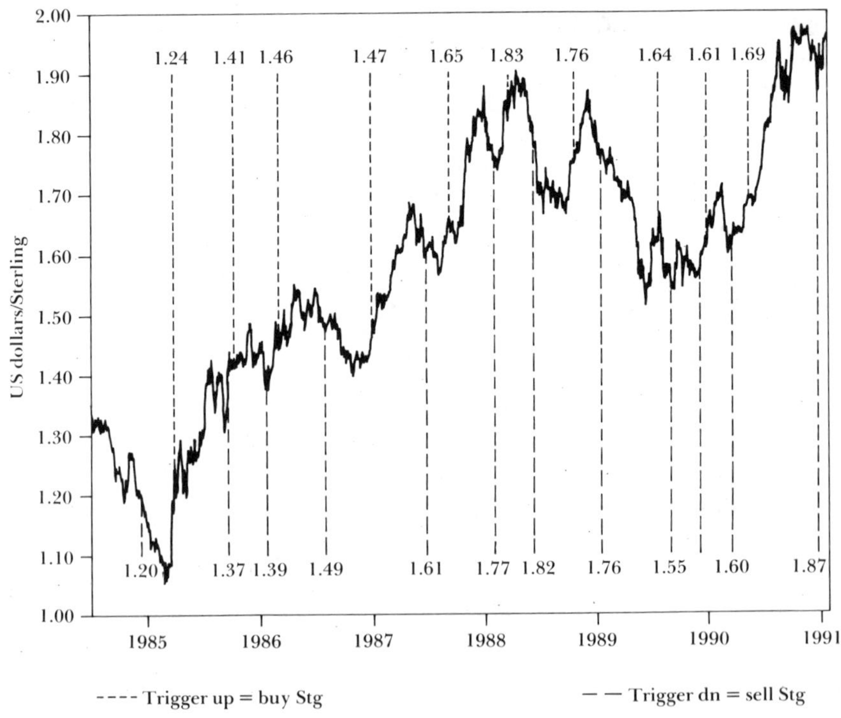

Figure 12.6 **Sterling v US dollar**

1.58 was not the bottom for sterling in this period (this being 1.50 in summer 1989), and the system is not designed to catch the extremes. However, it does seem to provide the balance between achieving early commitment to a favourable trend and the avoidance of expensive over-trading.

For the deutschemark, yen and sterling, the trigger point for action to buy or sell the currency is taken as the move through ±0.5 per cent from the zero direction. For the Australian dollar (Figures 12.7 and 12.8), where movements have been much more extreme and choppy, a ±0.5 per cent trigger point would be too negative in providing too many changes of decisions, making the model difficult to manage. Accordingly, a ±1.0 per cent trigger point is proposed as a more realistic alternative. Even so, some fourteen positive and negative decisions (purchase and sale) result, compared with fourteen positive and eleven negative decisions for the deutschemark with parameters of only 0.5 per cent.

If one wanted a more reactive signal than the 1-month v 3-month mav, one could use the 1-month v 2-month mav. The number of buy and sell signals would be increased, along with the feeling that the situation is under control at any time. However, the need for reactivity is also increased if the possibility of dealing losses when the currency 'turns' is to be reduced. Alternatively, one could move the 'buy' signal from −0.5 per cent to zero, thus accelerating the point at which relevant action would be taken, but at the same time improving the rate dealt. One could clearly make the signal zero for both, the buy or sell triggers being merely dependent on the movement of the momentum, but this would increase the likelihood of losses should the currencies go through a period of consolidation.

Although the longer term parameters are favoured for strategic progress, the object of this section has not been to promote the use of particular parameters for particular currencies, but to illustrate ways in which the underlying rates can drive out decision points to provide rational and, more importantly, changeable actions. These are not ends in themselves, but inputs into the decision-making process along with hitherto more conventional factors like forward interest differentials, budget rates, and comments from pundits paid and unpaid, professional and amateur. The parameters chosen will partly be a matter of the taste and stance of the relevant corporate, and partly a result of the feeling for the

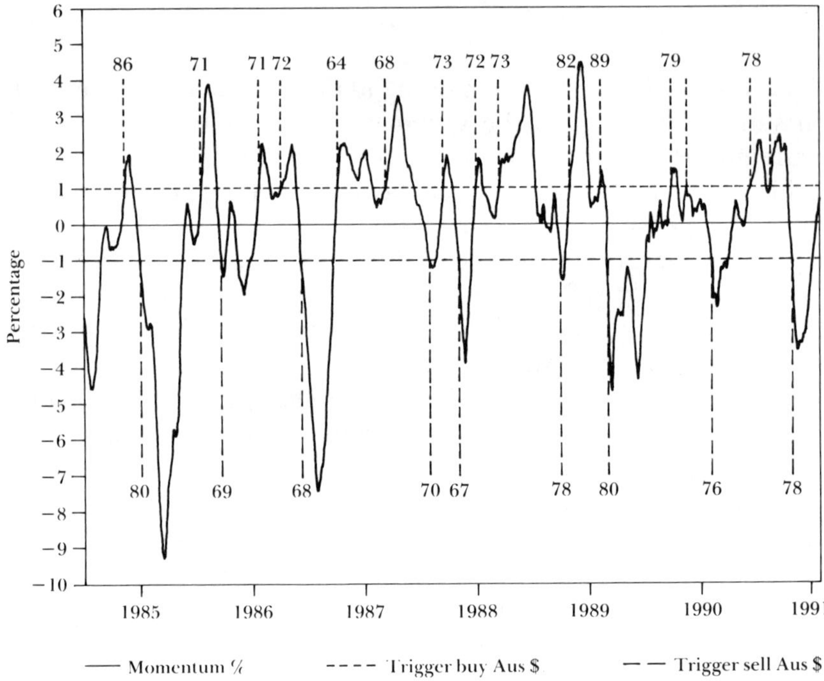

Figure 12.7 **Australian dollar v US dollar**

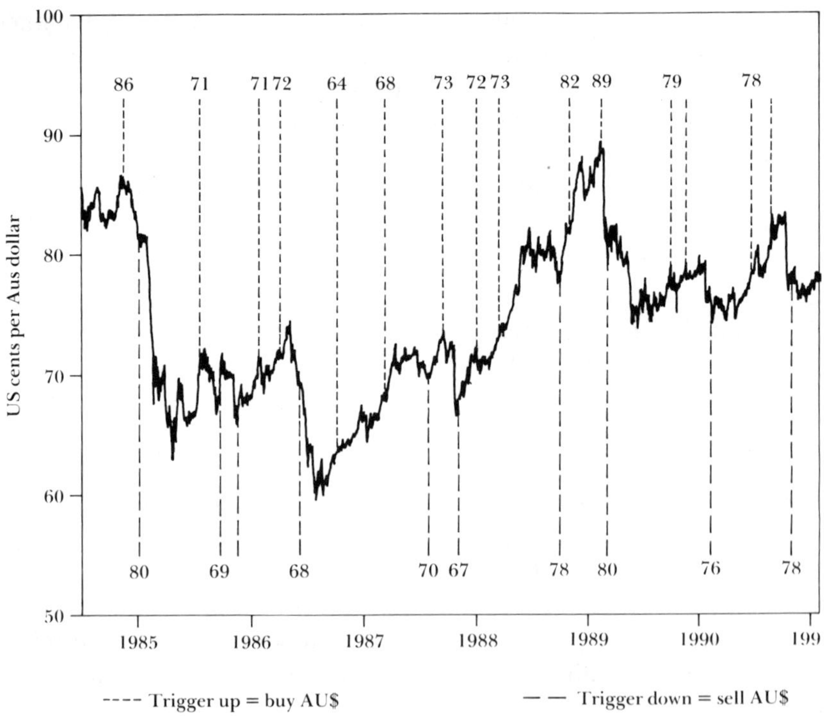

Figure 12.8 **Australian dollar v US dollar**

appropriateness of the relevant factors, and the response to the empirical question: Do they work? The author has a suspicion that there is more to moving averages and momentum models than might have been expected.

CHAPTER 13

Financial control

The object of financial control is to provide a framework for the management of key variables in the business, notably capital expenditure and working capital. The treasurer has a key role in the provision of the financial parameters and structures to enable financial control to be more than simply the adding up of returns provided to the centre. Financial control incorporates the following attributes:

- appraisal of business performance
- control over capital expenditure
- responsibility for working capital
- cash management
- structured funding.

Given that historical accounts can be misleading in not comparing like with like and in confusing funding with performance, a financial control system should see through the appearance of financial results to the underlying business reality.

For a multinational the structure of international businesses running their own national offices and operations can be superseded by a series of national groupings, each of which retains the requisite divisional structure enabling the main manufacturing operations to run their business. This can improve control, economize on administration and focus national attention on business strengths.

Each business, therefore, can comprise the national manufacturing centre plus its international network of selling operations. When all selling operations are integrated, the businesses have to be informed of the relevant stocks and capital tied up, and the financing costs that vary between countries. A common philosophy is required to be established, not to charge all businesses with the interest which historically derived from their operations—some being cash rich, and others being highly geared—but to eliminate financial flows from the scheme of appraisal for the businesses. In their place can be put notional flows relating the cost of capital of the company in each country to the total capital tied up in each business, averaged over time to avoid 'accidents' of lumpiness over specific balance sheet dates. Such flows in profit terms can be expressed as a charge on profits related to the capital used in the business.

This charge can begin as a flat rate fee for the first year and can then be changed to a weighted cost of capital related to local interest rates when the system can cope with this additional sophistication. For convenience the charge will be called the currency or cash utilization fee (CUF).

An example will illustrate that (as with inflation) formal books of account are not useful for intercompany comparison in the same group when current performance is compared after all costs, including conventional funding.

Consider a company that has grown by acquisition, owning three divisions, which are separate companies. Each company has \$50m of fixed capital and \$50m of working capital. Gearing varies from 100 per cent in A to 20 per cent in B to 50 per cent negative gearing (cash balances) in C.

Assume operating profits, as a percentage of assets employed, of 20, 15 and 10 per cent respectively, and interest rates of 10 per cent.

Example

	A	B	C
Asset	100	100	100
Liquidity	(200)	(50)	50
Equity	(100)	50	150
Operating profit	20	15	10
Interest	(2)	(5)	5
Profit before tax	Nil	10	15

Clearly, owing to the historic gearing position (which has nothing to do with the real current business performance), the order of performance shown by the businesses is diametrically opposite to the real performance. In decisions relating to funding and expansion, C might well be rewarded and A penalized even though current performance would not justify such a decision.

Now instead of the interest charge, insert the cash usage fee (for convenience at an 'average' rate of, say, 10 per cent). The real performance will be quite different.

Operation of CUF

	A	B	C
Operating profit	20	15	10
CUF at 10 % (flat rate)	(10)	(10)	(10)
Real performance	10	5	Nil

Now substitute a more sophisticated measure of CUF, dependent on the prevailing level of interest rates in each business.

Assuming weighted cost of capital is, for enterprises in the UK (at 15 per cent), USA (at 10 per cent) and Japan (at 5 per cent), the revised CUF charge would be:

	A	B	C
Revised CUF	(15)	(10)	(5)
Real performance	5	5	5

Provided that the highest returns are achieved in the businesses with the highest profits in high cost of capital countries, then the performances would broadly equate, as shown in the example.

The object of such a system is both to focus attention in the international business on the usage of that most scarce resource—cash—and to enable the reality of assets employed to guide actions on the allocation of funding. It might be argued that the autonomy of local management is prejudiced, since allocation decisions depend no longer on the local accounts and what the company can 'afford'. The response to this is in the affirmative. Indeed, one of the merits of such a system is that all companies are put on a level playing field (at least regarding financial costs), and they have to justify their performance in relation to commonly understood measures.

The refinement of local costs of capital is debatable. Is this overlay an unnecessary complication? Clearly, in the example shown, there was provision for a settling-in period, when the average cost of capital of the group was used. However, on a short period of time Germany might appear penalized and Australia rewarded if an average 10 per cent cost for capital used were deducted in each country. If the system is sensitive enough to deal with the sophistication of varying interest rates, then capital can migrate to where it is cheapest, thus enabling the system to produce a financially efficient result.

The scheme may be seen as ambitious, since it is clearly designed to supersede historical and local loyalties, and to make redundant (except for statutory reporting purposes) the funding side of local balance sheets for financial control purposes (as opposed to financing).

The following section illustrates the structure and guidance notes for such a system in a practical example of a financial control structure in a multinational manufacturing company.

Group financial control—a case study

XYZ plc

Introduction

The following instructions and attachments are designed to explain the group financial control structure.

Organization Each main country's operations are being consolidated into one legal entity, called a national holding company (NHC). This is explained and differentiated from a national controlling company (NCC) and ordinary subsidiaries.

Interest charges Funding is regarded as a central rather than a local function while the importance of interest charges is downgraded since they do not form part of the management incentive system.

Currency/cash usage fee (CUF) This is a cost taken as a deduction against operating profit at the unit level, which is calculated by reference to net assets employed. The philosophy and practice are explained.

Control accounts These are required where NHCs are established—their mechanism is explained.

Foreign exchange and trade finance The role of the different kinds of company in the group is explored.

Organization

Historically the company had been organized in the traditional business/ownership structure, as shown in Figure 13.1.

The changed organization gave scope for the operation of the new finance company as prime coordinator for cash and funding operations and the operation of the system of financial control. Liaison took place from all units direct with the finance company (Figure 13.2).

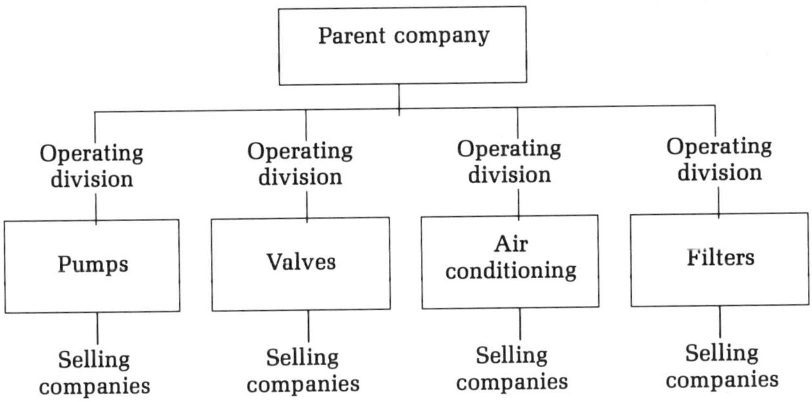

Figure 13.1

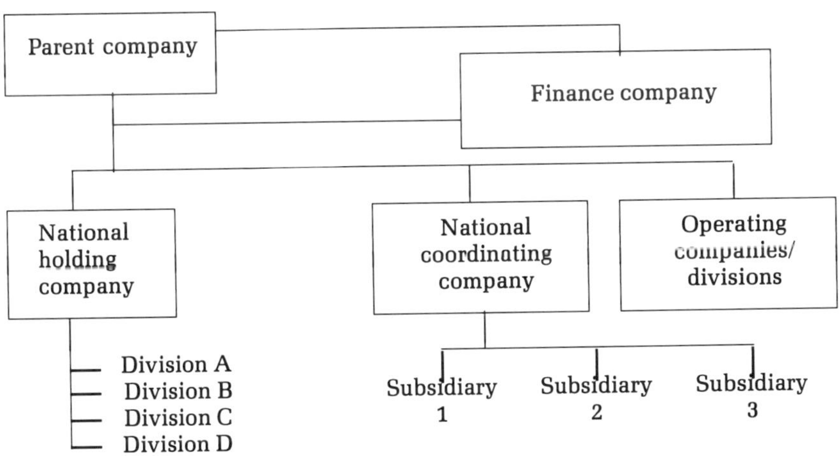

Figure 13.2

The centre

The centre performs the statutory consolidation functions and reports to the board on management results. It comprises XYZ plc, the ultimate holding company of all subsidiaries, and XYZ Finance Limited, the financing vehicle for the group. The role of the centre is:

- to coordinate funding for the group by borrowing efficiently under the group's multi-option facility (MOF)
- to guide the group in the evolution of its financial affairs, notably for foreign exchange and interest rate risk management, trade finance, and working capital control
- overall control of banking relationships, notably the avoidance of unnecessary proliferation
- to use the weight of the group to best effect in securing beneficial deals.

National holding companies

The NHCs are the amalgamation of XYZ operating units as the single legal representations of XYZ in a country. These act as:

- the conduit for funding to operating units in the territories
- the main coordination area for national operations.

National coordinating companies

These are junior to NHCs, but have a similar role in the funding process within their territory. Most national holding companies (NHCs) begin as national coordinating companies (NCCs), having authority within their territory for the funding and various central reporting aspects.

1 They act as the conduit of funds from the centre to their operating units.
2 Legally they do not have full ownership of them, except sometimes as subsidiaries.
3 In this structure, the operating units are separate companies, and for fiscal purposes they need to maintain their own statutory accounts.

Subsidiaries

These have independent legal status in their territory, and report either to their NCC, or directly to the centre if this has been agreed.

Branches

These are operating units with no independent legal status, and form part of the entity whose results are consolidated by the NHC.

Funding and interest charges

Funding is simply a mechanism for putting financial resources where they are needed, the drawing of external cash being a central and not a local function. Main funds are provided to the units from XYZ Finance Limited, using the MOF and other group funding facilities. Such funds are provided as required, but the position is reviewed at least monthly.

Banking by operating units is with one major clearer in each country, who can provide the advantages of pooling of debit and credit balances of the operating units daily, together with automatic notification of balances to the NHC/NCC.

The NHCs and NCCs are the conduits for funding from the centre to the operating units and have responsibility for coordinating local requirements outside delegated limits which operate for local banking on a daily basis.

Procedure—daily

1 NHC/NCC to monitor all the cash balances of all branches and subsidiaries by electronic methods if installed, or otherwise by telephone.
2 NHC/NCC to manage cash efficiently by pooling bank balances, to eliminate 'idle balances'.
3 NHC/NCC to submit daily fax of the national balance to the assistant treasurer at Central HQ for monitoring purposes.
4 NHC/NCC to notify centre of spare cash available or anticipated cash needs outside the delegated limits five working days before transfer is made.

Procedure—monthly

1 NHC/NCC to review delegated parameters for local borrowings/deposits with centre.
2 NHC/NCC to provide weekly forecast of cash for following month to centre.
3 NHC to remove cash balances from branches at month end.
4 NHC/NCC to provide one month's interest rate to apply to their borrowings/deposits with centre for following month—this to be agreed with centre.

Transfer of cash to from NHC/NCC

1 Should cash be needed by the national holding company, advance notice should be given of five working days to enable the centre to coordinate efficiently borrowings under centrally controlled term loan facilities.
2 Should an emergency injection of cash be needed locally, the notice period can be reduced (depending on the time zone) to no less than two days, but this route does involve short-term facilities and exposes group to possible foreign exchange risk, and is therefore not optimal.
3 Should extra cash be available for the centre to use, as many days' notice as practicable should be given of its remittance, but in any case not less than two working days, to enable the cash movement, with its foreign exchange implications, to be properly handled without the group losing value.

Interest charges

1 Between the centre and NHCs/NCCs/self-reporting subsidiaries, interest is charged at market rates and accrues from day to day.
2 Between NCCs and their subsidiaries, interest at arm's length is charged on loans and deposits.
3 There are no interest charges within NHCs (i.e., between the branch and its local head office).

Cash usage fee (CUF)

This is the charge at 10 per cent on average assets employed in each business and is calculated at the unit level each month. (This average charge to be refined by reference to notional costs of borrowing in Year 2 onwards.) The monthly CUF charge equals:

$$\text{Daily average assets employed} \times 10\% \times \frac{\text{Weeks in month}}{52}$$

The philosophy of CUF and a worked example are contained in the appendix.

Budget

The budgeted CUF charge is the result of annual budget forecasts of fixed assets and working capital employed in the business.

1 This is used as a measure of performance for the following year.
2 As the process becomes established this is expected to include phasing over the 12-month period.

Monthly procedure
The centre monitors the monthly CUF charge for the group, which equates to average assets employed for the period as annualized × 10 per cent.

NHC/NCC

- calculates funding adjustments for each branch/subsidiary and notifies branch within two working days of month-end—see worked example
- sends a summary of its adjustments to the centre (NHC monthly cash return).

The CUF disappears on consolidation within the NHC since the charge for CUF at a unit level is a credit at the NHC level (these being opposite entries in the control accounts). This leaves only the financing charge external and to the centre as visible for the NHC as a whole.

Operating unit
This calculates CUF charge for opening balance plus operating profit plus funding difference as notified by NHC/NCC. This forms part of monthly performance return to centre.

Control accounts in NHC

Control accounts

- are non-interest bearing, and simply reflect the assets employed in each constituent operating unit of the NHC
- provide the local unit with the ability to account for its assets and balance sheet on a full double-entry system, the opposite of their credits being debits in the books of the NHC
- are not vehicles for funding or controlling the business, which is a management function.

Management

Management of control accounts is primarily at a local level, but reconciliation with balances in the NHC needs to take place monthly.

Procedure

1 Establishment of control accounts—since these represent the assets of the branch, the liability is in the books of the branch, and the asset in the books of the NHC.
2 Structure: for ease of reconciliation it is recommended that the control account comprises three self-contained sections, as follows:
   (i) opening balance;
   (ii) profit for year to date (after deduction of CUF);
   (iii) funding movements, including monthly zero-izing of bank balances.
3 Charges to control accounts:
   (i) profit earned is an additional liability that can be monitored as a separate part of the control account;
   (ii) cash movements are reflected as additions to deductions for assets employed and, therefore, the control account;
   (iii) at month-end, spare cash on bank accounts is removed by those accounts being 'zero-ized' and deficits are made good in a similar way; the opposite entry occurs on the control account;
   (iv) no interest is charged on cash movements on balances, but the profit figure is quoted after the CUF charge (see below).

An example of the workings of the control account is shown in the appendix.

Foreign exchange and trade finance

Foreign exchange

This is a function with central and local aspects.

1 Local exposures are the net flows in foreign currency to and from the relevant country.
2 These can be aggregated by the national holding company and

managed nationally (as in the UK), or (less optimally) managed by each entity.

3 Spot deals, being delivery of flows of business cash, are often the preserve of each unit, while forward deals can be done at a national level.

The centre is involved in the following situations.

1 Long-term cover is contemplated (say over 12 months) or the NHC wishes to use the centre as a bank for its cover—this becoming more usual and enabling the group both to take advantage of economics of scale and to net internal exposures.
2 Strategic cover is required for some exposures which are forecasted but not yet secure as booked sales. The translation exposure of overseas profits into sterling is also managed for a one-year forward period.
3 Management is needed of the foreign exchange risk associated with intra-group loans where the currency borrowed might be different from that lent, and of balance sheet currency hedges where loans in currency are taken for policy reasons.

Trade finance

The initiative for accessing sources of government aid and insurance resides locally, where there is knowledge and expertise on governmental packages and arrangements.

Centrally there is the ability to channel local knowledge to other national companies, and to put group prestige behind local pressure. The central function is mainly a clearing house for trade finance, with some strategic and senior direction when required for group purposes.

Appendix

Summary

Instructions on procedure are dealt with in the main text, while this appendix is designed to cover:

- Philosophy of the CUF
- Calculation of the CUF
- Usage of control accounts.

Philosophy of the CUF

The CUF is designed to make operating units responsible for the cost of their average assets employed. This cost is the total cost to the group rather than the specific finance charge (whether via local interest or dividend) which would otherwise have applied.

By taking a deduction of CUF against trading profits for management purposes, management will have an immediate and lasting incentive to control their assets employed carefully, notably:

- fixed assets, to minimize excess capacity and optimize utilization
- working capital, to manage inventories actively and control debtors and disbursements.

By concentrating local attention on assets employed rather than financing, the responsibility of the centre for funding is reinforced, enabling the group to benefit from expertise at the appropriate level.

Calculation of the CUF

The CUF is calculated on average assets employed, using the following elements:

1 The prime figure is the net assets number at the beginning of the month, which is also reflected in the control account.
2 This is modified by the average balance at bank over the month, credit balances reflecting a reduction in the assets employed, and therefore providing a credit offsetting part of the monthly charge, and debit balances representing additional borrowing, and therefore an increase in the average assets for the month, and in the CUF.
3 Trading profits for the month are also part of the CUF calculation, since they are reflected by other movements in assets, for example, cash.

Daily balances at the bank are monitored by the NHC, and notified at month-end to the operating unit so that it can make an adjustment to the CUF calculation accordingly. Where funding (to or from the unit) takes place during the month, affecting the control account, this is removed from the calculation of the CUF adjustment, so that double-counting is avoided.

Example (4-week month)

Days	*Bank balance*	*Funding*	*Net for CUF*
1	30 000		30 000
2	153 000		153 000
3	150 000		150 000
4	102 000		102 000
5	102 000		102 000
6	102 000		102 000
7	50 000		50 000
8	43 000		43 000
9	27 000		27 000
10	20 000		20 000
11	22 000		22 000
12	22 000		22 000
13	22 000		22 000

14	4 000		4 000
15	−57 000		−57 000
16	−457 000		−457 000
17	100 000	500 000	−400 000
18	90 000		−410 000
19	90 000		−410 000
20	90 000		−410 000
21	100 000		−400 000
22	150 000		−350 000
23	200 000		−300 000
24	210 000		−290 000
25	220 000		−280 000
26	220 000		−280 000
27	300 000		−200 000
28	zero	300 000 Cr	−100 000
Total			3 295 000
÷ days 28			−117 000
CUF adj. @ 10% × 4/52			−905

It is acknowledged that the bank balance is not the same as the cash book owing to items like uncleared credits and unpresented cheques; for the purposes of this exercise it is assumed that over time the cash-book and bank-book figures will equate.

Usage of control accounts

While the control account could be regarded as one figure, it is considered to be three elements, that are accounted for separately in order to facilitate reconciliation at month-end:

- Net assets employed, start period
- Cash movements in period, average
- Profit earned in period, total.

Example

End Dec. Company A:	Net assets employed	GBP 356 000
	Control account	GBP 4 356 000 Cr
15 Jan.	Additional finance	GBP 500 000 Cr
15 Jan.	Control account	GBP 4 856 000 Cr
28 Jan.	Zero-ize bank account	GBP 300 000
28 Jan.	Profit for period	GBP 150 000 Cr
28 Jan.	Control account total	GBP 4 706 000 Cr
Comprising :	Opening balance	GBP 4 356 000 Cr
	Cash movements	GBP 200 000 Cr
	Profit for period	GBP 150 000 Cr

CUF charge compared

Therefore, using data provided in the example above, the total CUF charge for January, Company A, is as follows:

Opening balance	GBP 4 356 000
Average cash	GBP -117 000
Profit for period	GBP -150 000
Average net assets	GBP 4 623 000
CUF charge:	
×10% × 4/52	GBP 35 500

Since the CUF charge is a deduction from trading profit for management purposes, it is proper for it to be deducted from trading profit for accounting purposes in the operation of the control accounts. Therefore, control accounts will include the following items (from the viewpoint of the NHC):

Opening balance	Dr
Trading profit for period	Dr
CUF charge for period	Cr
Additional funding	Dr
Reduction in funding	Cr

A philosophical point to be made is that since the CUF charge is a flat financing fee on capital tied up, which would differ from the total of interest and dividend which might otherwise have been payable, the net reserves of branches will stray over time from what would have been the net reserves had they stayed as subsidiaries.

CHAPTER 14

The creation of a corporate treasury function

Part I
Recruitment, business, philosophy and relationships

International treasury departments have grown in line with the increasing internationalization of business. The modern treasury department in a UK corporate might seem to be a recent innovation, dating, dependent on your time horizon, either from the establishment of the Association of Corporate Treasurers coinciding with the indefinite supervision of exchange control in 1979, or from the breakdown of the Bretton Woods fixed exchange system in the early 1970s. However, functions currently performed by corporate treasury departments are very traditional. They include a wide range of specialisms that have always been needed by companies, but until recently have not been incorporated within one focused team.

Using the 'hard' and 'soft' labels that are applied to other modes of behaviour to differentiate between the mainstream treasury functions and those more peripheral functions that could be organized differently, we have:

Hard

Cash management The management of short-term funding for the business, including depositing surplus cash; this was once the preserve of former 'cashiers' sections in finance departments.

Foreign exchange management The management of the vulnerability of the business to adverse changes in exchange rates, mainly by the use of forward foreign exchange contracts.

Banking relationships The control of lines of credit and dealing lines with banks—both numbers of banks and the depth of each relationship.

Soft

Taxation Corporate taxation, including VAT, PAYE, overseas taxation, and relationships with revenue authorities; these can sometimes be the preserve of a separate taxation section.

Planning Often the preserve of a separate planning department which may not even report to the finance director, this is an area where the treasurer will at least need to advise, notably on financing for the future.

Capital structure A senior responsibility often discharged by the finance director or chief executive, this area includes working capital control, the raising of new equity and debt, the monitoring of gearing levels, etc.

Capital expenditure appraisal Establishment and monitoring of guidelines for large items, including appraisal of merger and acquisition prospects; this can be the responsibility of business divisions within the group, working within treasury/finance guidelines.

Financial control This is not the aggregation of numbers to produce accounts, but the establishment of parameters to appraise business. It often has a multinational aspect and requires all the skill that a treasurer can bring to bear.

Other aspects of corporate finance can be covered by the treasury function, including, for example, the custody of sales and purchase ledgers—notably in connection with working capital control and foreign exchange—and the preparation of annual accounts, particularly where the public profile of the company is perceived to be an important aspect. These are not included in this review since they are more commonly the preserve of the conventional accounting function.

It is probably true that the hard mainstream areas are those which finance directors seek primarily to be covered by treasury departments. Following on successful achievement in this area, other functions from the soft category might be added. The remainder of this chapter is therefore concerned with the strict treasury functions. Assuming that the corporate has decided that a professional approach and discipline needs to be applied to the management of the treasury function, how does a corporate establish one?

Recruitment

Firstly, the right man needs to be attracted to take the responsibility. Apart from the standard attributes of experience and integrity, the corporate should be looking for someone who is able to think clearly, keep calm in a crisis, and take the pressure of responsibility. There are no standard tests for these character points, though professional qualifications and previous experience should give a guide on the conscientiousness of the individual, which is at least the paper-guide for 50 per cent of the person needed.

Systems

An efficient department operates better with fewer rather than more people. Treasurers should not perceive the size of their empire as being judged by the number of people who report to them. Far better a small number of key professionals, both well remunerated and highly motivated, rather than vast banks of clerks performing dull routine tasks. To control large sums, particularly if the management style requires a positive contribution to be made by treasury instead of a passive role of simply, say, converting currency at spot on remittance, there needs to be a firm foundation of systems.

Since computerized systems are really just more efficient versions of manual systems, one should begin with a good appreciation of the structures necessary to enable the treasury operation to fulfil its functions properly. For example, a card index of all the active banks is a good starting point, containing the address, main contacts (client liaison officer, sterling dealers, currency dealers, back-up staff where known), phone numbers, and particular points to note, for example, on the routeing of funds or a particular weakness noticed on a prior occasion.

A full understanding of the company's banking system is also essential, and modifications may be needed to improve the efficiency of internal funding—for example, by rationalizing flows into one main clearer, who can concentrate funds into one master bank account on a same day basis, these funds then to be manipulated for greater efficiency of utilization overnight. Alternatively, if the enterprise is decentralized, a sound knowledge of the interrelationships between the businesses and the various banks is essential to enable the particular strengths of individual banks to be utilized to solve business problems—whether funding, cash handling or mergers and acquisitions.

On recruitment to a new company, the new treasurer will need to understand the new business to ensure that any ideas he or she may wish to apply are really suited to the new environment. Is there seasonality of cash flow for which special provision will need to be made, or are the cash flows unpredictable, requiring a different kind of flexibility? Are the foreign currency exposures quantified and categorized into economic, trading and liquidity? What are the major vulnerabilities of the business against which provision needs to be made? Are there structural or attitudinal impediments to particular approaches or institutions that require careful handling? When these questions have been answered the treasurer can concentrate on prioritizing problems in order to resolve issues in a logical way.

Efficient and workable systems are the basis of a good operation. They enable the treasurer to look up from the detail and concentrate on the rationale for a management approach and on the real decisions of management, on which eventually he or she will be appraised.

The computerization of the systems is a 'Mark II' process, effectively building on the foundation established in the manual system. A good computer system that is not relevant to the ground floor operations of the corporate may distort the workings of the function and be ultimately self-defeating and counterproductive. There are developments both in the treasury field and in systems that could help standardize operations in the longer term—one example is the 'cash management' terminal offered by many banks for monitoring accounts and moving funds world wide. Though many protocols are individual to the bank, the intense pressure for standardization is enabling data to be transferable between systems as a first step towards an 'industry standard'.

There are several packages marketed for corporates dealing with foreign exchange, and the exigencies of the marketplace will no doubt produce the better mousetrap which, with a few imitators, will perhaps become the accepted system for corporates. Since the market is still developing, some corporates have felt the need to produce their own systems rather than take an imperfect example on offer from outside, which might then require extensive customization to satisfy the needs of the company. This is certainly true of some of the bank-offered systems currently on offer, and applies also to some systems promoted by software houses—some of which are open to the charge of providing a solution in search of a problem. However the NIH (not-invented-here) syndrome is strong, and one should avoid the need perpetually to reinvent the computer disk.

Policies

It is not enough to recruit the person who installs the right systems, and simply leave it at that. What is that individual's goal? How is his or her performance to be measured? There needs to be established a clear framework for action by the treasurer, and a hierarchy of authority, so that what is delegated is clear, and, also as important, a process of action for what is not delegated.

The catalyst for the drive to create a new (or revitalize an old) treasury department may be a particular market experience, like rapid growth in exports, or privatization, takeover or management buy-out. Alternatively, in the absence of a firm philosophy or policy a department can atrophy and become ineffective and therefore unable to manage the inevitable funding, foreign exchange or business crises when they occur. The disaster, or disaster-avoidance rationale, is an important motivating factor for the corporate.

The approach to be taken depends fundamentally on the industry—for example, long production runs and lead times linked to fixed contracts require a correspondingly long time-frame for hedging activities. The norm in this environment would be for a fully hedged foreign exchange policy linked to long-term borrowing at fixed rates. Conversely, in an industry where profit margins are high and the ability exists to adjust prices at reasonably short notice, the economic exposure period is correspondingly shorter, and the normal treasury position can be much more aggressive and short term. Indeed, in this latter environment greater activity can appear rather avant-garde since, in the eyes of the board, it might be seen hardly relevant to the ongoing effort of the company to devote attention to sophisticated methods of hedging if healthy ongoing profits are seen to be pre-ordained as an integral part of the business. Why interfere with what the gods have ordained?

Not all companies will have the same philosophy on the scope to be given a treasurer, however able, articulate and trusted that person might be. All are influenced by the industry, many by their country of origin, some by past experiences of greater or less relevance to the present situation. Corporate culture is a fact of life, and the treasurer will need to ascertain (since it will seldom be consigned to paper) where the boundary exists between incisive and expeditious action and overextended authority. Suffice it to say that, in general, a written authority is of greater value than a verbal understanding, and the lowest common denominator for action (and reduction in personal vulnerability if that is a criterion of peace of mind) is that items not specifically delegated are outside one's powers.

It is better for the organization and for the treasury team if the powers and limits of authority at the various levels are clearly designated. This enables each level to act without compunction in its own area, and to relate openly with levels above its scope of authority. The final arbiter is the board, but since this only generally meets monthly or at irregular intervals, executive authority for large decisions needs to be delegated to either the chief executive, or the finance director, or an executive or management committee. Specific authority is preferable to a committee approach, as this gives crisper actions.

After a period of cautious and correct (in the organizational rather than results sense) activity, there will develop an understanding between the corporate entity and the treasurer, which should enable both to appreciate mutually the benefits of the function. Experience has shown that a lower profile of treasury activity increases effectiveness, and therefore, in general, the shorter this period of mutual acclimatization the better for all concerned.

Banking relationships

Banking relationships do not form part of a recognized examination syllabus in the same way as quantitative techniques or taxation, and therefore the subject is easy to dismiss as peripheral to the total treasury operation. Such an approach is short-sighted and even arrogant. The subject matter of good corporate banking is widening at a rate parallel to that of the corporate treasury function itself—indeed, it can be seen as the reverse of the same coin.

The scope of corporate banking seems in several respects to have been expanding on all fronts in the 1980s, with traditional business such as trade finance, syndicated loans and foreign exchange being overlaid with such new technologies as automated cash transfers and the new instruments of swaps, options and forward rate agreements. It is important that the corporate treasurer does not lose sight of the ball and become diverted onto relatively insignificant items that might appear the latest and the best, but do not address any real needs. Nevertheless, an appreciation should be maintained of the added value that some of these new approaches can really provide—as well as the risks involved for the unwary.

A word of caution is perhaps appropriate on some of the 'cash management' systems, which can offer impressive-looking facilities—e.g., printouts on-line of reported balances—or the ability to effect payment automatically out of an account. It might just be possible that the corporate has developed decent liaison and reporting mechanisms with the banks to enable the relevant information to be obtained in any case. Similarly, it might be perceived not to be in the company's best interests for payments outwards to be accelerated. An advantage of such systems is that they can instil a certain discipline into the dealing area, which increases control. For example, the requirement for a senior signatory to authorize via terminal the payments already input at a clerical level makes the process of authorization more structural than a file full of invoices and cheques to be signed, and is therefore more efficient and probably even safer from a control perspective.

Some of the financial instruments on offer might also be inappropriate for the corporate. For example, swaps are an excellent way to change a loans profile from variable to fixed rate, but the move from dollar borrowing to sterling involves several fiscal traps, including the taxation treatment of effective gains and losses on the unwinding of the transactions on maturity, and the tax treatment of the interest settlement payments in interim periods. Also, what might be a reasonable hedge at the outset could become a speculation should the underlying transaction (e.g., the dollar borrowing that was fixed by the swap) disappear or become diluted.

Caution is therefore advised on the novelty of some of the mechanisms and instruments on offer. Banks are becoming cast in the guise of the peripatetic door-to-door salespeople, with a bulging case of goodies and trinkets to tempt the unwary. This was certainly the impression in the years immediately after 'Big Bang' when banks were perceived to be establishing their rules and areas of marginal advantage. Treasurers are well advised to consider their needs carefully—including the span of their banking relationships—to establish where their best interests lie. Not to pursue the final sixteenth might be a better approach than to run the risk of upsetting long-established lines and relationships. To be slightly old-fashioned, even at the expense at the margin of perhaps employing an extra clerk, might help avoid some of the errors that could result from being first in new developments. Some businesses thrive on being a close second rather than being the trail blazer—the first over the top or over the cliff!

Within the area of foreign exchange, there is a series of banking services which the corporate should be able to tap. The perspective of the banking dealer is clearly much different from the standard corporate. The bank dealer sees virtually every move intra-day on the currency markets, and is very sensitive to sentiment, to resistance levels, and to large orders, whether from corporates or from central bankers (the dreaded 'intervention'). There is some advantage for the corporate treasurer to use the expertise offered by the bank trader. Clearly, it may not be too accurate from time to time, but advice as such is free, and its utility depends both on its quality and the ability of the corporate to react. Written advice from banks can also help the corporate, and there is a range of more or less glossy banking and economic publications issued by banks. For the corporate, this is a good source of specialized and intelligent comment; for the banks, this is a relatively cheap way of ensuring that their name is prominent in the eyes of the people who might be placing large transactions with them.

The familiarity of the bank dealer with options also helps underpin relationships with the corporate. Only a few years ago it was not uncommon for corporate treasurers to be in the position of tutors to their bank contacts in the structuring of their hedges. It is important for the bank dealer to speak in the same language as the corporate to underpin the confidence of mutual self-interest which is at the heart of a successful relationship.

Not to be underestimated is the importance of good, old-fashioned dealing back-up. Indeed, when there are occasional problems on delivery, or with the exchange rate quoted (e.g., premia treated as discounts), these can cause aggravation out of all proportion to the magnitude of the deal itself. The resolution of problems after the event (when no one is interested, except in proving it was not their fault) is tedious, inconvenient, and inefficient. No other item is so corrosive in its effect on banking relationships. As problems increase in magnitude and sensitivity, the more senior levels in the organization are brought into play. Arguably the more senior the involvement, the more intractable the problem, and the more damage to the relationship, which will be evident once the dust has settled. The trust resulting from the bank that quietly and without fuss gets it 'right first time' can almost be measured in its positive effect on the volumes of deals transacted.

The pendulum might swing back in due course towards the more traditional banking services, but at the time of writing such a trend is not yet in evidence, except perhaps in the area of lending where a premium is being placed again on relationships. The complexity of the banking services required by corporates has increased considerably, and this has been matched by the need for the treasurer to be up to and even ahead of the game. Treasurers must be able to define their evolving needs in a rapidly developing market, and the bank has to respond accordingly, since there is always another competitor waiting for an opportunity.

So that the corporate can appreciate the various strengths of its banks, where 'horses for courses' is the dictum that often operates, it is sometimes desirable to grade the banks. A range of the services offered, each of which has a different status, is illustrated in Table 14.1. Thus, a bank might be graded A to D depending on the depth of its relationship with the corporate. There is clearly more opportunity for long-term business the higher on the scale the bank is registered. However, banks are constantly moving up or down the scale,

Table 14.1 Grading banks

Categories	A	B	C	D
Banking	Main Clearer	x	x	x
Lines	Committed	Uncommitted	x	x
Terms	5 Years	1 Year	x	x
Forex	Yes	Yes	Yes	x
Specialist services	Yes	Yes	Yes	x
Advice:				
verbal	Yes	Yes	Yes	x
written	Yes	Yes	Yes	Yes

depending on performance. Alongside the grading of services is of course the credit assessment of banks, provided by the rating agencies such as Moody's, Standard & Poors and IBCA (International Bank Credit Analyst). As banks become regarded as corporate institutions that, just like their clients, can make mistakes, so loans and deposits to banks are regarded by the corporate as valuable and vulnerable. No matter how good the 'cash management' services provided by the banks, they are as nothing if the principal deposited is not repaid when due.

Therefore, galling though some corporate treasurers may find it, a high degree of attention needs to be devoted to banking relationships so that the corporate can be not only abreast of new developments in the banking world, but on top of them—in particular in their application to the corporate's own concern. The developments of only the last five years in options, swaps, futures, FRAs, caps and collars and other off-balance-sheet strategies and subtleties have, in the main, derived from the banking and brokerage sectors, and with the possible exception of OTC options have been bank-driven rather than driven by the demand of the corporate.

One of the most satisfying aspects of the job of corporate treasurer is the ability and requirement to interact with a wide range of institutions and people. The profile of the company in a day-to-day sense is in the hands of the treasurer who is in contact with the City constantly. A good banking and treasury profile could well lead to an improvement in the company's standing in the City and hence to a better share price—though, of course, the empirical evidence for this is thin. As new instruments are conceived the treasurer needs to keep abreast of the market, to compile a league table of banks for the various services required, and to maintain the longstanding relationships against the proverbial 'rainy day'. Therefore, much time needs to be concentrated on this important area, and the treasurer amasses dozens of City contacts in a standard year. Just as the treasurer might progress from company to company, banking contacts do likewise. This parallel growth in seniority and experience enables business to flourish between institutions which, historically, might not have been closely linked before.

The benefit of the relationships aspect of the creation of a treasury function is long term and not very apparent in comparison to the amount of time devoted in the early days especially. However, it is conceivable that the benefits could be of much greater significance in the years to come than ephemeral daily actions, even if these are underpinned by respectable computerized systems that stand the test of time.

Part II
Organizations, computer systems and procedures

Organizations

The style of organization of a treasury department is clearly related to the type of company, business and scope of operations. Three broad categories of companies can be identified: firstly, the national company, which has wide scope for funding operations and only a little for foreign exchange; secondly, the international company, with operations in different countries, but managed and controlled from one location; and, thirdly, the multinational company, with separate treasury operations in different countries, managing their own exposures and businesses.

Style is a matter of both form and content, and the implication is that different systems are appropriate for each. It is probably because of this that there are still many competing computer systems on the market. Some cater for banking-style operations, with the accent on the management of funds, nostro and correspondent accounts, and the maintenance of positions for a number of legal entities on the same system. These are most appropriate for international companies and multinationals, notably where a number of finance companies are involved.

International companies often work on a divisionalized basis, whereby international selling is standardized through special-purpose companies marketing the whole range of products (but possibly specializing in some division's product if the local market warrants this), but where production might be in different countries depending on their economies of scale and marginal advantage. In such an environment, treasury operations can be centralized in the headquarters of the main company, and possibly through the establishment of a separate finance company. In such a situation, the finance company will have the responsibility of ensuring that the positions of the individual operations are covered, and the total businesses are funded efficiently. It will therefore have relationships with the financial world and the City, in preference to the operations, who will relinquish this role. Funding and foreign exchange will become centralized and dealing will be aggregated in the one entity on behalf of the whole. The treasury system appropriate to this operation includes the maintenance of separate accounts with each of the operating units or divisions, as well as the monitoring of the positions of the finance company with the banks, and its own profit and loss and management accounts.

National companies might be very large—for example, some of the recently privatized utilities in various parts of the world. Their funding might be significant in volume, and impressive in the number of accounts and the capital employed. However, these companies and the small operator selling to a home market, share the common characteristic of a fairly simple foreign exchange operation. Foreign exchange is required only for the settlement of overseas invoices for supplies—often capital expenditure of a non-routine nature—or imports of raw materials for manufacturing purposes or, more commonly, finished goods for sale on the home market or, finally, for export purposes. In these instances, the requirement for foreign exchange is for a fairly simple system, robust and providing all the essentials, but not including the divisional allocations of the international company nor the quasi-banking characteristics of the true multinational.

Despite the different organizations, there are certain common characteristics in all treasury operations dealing with foreign exchange. All have to transact deals of different types: spots, forward, options. All have to produce confirmations of deals and maintain records. All have to account for and create accruals. The

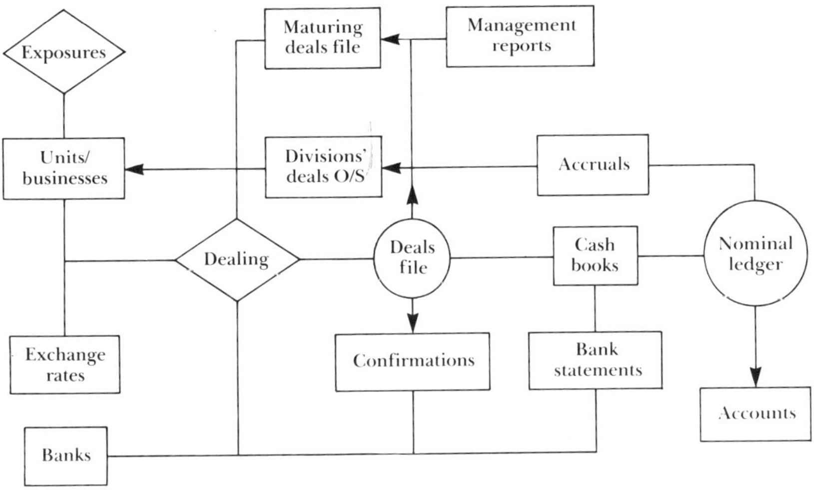

Flows as specified (mainly to right and centre)

Figure 14.1 **Dealing system flow chart: external, treasury, accounting**

organizational flow shown in Figure 14.1 illustrates the main interrelationships for an international company.

Deals originate from three sources: the main primary source is the underlying business or operating unit or division, and subsidiary sources are the banks and maturing deals, some of which require rolling forward or actions on maturity such as partial close-out or movement of funds.

The file of deals can be divided into current deals and matured deals, the latter growing in size as the year progresses. The deals file is used for a number of purposes, the creation of confirmations being the most immediate. It is also used for accounting, via updating cash books through entries passed through as a result of cash movement deriving from the deals, and via accruals created at period-ends (mainly month-ends). It is used as a source of management accounting information for the dealing and treasury operation, often integrating with the deals file other records of foreign exchange rate, either spot rates on the date of maturity of the deals, or the forward rate at the time the exposure was recognized (which could well vary from the forward rate booked, or budget rate for the year). It is also used to produce the 'ledger' of outstanding deals with divisions and units, which can also be a useful cross-check on their own records, and a reminder to them of the flows of currency and cash they are to expect. Finally, it is used to create a maturities files of deals outstanding, which, when arranged in date order, can provide a maturity ladder of deals awaiting action in, for example, the following week.

More in the accounting area, but also within the purview of the treasurer as he or she controls the flow of information on operations, is the impact of the deals as recognized in cash books and accruals on the nominal ledger. It is in this area that the proof of the performance measures adopted in appraisal of the dealing operation in the management accounting reports is cross-referenced with the final numbers. This can provide either a useful cross-check on the management accounting information, which is mostly more immediate and reactive to events, or a salutary reminder that the accountants might have a different view of the usefulness of a particular strategy. This is particularly apparent when budget rates are used for the conversion of all transactions for financial accounting purposes, and the ostensible effect of treasury deals is to depress performance as the budget fails to be met. It is also of interest when the accounts use spot rates on the day the cash moves, only to find that the treasury system drives out forward rates, and there is such an animal as an exchange difference between the two. The vexation this can cause the treasurer when the numbers are negative is almost as great as the consternation caused to the financial controller when the opposite is the case!

This organization flow is not very different for all the styles of organization mentioned above. Some have a more developed relationship with the subsidiaries via deals outstanding, notably when funding is combined with foreign exchange in a comprehensive treasury management package. Others have a particularly complex supplier relationship, with purchases of currency being channelled through a section with responsibility for aggregating currency requirements efficiently, this becoming another input into the dealing operation. Some have a highly developed banking network, with interactive lines and the ability to take risks and maintain positions on an intra-day basis, thus changing the dealing room into a quasi-bank or broking house, and therefore a profit centre in its own right (rather than a budget centre with the ability to contribute to total profits through the efficiency of bulk dealing or the aggregation of timely deals, which is what most corporate treasurers mean when they proudly refer to their operation as a 'profit centre'). Finally, in others, the accounting function is 'on top', with treasury relegated to moving the cash and slavishly covering on a one-by-one basis all the identified flows deriving from the units. Even in this pale imitation of a real treasury operation, when the management accounting role for example has been shorn of all rationale by the inability of treasury to contribute to total group performance, the basic flows of data are similar to that shown in Figure 14.1.

Systems

In order to relate to the company's need in foreign exchange management, a number of computer solutions have been created, and over time they are becoming specialized and refined. At the top level, and running on mainframes, are the banking systems. Having their origins in banks' dealing rooms, these are highly sophisticated, and specialize in the maintenance of a wide range of company and client information and, at the same time, maintain a real-time record of the ongoing position of dealers, making the bank responsive to the market and keeping the evolution of the dealers' positions under tight control. An aspect of such systems can be 'smart' methods of putting information onto the system, involving, for example, 'mouse' peripherals and dealing boards, thus obviating time-consuming screen-style manual input, at which dealers tend to claim to be not too proficient. These systems are clearly only partially relevant to the corporate. The 'dealing-room' aspects are a little rarefied for the corporates who know, for example, that their position is permanently 'long' dollars, and whose decisions are simply when to sell and how much. However, these systems—client ledger files, the confirmation systems often involving different methods of communication (letter, fax, telex), the database management systems, and the banking links and accounting—all share aspects with which the sophisticated corporate is familiar.

The blurred edges where such systems are available in the corporate area as well as banks, include money brokers and commodity dealers, insurance companies and investment houses, pension fund managers and a range of corporates whose preferred computer solution might sometimes be the biggest and most expensive rather than necessarily the most appropriate.

Medium systems tend to operate on smaller mainframes, minicomputers, or even some of the more powerful micros that are becoming very popular. Depending on the programming language, these can be difficult to modify and have generally evolved over a long period. Many are marketed by banks, but some are offered by software houses linked to computer manufacturers via an original equipment manufacturer (OEM) agreement, the hardware company providing worldwide offices for occasional use, while the software company, by its product, helps to move purchasers of hardware in the direction of its own OEM. Some systems are available as a complete package—the package being subject to revision and updating as the latest twist and rinky-dink to the evolution of the system is added. Others come in modules, with the corporate able to commence with a starter-pack of, say, forex and cash management, and then moving to options and swaps as capacity expands. All these systems are supported by trouble-shooters and development staff, and clearly if the company has a sufficiently significant operation, it is worth investing both money and time in a system that can cope with the complexities of the business.

It should be recognized, however, that no two businesses are alike, and that what is a minor concern to one company might be a real problem to another. Therefore, time and effort are needed to find the most appropriate system, and then even more commitment is required to put the ideas into operation and make the package work. In fact, it is not the purchase of the hardware and software, or the establishment of the files and databases and their required parallel running that causes the main effort and irritation in the adoption of new treasury systems. The main problems lie in the customization of the package to cope with the peculiar needs of the corporate. If such customization is then built into the original package, in order to sell an 'improved' version to other corporates, then the result can eventually look like the computer equivalent of the string and sealing-wax contraptions created by the late Heath Robinson. Alternatively, a Rolls Royce can be purchased when what one really needs is a tractor!

At the lower end of the spectrum is the work station, either provided by a bank, and possibly connected to its cash management system, or created by the corporate using a data-management package or a spreadsheet. The most simple is clearly the spreadsheet, where the sophistication of the treasurer or staff can enable quite robust systems to be built. Using macros in Lotus 'Symphony', for example, reactive models containing data for deals linked to exchange rates and revaluation tables can be created. These can produce the relevant accounting entries for both accrual and cash book purposes, as well as the data for management accounts. There is an upper level of approximately 250 deals per annum, above which such a system becomes unwieldy. Furthermore, since such a modest system does not produce its own confirmations, a part-time or full-time secretary is required. This system is therefore not cost-effective above a particular level, and requires considerable manual support. Finally, the more manual intervention needed, the less robust the system, and the greater the likelihood of errors. Needless to say, foreign exchange is not an area in which errors are permissible.

Between the spreadsheet and the mini-computer is the database package, often provided by banks but capable of development by a software house or in-house by the company. The following pages illustrate a typical system operational for an international company and capable of being transplanted to a number of locations. This comprises a series of modules, of which foreign exchange is the one discussed. The system works via input screens accessed by menus, creating a database of numbered deals. Confirmation files are created, together with financial and management accounting reports. Additional information to enable the system to work includes files of data on banks, subsidiary companies, exposures, and exchange rates. This system works on IBM micros supported by Hewlett-Packard peripherals.

Procedures

It is not difficult for treasurers to be preoccupied with the higher level and more glamorous parts of the job—for example, the provision of information to the board, the entertainment of bankers, or the creation of particular schemes to add value to the enterprise. In fact, if treasurers are not interested in these areas, they should probably examine carefully whether they have the right calling and whether there is not a 'back-room boy' striving to get out!

However, a treasurer ought to be interested in, but not preoccupied with, his or her 'back office'. This is the engine room where, if things go wrong, the result can be terminal! Much depends on trust—the banker's trust of the client's word and, in reverse, the corporate's trust of the advice, impartiality and efficiency of the banker. One also trusts the systems and operations to produce the correct result from the deals transacted, and indeed to transact the right deals. This is not just a matter of ensuring that the premia in forward deals, for example, are treated correctly, but that the audit trail is maintained properly, that proper controls on operations are in place, that speculative positions are not knowingly (or even worse, unknowingly) built up, and that the procedures are tight and understood.

At the heart of a good treasury operation is the treasury manual—a record of authorities, policies and procedures. Each operation needs to be fully thought through, for its relevance to the whole to be appreciated and for the total treasury function to be controlled properly. The results of an insecure operation can be dire indeed, whether resulting from changed personnel, clerical error, lax operation of old software, or the inevitable dislocation resulting from the introduction of new. Waiting in the wings are management consultants and auditors, ever eager to prove their worth by actually interfering in the operations of a vital centre or, better still, bringing such operations to a stop through the application of *post factum* rationalization to a fast-moving situation. Therefore, it is best to ensure that the systems are working properly, and that the treasury function has clear guidelines and procedures before the advisers are called in, since possibly afterwards may be too late.

At the simplest, procedures may seem to be somewhat simple or simplistic. It should be remembered that they are there not only as a point of reference for senior staff and as a reassurance for the company via the auditors, but also for the day-to-day guidance of the clerical staff who make the system work. It is much better for such guidance notes to be prepared by those who actually created the system than be imposed as an afterthought or, worse still, be imported from some external adviser whose motives might not be pure.

The following section is a procedures manual for the computer system outlined above. This talks the operator through the various steps required to make the system work, as well as explaining some of the practical workings of some of the financial instruments. The various files are explained, together with the accounting and management reports. Examples are included for reference purposes.

User Guide
The Jonathan Robin Company Limited
Treasury Dealing System

FOREIGN EXCHANGE

Preface

This user guide is designed to enable someone not familiar with the operation of the dealing system to:

- understand the current foreign exchange position
- find out which deals are currently in place and whether they are showing a profit or a loss when compared with current market rates
- undertake foreign exchange forward deals and currency options.

The layout of the guide should provide the user with comprehensive help in either understanding what particular screens are used for or how particular daily, weekly or monthly procedures are accomplished.

Contents

7 **Management reporting**
   1 Treasury exposure management (TEM) report: description
   2 Maturity ladder: description
   3 Deals to date report
   4 Confirmation exception reports

8 **Internal controls**
   1 Password/user ID
   2 Confirmation exception reports
   3 Cash office/sales ledger reports
   4 Bank confirmations

9 **'Change'**
   1 Signatories
   2 Subsidiaries
   3 Deals
   4 Foreign exchange exposures
   5 General ledger codes
   6 Month-end rates
   7 Adding or changing bank details
   8 Current and forward exchange rates

10 **Export data to Lotus 1-2-3**
   1 The export data function

11 **Programming changes**

CHAPTER 1

Preliminaries

There may be occasions when an inexperienced member of staff is called upon to use the dealing system to produce reports, undertake deals or establish the current dealing position.

These occasions should be rare and in most circumstances a period of training would be provided using the dealing test system on the micro-computer.

1 Get into the system

- Switch on micro using security and quote password key (consult treasury staff).
- Select dealing system box from screen menu, using cursor key < >. Press the 'enter' key.
- The dealing system will now load and show the current date (Figure 1). Press enter. Next a user ID will be requested (Figure 2). This can be obtained from an authorized user (e.g., the group treasurer, group controller or director of finance). Input the appropriate user ID and press 'enter'. A password will now have to be entered (Figure 3). This is also available from the senior staff mentioned above. There is also an option to change any of the previous information (Figure 4). Press the 'enter' key. You will now be in the treasury dealing system. The main menu (0.0) will be displayed.

2 Find out current dealing position

- Type 7, press enter. Type 1, press enter. Type 1, press enter. You are now in the maturity ladder screen. Type Y. Press

```
        JJJJJJJRRRRRRRRR
            JJRR         RRR        THE
            JJRR           RR
            JJRR           RR       JONATHAN
            JJRR         RRR
            JJRRRRRRRRRR            ROBIN
            JJRR     RR
            JJRR       RR           COMPANY
   JJJ      JJRR        RR
    JJJ    JJJRR          RR        LIMITED
      JJJJJ  RRR           RRR

T R E A S U R Y   D E A L I N G   S Y S T E M
```

```
ENTER DATE....... 08/09/90
```

Figure 1

```
        JJJJJJJRRRRRRRRR
            JJRR         RRR        THE
            JJRR           RR
            JJRR           RR       JONATHAN
            JJRR         RRR
            JJRRRRRRRRRR            ROBIN
            JJRR     RR
            JJRR       RR           COMPANY
   JJJ      JJRR        RR
    JJJ    JJJRR          RR        LIMITED
      JJJJJ  RRR           RRR

T R E A S U R Y   D E A L I N G   S Y S T E M
```

```
ENTER DATE....... 08/09/90
USER I.D.........
```

Figure 2

```
        JJJJJJJRRRRRRRRR
            JJRR         RRR        THE
            JJRR           RR
            JJRR           RR       JONATHAN
            JJRR         RRR
            JJRRRRRRRRRR            ROBIN
            JJRR     RR
            JJRR       RR           COMPANY
   JJJ      JJRR        RR
    JJJ    JJJRR          RR        LIMITED
      JJJJJ  RRR           RRR

T R E A S U R Y   D E A L I N G   S Y S T E M
```

```
ENTER DATE....... 08/09/90
PASSWORD.........
```

Figure 3

```
               JJJJJJJRRRRRRRRR
                   JJRR        RRR        THE
                   JJRR          RR
                   JJRR          RR       JONATHAN
                   JJRR        RRR
                   JJRRRRRRRRRR           ROBIN
                   JJRR     RR
                   JJRR       RR          COMPANY
         JJJ       JJRR        RR
          JJJ     JJJRR         RR        LIMITED
            JJJJJ  RRR           RRR

     T R E A S U R Y    D E A L I N G    S Y S T E M

                    ENTER DATE....... 08/09/90
                    PASSWORD......... ROBIN
                    CHANGE ? (Y/N)... N
```

Figure 4

enter, this leaves the current date as originally displayed. Changing this date will make the report print out deals outstanding up to the new date selected.

- The micro will now calculate which deals are still current and will print them out. Press enter escape 4 enter 7 enter 8 to get back out of the dealing system.
- The report called 'FX maturity ladder' shows deals that are coming up for settlement on particular dates. These deals should be addressed, i.e., rolled or closed out at least two business days prior to the settlement date. If the letters CL (which stand for 'closed') appear after the deal type TRAN or LIAB, this means that the particular deal or deals have been addressed and no further action is required on them. They only remain on the maturity ladder because the base currency (sterling) and foreign currency funds that are moving as a result of the deals have yet to move, e.g., two business days away. A fuller description of the FX maturity ladder and its interpretation can be found in Chapter 7.

3 Produce treasury exposure management (TEM) report

From the main menu (0.0) type 1, press enter, type 5, press enter, type 1, press enter. You are now in screen 1.5.1. The prompt on the screen asks whether you wish to continue with the report. Select the Yes option after you have ensured that the printer is switched on and correctly connected. Once the report is started it will take some 10 minutes to run. Each currency is calculated individually (and then printed on a separate line of the report). It is therefore important that no other documents are printed while the report is being produced or the report will be printed partially complete. This is the simple version for running the TEM report.

A more accurate procedure should normally be followed—see the routine used in Chapter 4, 'Weekly procedures'. A full description of the terms found in the TEM report can be found in Chapter 7. The three-letter code is the standard SWIFT currency coding. Under 'type' in the report it will state New, Sim or Cyl. New is a straight foreign exchange contract. Sim or Cyl correspond to simple and cylinder currency options which may or may not be in-the-money and therefore exercisable. TRAN or LIAB correspond to whether the deal is covering a trading (TRANsaction) exposure or Liquidity (LIAB-ility) exposure. The latter are only used when taking hedging action or deposits/borrowings the parent company has with its subsidiaries. These deposits are made in currency and therefore there is a currency risk for the parent company.

The counterparty refers to the bank that was used for the deal. The S and B indicators in the 'type' column of the report indicate whether currency (i.e., other than sterling, the base currency for this system) has been sold or bought. This is further emphasized by the 'currency amount' column which shows a figure in brackets if the currency has been sold and without brackets if it has been bought. The currency amount always refers to the currency denoted in the 'currency' field of the report.

The exchange rate is the all-in rate for which the deal was struck. This rate is made up of two components.

(1) The 'spot rate' for the currency, which is expressed as the value of one currency in terms of another for a delivery of that currency two business days away.
(2) An interest rate adjustment ('forward points') to correct for the disparity between interest rates for the base currency (pounds sterling) and interest rates of another currency. The interest rate adjustment will always be necessary if a deal has been struck for other than two business days away. The sterling value is the amount of sterling (currency amount divided by exchange rate) that will be paid or received on the settlement date of the deal.

The profit/loss on current rate is the valuation of the deals already outstanding against a market rates valuation. Effectively, if the currency has been sold and therefore sterling will be received, this column values how much it would be to reverse this deal, i.e., buy the currency and sell sterling. In doing so it mimics how much it would cost/gain if all the present FX contracts were removed. This column uses the 'current and forward rates' that are currently in the system. To check whether these rates are approximately correct, go back to the main menu (0.0) and input 5 enter 3 enter 5 enter A enter ZZZ enter. This will print out the current rates for each currency in the system. These can then be checked against daily rates in a newspaper or up-to-the-minute rates using Reuters or Telerate. Forward rates are also used in the calculation of the profit/loss column. These can be checked for each currency by typing from the main menu (0.0) the following: 1 enter 4 enter 3 enter and then the appropriate currency code. The buy and sell forward points should then be checked and adjusted against Reuters or Telerate.

CHAPTER 2

Quick menu guide

The dealing system structure (Figures 5 and 6) is made up of a series of linking menus, a concept also found in spreadsheet packages, e.g., Lotus 1-2-3.

The next few pages show the hierarchical structure of these menus. They are all accessible from the main menu (0.0).

The numbers quoted above the description, e.g., 4.4 'confirmation', are the numeric keystrokes required to get into that particular screen when starting from the main menu (0.0).

In the example above, a combination of keystrokes of 4 enter 4 enter, starting with the main menu on the screen, would pull up the confirmation verification menu.

If a screen is called up that is not a menu, and therefore does not have an exit function, the user can return to the previous menu by pressing the ESC-ape key on the keyboard.

THE JONATHAN ROBIN COMPANY LIMITED
TREASURY DEALING SYSTEM – FOREIGN EXCHANGE

SYSTEM:	1.0	FOREIGN EXCHANGE	
	2.0	MONEY MARKET	} MODULES NOT
			} AVAILABLE IN
	3.0	BORROWINGS	} THIS VERSION
FACILITIES:	4.0	CONFIRMATIONS	
	5.0	MAINTENANCE	
	6.0	ACCOUNTS	
	7.0	REPORTS	
	8.0	EXIT	

CHOOSE ONE OPTION ⇒

Figure 5 : Screen 0.0

THE JONATHAN ROBIN COMPANY LIMITED
TREASURY DEALING SYSTEM

1.0 NEW DEAL

2.0 OPTIONS

3.0 DELIVERY

4.0 FX RATES

5.0 FX EXPOSURES

6.0 EXIT

CHOOSE ONE OPTION ⇒

Figure 6 : Screen 1.0

THE JONATHAN ROBIN COMPANY LIMITED
TREASURY DEALING SYSTEM - FOREIGN EXCHANGE - QUICK MENU GUIDE

SCREEN REF

1.0 FOREIGN EXCHANGE

1.1 NEW DEAL

1.2 OPTIONS

1.3 DELIVERY

1.4 FX RATES
- 1 CURRENT
- 2 MONTH END
- 3 FORWARD POINTS
- 4 BUDGET RATES
- 5 AVERAGE DEAL RATES

1.5 EXPOSURES
- 1 BUDGET TEM
- 2 LATEST FORECAST
- 3 CURRENCIES
- 4 LATEST FORECAST
- 5 RECEIVABLE
- 6 PAYABLE

1.6 EXIT

REF

4.0 CONFIRMATIONS

4.1 FOREX
- 1 NEW DEAL
- 2 REPRINT
- 3 SIMPLE OPTION
- 4 REPRINT
- 5 CYLINDER
- 6 REPRINT

4.4 VERIFICATION
- 1 NEW DEAL
- 2 SIMPLE OPTION
- 3 CYLINDER OPTION

4.5 EXIT

Figure 7

THE JONATHAN ROBIN COMPANY LIMITED

TREASURY DEALING SYSTEM - FOREIGN EXCHANGE - QUICK MENU GUIDE

SCREEN REF

5.0 MAINTENANCE

5.1 BANK FILE
- 1 DISPLAY
- 2 CHANGE
- 3 ADD ITEM
- 4 REMOVE
- 5 PRINT

5.2 CORRESPONDENT
(SUBHEADS AS 1)

5.3 CURRENCY FILE
(SUBHEADS AS 1)

5.4 DEAL
- 1 DISPLAY
- 2 MODIFY
- 3 PRINT

5.5 ACCOUNTS
- 1 SUBSIDIARY
- 2 TREASURY

5.6 SUBSIDIARY
(SUBHEADS AS 1)

5.7 SIGNATORY
(SUBHEADS AS 1)

5.8 EXIT

REF

6.0 ACCOUNTS

6.1 FOREX

6.4 CASH OFFICE

6.5 EXIT

REF

7.0 REPORTS

7.1 FOREX
- 1 MATURITY LADDER
- 2 DEALS TO DATE
- 3 TEM REPORT
- 4 POSITION CHANGE

7.2 EXPORT DATA

7.3 CONFIRMATIONS
- 1 BANK CONF REFS
- 2 DEALS WITH NO CONF
- 3 DEALS NOT CONFIRMED BY THE BANK

7.4 CASH OFFICE

7.5 SALES LEDGER

7.6 MONTH END

7.7 EXIT

Figure 8

CHAPTER 3

Daily procedures

Detail These daily procedures are illustrative of the routine daily tasks that should be performed using the dealing system. They are not exhaustive and would be supplemented by additional tasks discussed under the weekly and month-end procedures (Chapters 4 and 5) at the appropriate time of the month. In addition, there may be ad hoc procedures and reports that are required for a special exercise.

1 Current foreign exchange rates

It is important that the current exchange rates are input into the system on a regular basis (usually daily is sufficient—first thing in the morning) so that the maturity ladder column 'profit/loss on current rate' and the TEM report columns 'gain/loss v plan' and 'gain/loss v spot' are calculated correctly.

The rates that are currently in the system can be checked by printing them out using screen 5.3.5—see Chapter 9 for instructions to change current rates.

2 Maturity ladder (FX deals outstanding)

This report needs to be produced each working day by 11.00 am to ensure that:

- FX deals approaching maturity are addressed and action is taken;
- base currency (sterling) cash that is expected to move on a

particular day is recorded in the dealing diary so that appropriate actions can be taken when placing or receiving overnight money market funds;

- management (in particular the group treasurer) can assess the current worth or liability against forward rates of those foreign exchange deals currently in place.

This report can be selected using screen 7.1.1. For fuller understanding of the terms used in the FX maturity ladder, see the description given in Chapter 7.

3 Back-up routine

At the end of each day the dealing system that resides on the Winchester hard disk of the IBM/compatible micro should be 'backed up' onto 5.25 in. or 3.5 in. floppy disks and kept in safe storage. This procedure is necessary to ensure that the database that contains details of all the FX deals, together with their appropriate codes, remains intact.

This back-up routine should be regular and automatic. To this end, there should be installed on the main menu on the computer an option called 'back-up'. This should be selected and the appropriate back-up disks used, which should be utilized as a hierarchy (see below).

These disks should be kept in a safe and fireproof lock-box. A table can be maintained showing which set of disks should be used for the daily back-up for each day, these being used chronologically. For example, three sets of disks (perhaps in pairs) called Monday, Tuesday and Wednesday (back-up 1 and 2), may be used in rotation. This is known as the grandfather, father, son routine. Thus if Tuesday's disks were used yesterday, Wednesday's disks would be used as back-up today.

As a check to which set of disks are next, refer to the table mentioned with the floppy disks, e.g.:

	September							
Monday	3	8	11	16	19	24	29	
Tuesday	1	4	9	12	17	22	25	30
Wednesday	2	5	10	15	18	23	26	

Monday's disks are next and today's date is 8 September. After the back-up routine has been selected the following message might appear on the screen:

C>BACKUP C:\DEALING.SYS A:

Insert Archive Diskette 01 in Drive A: WARNING! All files in the \root directory WILL BE DELETED! Press Any Key To Continue, Control-C To Abort.

The first part of the message refers to the direction of the archiving, i.e., the back-up routine held in the 'C' directory is backing up the entire C:\Dealing.SYS directory onto the floppy disk held in the A drive of the micro.

The second part of the message should be heeded. Ensure before striking any key that:

- the correct set of disks have been chosen
- the first of those disks marked 1 has been correctly inserted into the A drive.

Press enter. The files currently held on the floppy disk will be deleted. The system will then back up files from the hard disk until the floppy disk is full. If there are more files to back up, the system will ask you to insert 'Diskette 02' and once this has been done the system will continue backing these up. At first only two back-up disks might be required to back-up all of the dealing software together with transaction details. As the files grow with dealing, additional back-up disks may need to be added.

Once the back-up routine is finished the most recently backed-up disks should be placed behind the latest previous back-up disks used in the lockable disk box.

The system should always be backed-up on separate disks to the daily back-up in the following circumstances:

(1) if the micro is giving periodic disk error messages (an indication that the hard disk may be failing);
(2) at the month-end (never overwritten);
(3) before any programming changes are made by the software maintenance company;
(4) if the operator is unhappy with the performance of the dealing system in any way.

In cases (1) and (4) the user should inform the software support staff immediately.

4 Checking third party confirmations

The dealing system is essentially a deal-logging system with the key data being held in the computer memory in a database form. It is not sufficient that the user accepts that everything that has been input to the system is correct. Therefore, when bank confirmations are received from the counterparty bank from, or to whom, foreign currency has been bought, or sold, these should be compared to the company's own perception of the deal recorded in the dealing system databases.

There might be occasions when the bank's perception is different from the company's. Almost exclusively such differences are accounted for by clerical errors on the part of the bank. There may, however, be the possibility that the company and the counterparty believe they have both bought or sold the currency due to mistake at the time of the deal. In these circumstances neither party's confirmation is correct and in English law the deal would be treated as null and void. It is not possible in most circumstances to correct a dealing misconception without an inherent loss to the company. This may be large and could total many thousands of pounds, solely because the rates for a particular currency have moved from the levels achievable at the time of the original aborted deal. It is therefore crucial that the third party confirmations are checked as soon as practicable after they have been received by the company, and preferably by a different section from the one that performed the original deal on behalf of the company.

This is achieved using the confirmation verification menu (4.4). Once this has been selected the user types in:

- the reference of the deal that is being checked
- the code of the counterparty.

Without referring to the database, the user will then type in exactly what is said on the counterparty confirmation, e.g., currency, amount, rate, bought/sold sterling value and settlement date for new deals (straightforward foreign exchange contracts). After typing these in the user will get a series of messages on the right-hand portion of the screen detailing whether it matches with the record on the system (MATCHED) or it does not (ERROR).

Errors will then have to be investigated immediately by referring to the hard copy of the company's deal held in the dealing file. If all fields checked receive a MATCHED message the system takes the user to the bank reference line. Here the user should input the counterparty's reference shown on the foreign exchange deal. This reference will later be used in any confirmation letters subsequently sent to that counterparty referring to that particular deal.

After this has been input a MATCH reference will appear on the screen. This should be written on the face of the counterparty confirmation to show that it has been input and checked by the system.

It is vitally important that this checking exercise be performed 'blind' (i.e., without prior reference to the company's detailed files), also only what is said on the confirmation should be input. This ensures that no problems arise in trying to interpret a confirmation in the company's terms. Thus, if the user inputs the bank sold currency, it would check to see whether the dealing system has a record of the company buying that currency.

This confirmation verification routine should be used in all circumstances. As an additional check, large value items might be subject to extra scrutiny. For example, when 'new' cover (i.e., excluding deal rollovers) is being taken all deals of value greater than, say, \$3 000 000 might be additionally checked manually by a senior treasury/finance officer, who should sign his approval on the face of the third party confirmation.

The same principle should be applied for options and for forward contracts (slightly different verification screens would, however, be used).

CHAPTER 4

Weekly procedures

1 Dealing procedures

A period of training on the test dealing system should be provided by treasury staff before any other person is allowed to use the dealing system. In most circumstances this should be possible. However, on the rare occasions when this is not possible the routine stated below should be used.

A brief overview of the dealing procedures can be illustrated, as follows:

(a) Establish which foreign exchange deals need to be undertaken.
(b) Undertake deals using screen 1.1—agree settlement dates, currency flows and funds routeing with counterparty dealer.
(c) Confirmations: Print using screen 4.1.1. Pass to signatories for signing and have envelopes typed by departmental secretary. On return have confirmations copied, the copies filed and the originals sent out.
(d) Code currency and sterling flowing in deal using screen 6.1.
(e) Produce cash office report using screen 7.4, and sales ledger report using screen 7.5.

(a) Establish deals to be undertaken

This can be done by accessing a variety of sources.

(1) Foreign exchange maturity ladder (see daily procedures in Chapter 3 and description in Chapter 7).
This report should be examined to see which deals have settle-

ment dates within the next three business days (excluding weekends and bank holidays) which are not 'closed', i.e., have the CL reference displayed under deal type. If any are found, each deal should be examined in the current dealing file (lever arch file of manual records) to see what action should be taken. If currency has been sold for a particular day, e.g., 30 September, and no currency is available for delivery to meet this contract, the deal should be 'rolled'—that is, buy and sell currency simultaneously such that the deal maturing on 30 September is closed out and a new deal for a later date substituted in its place. In practice this would be achieved as follows:

US$ 5 000 000 sold for settlement 30 September.
New deal required:
Co. buys US$ 5 000 000 for settlement 30 September and simultaneously sells US$ 5 000 000 for a later date when some US dollar funds are expected (usually a month-end), e.g., 31 October.

(2) Dealing diary for the current year.
The first job every morning is to review the dealing diary to establish which deals are maturing. This check is in addition to the foreign exchange maturity ladder. The diary will include such other items as maturing deposits/borrowings, e.g., money market and acceptances. In addition it may be necessary to purchase currency to fulfil the interest payments that need to be made to service the company's currency borrowings, which may be mostly external items, but can be intra-group. These will be diarized where appropriate.

(3) Review any telexes or faxes which arrive FAO the treasurer or assistant treasurer.
Throughout the month and more normally at the month-end telexes arrive from subsidiaries and main distributors indicating they wish to pay their sales ledger debts with the company. In the case of subsidiaries they would mention how much they are paying on their current, materials or deposit accounts together with the 'date funds available'. This is akin to the settlement date of a contract. However, it should be noted that no funds will actually move until treasury instructs the subsidiary/distributor to deliver the funds to a particular bank to settle the company's part of a foreign exchange contract.

Generally if subsidiaries mention they have funds available, treasury will sell these currency funds to a bank and then receive base currency (sterling) funds to the company's bank account. Treasury will instruct the subsidiary/distributor by fax/telex to deliver the funds sold to where the purchaser requires those funds.

It should become apparent after reviewing these three areas which deals need to be undertaken.

In addition, the group treasurer or senior finance staff may require the company to take action on the foreign exchange market to protect the company from the appreciation of the base currency (pound) against other currencies. For example, when the pound appreciates in value the company receives less in sterling terms for the sales of currency that it has to make throughout the year.

This final need for a foreign exchange deal will be informed to the user on an irregular nature dependent on the foreign exchange market for that particular day.

All the above categories would require the user to undertake foreign exchange dealing transactions. Having established which deals need to be undertaken, the following procedure should be used when dealing:

(b) Undertake deals

Get into the dealing system. From the main menu go into screen 1.1.

You are now in the foreign exchange dealing screen. A new, unique deal reference will appear at the top of the screen.

The user should now input the currency (i.e., other than base currency, e.g., yen) using the three-lettered currency code shown on 5.3.3.

Input the direction of the deal, i.e., to sell or to buy the currency, as an S or a B. The type of foreign exchange deal should then be input. This is either a T (transaction/trading) or an L (liquidity) management deal. In most circumstances this will be a T as most deals are undertaken to protect the company's trading position not to hedge any currency deposits or borrowings it may have. The currency amount should then be inserted after it has been determined using the routine mentioned earlier.

Next, a bank should be inserted using its alphanumeric code

(see 5.1.5). The bank to be used is determined by a number of factors, the most important of which are:

- the current deal being rolled is with this bank (ease of administration)
- the quotes given are the most competitive (best price)
- the subsidiary/distributor can deliver the funds easily using the bank, without mistakes (practicality, confidence).

In practice, if a deal is being quoted competitively, i.e., when more than one bank is simultaneously asked for a price, the bank code will only be inserted when the outcome of the 'auction' is known. Once this is known the dealer's name can be inserted. The rest of the procedure can be seen by referring to Chapter 6.

The 'new deal' screen should provide the user with comprehensive help when undertaking the deal with the bank. Features of the system include:

(1) relating the new deal being undertaken with maturing deals for the sold/purchased currency, counterparty and settlement date and informing the user of net currency and sterling which will flow as a result of the netting of those deals;
(2) giving the sterling equivalent of the new deal struck so that it can be agreed with the bank's dealer;
(3) using colours to indicate direction, enabling the user to know instinctively whether 'money' is coming in or going out: red means out and blue means coming into the parent company.

(c) Confirmations

A deal is a verbal undertaking to exchange one currency for another at a given and agreed rate, for a determined future date, or a deposit of borrowing of a given principal at a given rate of interest. All deals need to be confirmed in writing so that the amounts, rates, dates and delivery can be checked by both sides. Lack of agreement on the details implies a need to correct the deal, in case it is made void by the non-agreement of the parties at maturity. Accordingly, confirmations are a crucial part of the dealing process although naturally they occur after the verbal dealing itself. Counterparties provide reciprocal confirmations, which should be checked independently.

The dealing system enables the user to print confirmations without inputting any further information, apart from the reference and signatories, after the deal has been struck and recorded.

It is usual to print all confirmations for deals undertaken during the day as one of the last tasks of the day. The following routine should be followed.

Select screen 4.1.1 if it is a new deal; use 4.1.3 and 4.1.5 for simple and cylinder options. Input the deal reference of the deal to be printed and press enter. Input the two signatories to be used on letter using the three-letter alphabetic code (see 5.7.5). The signatories should be members of staff on the current financial (list B) signatory list who will be available to sign the letters when produced.

The confirmation will now be built on the screen in two halves. Once the first half has been displayed on the screen, press enter. The second half will be displayed. A prompt Y/N will then ask if the user requires the confirmation to be printed. This should be answered Y only when the printer has been checked and that it has sufficient headed notepaper. The confirmation will then be printed. If a further print of the confirmation is required (e.g., a bank requests it or different signatories are required) the reprint screens will be required, i.e., 4.1.2, 4.1.4 and 4.1.6).

All confirmations required for signing should be sealed in a plastic file together with a copy of the dealing screens used by the dealer when undertaking the deal. The plastic folder should then be passed to the appropriate signatories. Once signed, the confirmation should be passed to the departmental secretary who will type appropriate envelopes and dispatch the confirmation after retaining a photocopy. The signed confirmation photocopies, together with any dealing back-up papers, should be returned to the treasury unit for filing in the manual dealing files by currency.

(d) Coding of deal

Any deal undertaken by treasury which has 'net sterling' flowing either out or into the company's bank account has to be reported to the cash office so that appropriate nominal ledger entries can be made. As part of the dealing procedure, therefore, any sterling flowing as a result of foreign exchange deals will need to be coded. The dealing system 'accounts' program is structured to help the user code the currency flowing to the correct account with the minimum of effort.

Select screen 6.1. The screen asks if the user wishes to continue with the 'allocations of transactions'. Select the Y option. The system will now scan to find deals that have been 'closed' since last time for which the sterling flowing has yet to be coded (allocated). Once the file has been scanned the next unallocated deal reference will appear on the screen. The user should then look this up in the dealing file. The questions appearing on the screen should then be answered. The series of prompts should take the user through the coding of that particular deal without any direct knowledge of the codes used in the general ledger. At the end of coding that particular deal, the system will save the information and then ask if the user wishes to continue allocating deals. If all deals have been coded a message will be shown on the screen to this effect.

(e) Cash office and sales ledger reports

When new deals have been coded the cash office needs to be informed of the sterling that will flow on a particular day from/to a particular bank. The screen to be used is 7.4. This enables the bank account movements to be reconciled and the accounts to be posted correctly. Errors in transmission can be located at this point, and corrected speedily.

Similarly, the sales ledger report should also be printed, using screen 7.5. The purpose of the sales ledger report is to notify the sales ledger of which customers/subsidiaries are paying and how much currency is being remitted. This is then posted to the sales ledger at the relevant budget rate, and the exchange difference is driven out to a separate account for monitoring and control purposes.

2 Forward foreign exchange rates

In world markets there is always a difference in the price of commodities. In the case of 'money' the difference is reflected in the value of one currency compared to another and the difference between one currency's interest rate compared to another. The cost or benefit of holding or owing one currency as compared to another can be expressed in terms of the price of that currency *vis-à-vis* the other. This can be shown using the following example:

Assume the current rate for the pound sterling (Stg) in US dollars (US$) is 1.65 and one year interest rates are 8 per cent for the US$ and 11 per cent for the Stg. The user should then decide whether it would be better to have Stg 100 worth of sterling (i.e., Stg 100), or Stg 100 worth of US$ (in this case $165). The user would be indifferent if the currency markets were stable and there was no difference in the earning capacity of both investments. However, in this example the holder could put the US$ on deposit at 8 per cent or could put Stg on deposit at 11 per cent. At the end of a year the position would be as follows:

Stg	US$
111	178.20

Given that the rate of US$/Stg is still $1.65 : Stg 1, the dollar holdings in terms of sterling would only be Stg 108.

If there were no allowance on the foreign exchange markets for the difference of yield, depositors would always favour high yield/interest bearing countries (e.g., Australia) while borrowers would favour the opposite (e.g., Switzerland).

The currency markets are in true equilibrium so that an adjustment is made in the price of one currency for another to make allowance for the difference in earning capacity. In the above example this equates to 3 per cent. This adjustment is necessary or else the sharp investor could:

Day 0:	Borrow $165 at 8 per cent Sell $165 at 1.65 to give Stg 100 on Day 0 Buy $178.20 at 1.65 to give Stg 108 for Day 365 Place Stg 100 on deposit at 11 per cent
Day 365	Receive interest on Stg deposits of Stg 11 Total funds now Stg 111 Deliver $178.20 bought on above foreign exchange Contract to lender and pay Stg due at Stg 108 Net Stg left in bank (111–108) = Stg 3

Thus the investor who did not have any funds at the start made Stg 3 without trying.

This example shows that markets once in equilibrium will not allow this inequality to exit. Thus in the example above, the 'investor', when asking to buy US$ forward on the foreign exchange would not be able to do it at par, i.e., $1.65 in this case. It would be at a rate that would ensure that there is a zero sum total to the above example. Using the above example this would be at a rate of $1.6054. The difference between this rate and the 'spot rate', i.e., the date available for Day 0, is called the forward points. In this example it would be $1.6500 – $1.6054 = $0.0446, known as 446 forward points.

The forward points are input into the dealing system as part of the weekly routine. It is important that they are updated on a regular basis so that the column 'profit/loss against current rate' in the foreign exchange maturity ladder (7.1.1) correctly reflects the true cost of completely closing the foreign exchange deals which are currently held in the system.

Example

Deal currently held in the system:

Settlement date
US$ sold 5 000 000 @ 1.55 = Stg 3 225 806.45 31 December

To buy back the current deal the reverse would have to be undertaken.

Buy US$ 5 000 000 for 31 December

Current spot rate: 1.65 Spot date: 30 September

Forward point adjustment to buy forward to 31 December from a start point of 30 September = 52 points.

'All in forward rate' = 1.65 − 0.0052 = 1.6448

Cost of buying back $5 000 000 @ 1.6448 = 3 039 883.27

Gain to be shown in last column of foreign exchange maturity ladder

Stg (3 225 806.45 − 3 039 883.27) = Stg 185 923.18

The forward points for each currency are input into the system using screen 1.4.3. Both sides of the market, i.e., buy and sell, are input for a number of months hence (e.g., 1, 2, 3, 6 and 12 months). The system will pro rata how many points are required by first evaluating how many days to the future the settlement date is compared to the current spot date and then using the appropriate nearest indices: 45 days in the future would use the average of the one- and two-month rates.

Once the forward points have been input for each currency the system becomes totally automatic. A weekly review of the forward point screen for each currency should be sufficient to ensure that the dealing system is not too far out of line with the interest rate market.

3 Treasury exposure management (TEM) report

The TEM report is produced by using a number of the databases within the dealing system. To produce an accurate report it is therefore necessary to ensure that these databases are current.

The sequence of the automatic TEM report program is detailed below.

(1) Select a currency.
(2) Find out which deals are outstanding at the date of the report. Compare total of currency deals outstanding with that of the total exposure for a year for that currency. Express the result in terms of 'months' value of residual cover.
(3) Total the currency field for all deals of that particular currency year to date ('total currency'), together with the total sterling ('total sterling') on such deals. Sold and bought are netted as negative and positive when summing. Divide total currency by total sterling, producing an average exchange rate per currency, for all deals in the year to date.
(4) Compare 'total currency' with currency exposure for year. Calculate difference. This is equivalent to amount of currency not yet sold. Divide the result by the 'current rate'. Store result ('residual sterling'). Add 'residual sterling' to 'total sterling'. Result equals 'total expected sterling'. Compare result with 'plan sterling' (i.e., total currency exposure divide plan rate for currency). Resulting difference expressed in terms of StgK in the 'gain/loss v plan' column of report.
(5) Total currency received in year that has been posted to current/materials account on the sales ledger calculated from the currency received screen (1.5.5). Subtract from with total currency exposure for year. Divide result by current rate and store ('current sterling'). Divide currency received by plan rate. Add to this result the total posted for that currency to treasury exchange difference fields 'SLM and SLC'. This gives the total sterling achieved by just selling for spot so far. Add to this 'current sterling' to give total expected sterling using the spot rate sale only option. Compare the result with 'total

expected sterling'. As above, the difference is expressed in terms of StgK in the 'gain/loss v spot' column of the report.

(6) Print out report currency by currency. Static databases also accessed for printing the report are as follows:

- currency file (5.3)—selects all currencies inserted in system
- currency exposure file (1.5.3)—'total currency exposures' column
- budget rates (1.4.4)—'AOP' column
- current rates (1.4.1)—'current spot' column.

If any of these databases do not hold the latest information the TEM report will not be totally accurate. The first three databases will probably only require revision annually; the last should be changed immediately prior to running the report.

Summary of TEM report procedure:

(1) Call up screen 1.5.5 'currency received' for each currency that has had a delivery since the last TEM report was run and save the result by responding Y-es to the question at the bottom of the screen.
(2) Update current foreign exchange rates (see 'Change', Chapter 9).
(3) Ensure currency, exposures and budget rate databases are accurate.
(4) Print TEM report. This can take up to around 10 minutes, depending on the number of deals and the memory of the computer.

In practice, (2) above provides the largest single effect on the report. A fuller explanation of the terms used in the TEM report can be seen in Chapter 7 under TEM report description.

4 Confirmation exception reports

Three reports (7.3.1, 7.3.2 and 7.3.3) are available from the system and are designed to ensure that:

- the audit can match third party confirmations with company confirmations on a test check basis;
- the company sends out a copy of the deal confirmation;

- a reciprocal confirmation is received from the counterparty.

The last two, 7.3.2 and 7.3.3, are designed to run on an exception basis, i.e., they only report the deals that have not been notified to the company or confirmations from third party not received.

The user should print at least two of these reports—7.3.2 and 7.3.3—on a weekly basis at minimum. This will ensure that there is timely checking of company confirmations with the counterparty's own confirmations. A copy of each report should be provided to the internal audit department on request. The treasury function should ensure that within one working day of the deal being struck the company's own confirmation is dispatched and that within four working days the counterparty's confirmation has been received and checked using the confirmation verification system (4.4). Regular printing of reports 7.3.2 and 7.3.3 will help this to be achieved.

Report 7.3.1 prints all deals year to date in deal reference order together with the bank references which were received on the counterparty's matching confirmation. A reference cannot be input into the system until the deal has been matched with the company's own perception. This report could be used by internal audit to test check confirmations received by the company.

CHAPTER 5

Month-end procedures

1 Monthly back-up

Chapter 3, 'Daily procedures', explained the use of the back-up function on the main menu of the micro and the importance in maintaining an accurate version of the dealing system. The grandfather, father, son technique of saving the dealing system is adequate in most circumstances to maintain a corrupt-free version of the dealing system. However, there may be occasions when, due to a hard or software fault, the database becomes corrupted over a period of time without being brought to the user's notice. Obviously, if it happens over a period of more than three days (the length of the revolving back-up period) a corrupt version of the system will overwrite a previously corrupt-free version.

For this reason a separate monthly back-up disk is used to back up the dealing system. This disk is NEVER overwritten. If a chronic fault occurs it will be possible to restore the system to a previous fault-free mode once the fault has been determined. The monthly back-up should be taken to coincide with the month-end after most/all of the month-end deals have been recorded, coded and confirmed. To restore to this point on Day 25 of the next month, therefore, will not entail too many deals being re-input as Days 0–22 of the month form the 'lean period' for foreign exchange dealing.

The back-up routine is identical in nature to that described under the procedure in Chapter 1 except that a previously unused set of disks are used. These disks are then saved in safe storage NEVER to be overwritten.

2 Month-end journal

At the end of every month the treasury unit provides between eight and ten journals for the month-end accounts. Most of these are minor in nature, e.g., overdraft interest accrual, capital additions interest accrual, but a number may impact on the month-end accounts substantially.

One of these is the evaluation of the foreign exchange contracts at the end of the month when 'marked to market'—in this case, month-end rates.

This journal is made up of a number of components. The principals which this foreign exchange (standard journal 7) journal is designed to address are as follows:

(1) *On liability* ('L') *deals, revalue all contracts to month-end rates.*

Take all gains or losses on such deals into the month-end accounts to offset gains or losses arising on the revaluation of currency deposits/borrowings held in the nominal ledger.

(2) *Revalue transaction* ('T') *deals outstanding at the month-end.*

Reflect in the monthly accounts that proportion of the gain or loss arising which the month-end debtors in currency terms bear to the total currency foreign exchange deals outstanding at the month-end. Foreign exchange transaction cover is used by the company so that any adverse revaluation of assets at the period end, e.g., currency debtors, are offset by benefits accruing on underlying protective foreign exchange deals. To protect the company for an extended period a large amount of foreign exchange cover may be required for, say, 12 months.

If the currency assets held in the ledger at the month-end equate to only 3 months there would be a mismatch in the accounts if the full 12 months' revaluation was taken into account. It is to this principal that only 3/12 of the gain or loss is taken into account at the month-end in the above example. Obviously if no cover was in place the full revaluation of the debtors to new rates would go ahead unabated.

(3) *Ensure that cash settlements received or made on deal 'rolls' are within the correct period.*

For the same reason in (2) above, it is incongruous to take out cover for 12 months to protect the company and then reflect the results in one monthly period. For administrative ease, deals are carried out in bulk, e.g., 12 months together not as 12 individual month-end deals. In addition, the deals are dealt first for each of month 1 and then rolled *vis-à-vis* base currency (say sterling), and also dealing lines do not become congested with outstanding deals. A consequence of this practice is that, at the month-end when deals are rolled, large amounts of sterling are received or paid reflecting the benefit or otherwise of the full 12-month protection. Technically these are realized gains and losses and normal accounting prudent practice would expect these to be reflected in that month's accounts. However, because 'cover' is still in place as the deal was rolled it would seem inexplicable to reflect a realized loss in the accounts when there is an inherent unrealized gain in the deal that is now outstanding. For this reason, accruals on the foreign exchange gains and losses account are related to the timing of the underlying cash flow.

The rest of the month-end journal therefore reflects in the accounts only a proportion of the gains or losses realized (i.e., sterling received or paid) year to date. The proportion taken into the accounts cumulatively will rise as the year progresses, reflecting the delivery of the underlying currency exposure so that at the end of the year all realized gains or losses applicable to that year are included in that year's accounts.

If the underlying foreign exchange cover is removed, the prudence accounting concept is met by ensuring that all realized gains and losses are taken into account.

The fraction used when determining the extent to which realized gains/losses are taken into account is as follows:

$$\frac{\text{Currency received year-to-date} + \text{Currency debtors outstanding at month-end}}{\text{Total cover outstanding at month-end} + \text{Currency received year-to-date}}$$

From the user's point of view this may appear complex. This approach is, however, necessary to ensure that if the company sells the US\$ at 1.50 for a year the underlying effect for the US\$ in the accounts is that an underlying protective rate of \$1.50 is felt in the accounts every month from January through to December. Without this approach large deals would distort the accounts when the whole need for the deals is to provide simplicity, stability and protection.

Management should get the message that the underlying protection is at a particular level and this should not be changed unless a new position is taken or reversed.

Procedure

Although the principles are complex, the practice of producing the journal is simple. The system has a highly automated process which produces the month-end journal. The user need only key in the following items to produce the month-end journal:

- Month-end rates for each currency (use screen 1.4.2)
- Debtors by currency (use screen 1.5.6)

In addition, the user should ensure that all deals have been allocated/coded for accounts purposes (see 6.1). Keep coding deals until the message 'all deals have been allocated' is displayed.

After the user has ensured the above are up to date, screen 7.6 should be selected. The date selected should then match the month-end that is being run. The Y/N query 'Continue with month-end report?' should be answered once it is certain the printer and peripherals are switched on.

The report may take 12–15 minutes to run, with all five pages of the report being printed once the program has been run.

3 General ledger

The treasury standard journals all have to be checked against the general ledger printout at the end of each month. This is necessary to ensure:

- that all cash movements expected to occur in the month have in fact occurred
- that the month-end journal has been correctly posted.

The structure of the general ledger for treasury foreign exchange differences is as follows:

Budget code	*Account code*	*Third field*	
XXX	123	abc	Exchange difference between the spot and budget rates for currency received/paid on current (SLC) accounts with subsidiaries.
XXX	234	def	As above, but for the sales ledger materials (SLM) account for both subsidiaries and currency-paying distributors.
XXX	345	ghi	Exchange difference between treasury forward rates achieved on deals and the spot rate that would have been achieved without treasury action. This difference refers to trading (transaction) deals only.
XXX	567	jkl	Any exchange differences due to treasury on liquidity (or group liability) hedging operations.
XXX	678	mno	Costs/benefits (premia) of undertaking currency options.

Within the general ledger each account for exchange difference has a general account with a third field together with individual accounts for each currency. Each currency account is denominated by the currency code used in the system (see 5.3.5).

Example
For Australian dollars the treasury exchange difference account for material account would be:

XXX 345 ghi/AUD

The individual currency accounts are used for posting sterling realized (i.e., paid out or received) on foreign exchange deals that have been closed or rolled. The 0 third field is used to post the month-end accruals and these reverse every month. In this way it is obvious to the user of the general ledger which differences are realized and which are unrealized. In addition, this provides a valuable benefit to the user in checking that all cash expected to be received or paid on a currency has in fact been received and correctly posted.

One sheet of the foreign exchange journal (entitled 'swaptions') produced by the system produces a column called 'cumulative' (recvd/paid). This column represents realized exchange differences (equivalent to sterling received or paid) and should agree with the individual cumulative totals in each of the XXX 345 ghi/— accounts.

Example
Per journal printout for the month-end August:

French francs	GBP 486 968.37

Per general ledger code XXX 345 ghi/FRF:

Opening balance	movement in months	Closing balance
GBP 494 544.89 CR	7576.52 DR	GBP 486 968.37 CR

Any disparity between the general ledger accounts and the journal should be investigated. Such disparities normally arise because a payment or receipt expected on the last day of the month does not actually arrive until the first day of the following month. As the cash office closes the cash book, and postings to the monthly ledger, on the last day of the month, the entry is therefore not passed in the ledger. If this occurs a reversing cash book journal should be raised by treasury to ensure that the relevant receipt of payment is correctly reflected in the monthly accounts.

The treasury exchange difference accounts codes may change from time to time. If they do it is important that the codes held by the dealing system are also changed. See Chapter 9.

CHAPTER 6

Foreign exchange dealing

1 Forward contracts

Detail In general terms, the dealing procedures required when undertaking a foreign exchange deal are explained in Chapter 4. However, it is important to have knowledge of a number of the different permutations that are available to the user of the dealing system. These are graded, starting with the simplest to understand.

(a) Selling currency for 'spot'

The company can sell any currency remitted arising from sales invoiced in currency solely as it arrives. This practice is usually called selling for 'spot', which equates to obtaining value for currency sales two business days hence.

The user should use screen 1.1, new deal, and follow through the screen as explained in Chapter 4 until part of the screen called 'exchange rate detail' becomes visible. At this point the 'spot race' quotation obtained from the bank should be inserted and the enter key pressed twice. This will show the sterling that will be received by the company. Enter the correct spot settlement date (agreed with the bank). Press enter.

The user should now press Y in answer to the 'deal close' question. Answering 'yes' to this question means that the user is happy to flow the currency and sterling due on the settlement date. After answering 'yes' to the question of whether the entries are correct, the system will search for any 'related deals'. These are deals, held in the system, which have all the following characteristics:

- unclosed
- with the same counterparty
- using the same currency against base currency (e.g., sterling)
- having a settlement date coincident with the deal just struck.

Any related currency and sterling flows will be netted against the flows of the deal just completed. For a straight spot rate sale there would usually be 'no related deals'.

After this search has been completed the system will display the total net currency and sterling that will flow on the settlement date.

The usual colour conventions apply. A red background indicates movements of currency and/or sterling outside the group. Blue indicates a movement within the group. Next, by pressing any key the normal delivery instructions that apply to these movements will appear on the screen. Any changes to these instructions should be agreed with the dealer at the time of the deal by overtyping the screen. The exception to this is when sterling is coming into the group. This will generally be received into the company's clearing account, but might go to an account of a specified finance company (subsidiary). This routeing is driven by the bank details screen, and the detail cannot be changed while on the dealing screen (see Chapter 9 for permanent changes to bank details). Once everything is agreed the deal can be added to the database by answering 'yes' to the final screen question. If something is noticed as incorrect at this stage, a 'no' answer will ensure that the deal is aborted, and the details can be re-input.

Accounts coding and confirmation printing should be achieved using the routine explained in Chapter 4. (See Figures 9–13 and 14–21 for details of the various stages in new deal transactions.)

New forward contract

This is a deal to sell currency against sterling for any time more than two business days hence. In many respects this is similar to a 'spot sale'. The major differences are that on the exchange rate detail part of the screen an entry should be placed in the forward points line. These should be typed in to give the correct all-in forward rate quotation agreed with the bank. The convention used is if the points 'come off' the spot rate, i.e., when dealing with currency

```
          THE  J O N A T H A N  R O B I N  C O M P A N Y  LIMITED
                    Foreign Exchange Dealing - New Deal

+===================================+ +--------------------------------------
|DEAL REF......      49             | |Co BANK CODE.
+===================================+ |BANK NAME....
|CURRENCY......                     | |ADDRESS......
|BUY/SELL......           T/L...... | |       ......
|AMOUNT........                     | |BANK DEALER..
+-----------------------------------+ +--------------------------------------
```

Figure 9

```
          THE  J O N A T H A N  R O B I N  C O M P A N Y  LIMITED
                    Foreign Exchange Dealing - New Deal

+===================================+ +--------------------------------------
|DEAL REF......      49             | |Co BANK CODE. DEM001
+===================================+ |BANK NAME.... Demo Banking Corp Ltd
|CURRENCY...... USD                 | |ADDRESS...... Demonstration House
|BUY/SELL...... B        T/L...... L| |       ...... Testing Lane
|AMOUNT........      10,000,000.00  | |BANK DEALER.. Felicity
+-----------------------------------+ +--------------------------------------
```

Figure 10

```
          THE  J O N A T H A N  R O B I N  C O M P A N Y  LIMITED
                    Foreign Exchange Dealing - New Deal

+===================================+ +--------------------------------------
|DEAL REF......      49             | |Co BANK CODE. DEM001
+===================================+ |BANK NAME.... Demo Banking Corp Ltd
|CURRENCY...... USD                 | |ADDRESS...... Demonstration House
|BUY/SELL...... B        T/L...... L| |       ...... Testing Lane
|AMOUNT........      10,000,000.00  | |BANK DEALER.. Felicity
+-----------------------------------+ +--------------------------------------
|EXCHANGE RATE DETAIL               |
+-----------------------------------+
|SPOT..........        1.90000      |
|FWD POINTS....        0.04000      |
|FWD RATE......        1.86000      |
+-----------------------------------+
|STERLING VAL..        5,376,344.09 |
|S'MENT DATE... 31/12/90            |
+-----------------------------------+
|DEAL CLOSE ?.. N                   |
+-----------------------------------+

                Are the above entries correct ? (Y/N) Y
```

Figure 11

```
          THE  J O N A T H A N  R O B I N  C O M P A N Y  LIMITED
                    Foreign Exchange Dealing - New Deal

+===================================+ +--------------------------------------
|DEAL REF......      49             | |Co BANK CODE. DEM001
+===================================+ |BANK NAME.... Demo Banking Corp Ltd
|CURRENCY...... USD                 | |ADDRESS...... Demonstration House
|BUY/SELL...... B        T/L...... L| |       ...... Testing Lane
|AMOUNT........      10,000,000.00  | |BANK DEALER.. Felicity
+-----------------------------------+ +--------------------------------------
|EXCHANGE RATE DETAIL               |
+-----------------------------------+
|SPOT..........        1.90000      |
|FWD POINTS....        0.04000      |
|FWD RATE......        1.86000      |
+-----------------------------------+
|STERLING VAL..        5,376,344.09 |
|S'MENT DATE... 31/12/90            |
+-----------------------------------+
|DEAL CLOSE ?.. N                   |
+-----------------------------------+

                Deal has been added to database - Press Any Key -
```

Figure 12

Demo Banking Corp Ltd
Demonstration House
Testing Lane
London

8 September, 1990 Our Ref : 49

Dear Sir,

We confirm our telephoned instructions for the following foreign exchange transaction.

Currency purchased by us :-

Currency	:	US Dollar
Amount	:	*****10,000,000.00
Exchange Rate	:	*****1.86000
Sterling Value	:	*****5,376,344.09
Settlement Date	:	31 December, 1990

Delivery Instructions will be agreed closer to maturity.

Yours faithfully,

S Smith
Finance Director

T Taylor
Group Treasurer

Figure 13

```
              THE  J O N A T H A N  R O B I N  C O M P A N Y  LIMITED
                         Foreign Exchange Dealing - New Deal

+==================================+ +-----------------------------------
|DEAL REF......      55            | |Co BANK CODE. DEM001
+==================================+ |BANK NAME.... Demo Banking Corp Ltd
|CURRENCY...... USD                | |ADDRESS...... Demonstration House
|BUY/SELL...... B       T/L...... L| |       ...... Testing Lane
|AMOUNT........       1,000,000.00 | |BANK DEALER.. Felicity
+----------------------------------+ +-----------------------------------
|EXCHANGE RATE DETAIL              |
+----------------------------------+
|SPOT..........       1.90000      |
|FWD POINTS....       0.00000      |
|FWD RATE......       1.90000      |
+----------------------------------+
|STERLING VAL..          526,315.79|
|S'MENT DATE... 12/09/90           |
+----------------------------------+
|DEAL CLOSE ?.. Y                  |
+----------------------------------+
```

Figure 14

```
              THE  J O N A T H A N  R O B I N  C O M P A N Y  LIMITED
                         Foreign Exchange Dealing - New Deal

+==================================+ +-----------------------------------
|DEAL REF......      55            | |Co BANK CODE. DEM001
+==================================+ |BANK NAME.... Demo Banking Corp Ltd
|CURRENCY...... USD                | |ADDRESS...... Demonstration House
|BUY/SELL...... B       T/L...... L| |       ...... Testing Lane
|AMOUNT........       1,000,000.00 | |BANK DEALER.. Felicity
+----------------------------------+ +-----------------------------------
|EXCHANGE RATE DETAIL              | |RELATED DEALS
+----------------------------------+ +-----------------------------------
|SPOT..........       1.90000      | |REF.          REF.          REF.
|FWD POINTS....       0.00000      | |REF.          REF.          REF.
|FWD RATE......       1.90000      | +-----------------------------------
+----------------------------------+
|STERLING VAL..          526,315.79|
|S'MENT DATE... 12/09/90           |
+----------------------------------+
|DEAL CLOSE ?.. Y                  |
+----------------------------------+

             No related deals were found - Press any Key - ......
```

Figure 15

```
              THE  J O N A T H A N  R O B I N  C O M P A N Y  LIMITED
                         Foreign Exchange Dealing - New Deal

+==================================+ +-----------------------------------
|DEAL REF......      55            | |Co BANK CODE. DEM001
+==================================+ |BANK NAME.... Demo Banking Corp Ltd
|CURRENCY...... USD                | |ADDRESS...... Demonstration House
|BUY/SELL...... B       T/L...... L| |       ...... Testing Lane
|AMOUNT........       1,000,000.00 | |BANK DEALER.. Felicity
+----------------------------------+ +-----------------------------------
|EXCHANGE RATE DETAIL              | |RELATED DEALS
+----------------------------------+ +-----------------------------------
|SPOT..........       1.90000      | |REF.          REF.          REF.
|FWD POINTS....       0.00000      | |REF.          REF.          REF.
|FWD RATE......       1.90000      | +-----------------------------------
+----------------------------------+ +-----------------------------------
|STERLING VAL..          526,315.79| |  NET CURR. FLOW.        1,000,000.00
|S'MENT DATE... 12/09/90           | +-----------------------------------
+----------------------------------+ +-----------------------------------
|DEAL CLOSE ?.. Y                  | |  NET STER. FLOW.(        526,315.79)
+----------------------------------+ +-----------------------------------

               * Press any key for Delivery instructions *
```

Figure 16

```
        THE  J O N A T H A N  R O B I N  C O M P A N Y  LIMITED
                    Foreign Exchange Dealing - New Deal
______________________________________________________________________________
+===================================+ +-------------------------------------
|DEAL REF......      55             | |Co BANK CODE. DEM001
+===================================+ |BANK NAME.... Demo Banking Corp Ltd
|CURRENCY...... USD                 | |ADDRESS...... Demonstration House
|BUY/SELL...... B        T/L...... L| |             ...... Testing Lane
|AMOUNT........         1,000,000.00| |BANK DEALER.. Felicity
+-----------------------------------+ +-------------------------------------
|DELIVERY INSTRUCTIONS              | |STERLING....(         526,315.79)
+-----------------------------------| +-------------------------------------
|CURRENCY..      1,000,000.00       | |BANK........Demo Banking Corp Ltd
+-----------------------------------+ |ADDRESS.....1 High Street
|BANK......USD Receiver Int'l       | |       .......New Town
|ADDRESS...New York                 | |ACCOUNT.....The Corporate Limited
|      ...                          | |ACCOUNT NO..12345678
|ACCOUNT...Corporate Subsidiary Inc | |SORT CODE...01-02-03
|      ...                          | +-------------------------------------
|A/C NO....00001111                 | |SECURITY....Code XXX987
+-----------------------------------+ +-------------------------------------
______________________________________________________________________________
                    ** PLEASE CONFIRM WITH LOCAL BANK **
```

Figure 17

```
        THE  J O N A T H A N  R O B I N  C O M P A N Y  LIMITED
                    Foreign Exchange Dealing - New Deal
______________________________________________________________________________
+===================================+ +-------------------------------------
|DEAL REF......      55             | |Co BANK CODE. DEM001
+===================================+ |BANK NAME.... Demo Banking Corp Ltd
|CURRENCY...... USD                 | |ADDRESS...... Demonstration House
|BUY/SELL...... B        T/L...... L| |             ...... Testing Lane
|AMOUNT........         1,000,000.00| |BANK DEALER.. Felicity
+-----------------------------------+ +-------------------------------------
|DELIVERY INSTRUCTIONS              | |STERLING....(         526,315.79)
+-----------------------------------| +-------------------------------------
|CURRENCY..      1,000,000.00       | |BANK........Demo Banking Corp Ltd
+-----------------------------------+ |ADDRESS.....1 High Street
|BANK......USD Receiver Int'l       | |       .......New Town
|ADDRESS...New York                 | |ACCOUNT.....The Corporate Limited
|      ...                          | |ACCOUNT NO..12345678
|ACCOUNT...Corporate Subsidiary Inc | |SORT CODE...01-02-03
|      ...                          | +-------------------------------------
|A/C NO....00001111                 | |SECURITY....Code XXX987
+-----------------------------------+ +-------------------------------------
______________________________________________________________________________
           Do you wish to record this deal ?(Y/N)  Y
```

Figure 18

```
        THE  J O N A T H A N  R O B I N  C O M P A N Y  LIMITED
                    Foreign Exchange Dealing - New Deal
______________________________________________________________________________
+===================================+ +-------------------------------------
|DEAL REF......      55             | |Co BANK CODE. DEM001
+===================================+ |BANK NAME.... Demo Banking Corp Ltd
|CURRENCY...... USD                 | |ADDRESS...... Demonstration House
|BUY/SELL...... B        T/L...... L| |             ...... Testing Lane
|AMOUNT........         1,000,000.00| |BANK DEALER.. Felicity
+-----------------------------------+ +-------------------------------------
|DELIVERY INSTRUCTIONS              | |STERLING....(         526,315.79)
+-----------------------------------| +-------------------------------------
|CURRENCY..      1,000,000.00       | |BANK........Demo Banking Corp Ltd
+-----------------------------------+ |ADDRESS.....1 High Street
|BANK......USD Receiver Int'l       | |       .......New Town
|ADDRESS...New York                 | |ACCOUNT.....The Corporate Limited
|      ...                          | |ACCOUNT NO..12345678
|ACCOUNT...Corporate Subsidiary Inc | |SORT CODE...01-02-03
|      ...                          | +-------------------------------------
|A/C NO....00001111                 | |SECURITY....Code XXX987
+-----------------------------------+ +-------------------------------------
______________________________________________________________________________
           Deal has been added to database - Press Any Key -
```

Figure 19

Demo Banking Corp Ltd
Demonstration House
Testing Lane
London

8 September, 1990 Our Ref : 55

Dear Sir,

We confirm our telephoned instructions for the following foreign exchange transaction.

Currency purchased by us :-

Currency	:	US Dollar
Amount	:	******1,000,000.00
Exchange Rate	:	*****1.90000
Sterling Value	:	*******526,315.79
Settlement Date	:	12 September, 1990

Currency will be paid to our instructions as follows :-

Bank	:	USD Receiver Int'l New York,
Account	:	Corporate Subsidiary Inc
A/C No.	:	00001111

Sterling to be paid as follows :-

Bank	:	Demo Banking Corp Ltd 1 High Street New Town
Account	:	The Corporate Limited
A/C No.	:	12345678

Yours faithfully,

S Smith
Finance Director

T Taylor
Group Treasurer

Figure 20

Own Clearing Bank Ltd
1 Victoria Street,
Westminster,
London SW1

8 September, 1990 Our Ref : 55

Dear Sir,

This is to confirm our telephoned instructions of today to make the following transfer :-

Amount	:	£*******526,315.79
Bank	:	Demo Banking Corp Ltd 1 High Street New Town
Sort Code	:	01-02-03
Account	:	The Corporate Limited
A/C No.	:	12345678
Security Ref	:	Code XXX987
Date	:	12 September, 1990

Yours faithfully,

S Smith
Finance Director

T Taylor
Group Treasurer

Figure 21

that has lower interest rates than sterling (see Chapter 4 for explanation of forward exchange rates).

Example
Selling or buying US$ v Stg.

Spot rate = 1.6510
Forward points for one month = 55 points
All in rate = 1.6510 − 0.0055 = 1.6455.

This would be input into the exchange rate detail screen by typing in:

Spot 1.651
Fwd points 0.0055
Fwd rate 1.6455 (calculated by system automatically).

No negative is required as the program automatically subtracts the points. If the points 'go on' or are 'against us' the opposite is true. In the example above, a negative would have to be put in front of the forward points.

Example
Selling or buying A$ v Stg.

Spot 2.2965
Fwd points −0.0135
Fwd rate 2.3100 (calculated by system automatically).

The only other major difference to the 'spot rate' selling mentioned in 1(a) above is that the deal is not treated as closed (answer 'no' to 'deal close'). This means that at the moment that the deal is struck, delivery instructions will be agreed closer to the maturity of the deal and are not known at present.

After this question has been answered the deal will be saved as usual once the entries have been established as being correct.

(c) Delivering an existing forward contract

If nearer the maturity date of an FX contract it becomes apparent that the contract can be fulfilled, it will need to be delivered. This means that the currency and sterling delivery instructions that were not agreed at the time of the original deal will now be addressed.

This is achieved by using screen 1.3. When this is selected input the deal reference of the forward contract that is to be delivered. All the deal details will now be displayed on the screen and the user will have to answer the 'deal close' question again. This will be answered 'yes' as the deal is being delivered. The procedure is then as illustrated in 1(a) above.

(d) Rolling an existing forward contract

The mechanics of rolling an existing forward contract are mentioned in Chapter 4, section 1(a). In simple terms, an existing forward contract for one settlement date is substituted for a new contract on a different date (usually later than the first date). The new contract is exactly the same as the previous deal apart from the rate and the settlement date. To achieve this the original deal should be netted by doing an opposite deal, i.e., in all respects the same apart from the buy/sell directions and exchange rate. See Chapter 4, section 1(a), for an example.

When netting a previous FX deal the user will:

- use new deal screen 1.1 set up with the same currency, bank, currency amount and settlement date;
- select the 'deal close' option—'yes';
- agree that the net currency flowing on related deals (there should be at least one in this example; equivalent to the previous maturing deal) total zero;
- agree the delivery instructions for the net sterling due with the counterparty dealer;

(e) Delivering part currency against an existing forward contract

Procedure is as for (d) above except the reversing deal does not match totally the original deal in currency amount terms.

Example

Settlement date: 31 August

Original deal:		
Sell	US$ 5 000 000 @ 1.50	GBP 3 333 333.33
31 August—Deal reversal:		
Buy	US$ 3 000 000 @ 1.60	GBP 1 875 000.00

Currency to be delivered		Sterling delivered outside group
	US$ 2 000 000	GBP 1 458 333.33
30 September—New deal:		
Sell	US$ 3 000 000 @ 1.5950	GBP 1 880 877.74

Delivery instructions for the net currency and sterling flowing on 31 August will then be agreed in the usual way.

The new deal for 30 September will be set up as in (b) above.

(f) Closing out an existing forward FX deal

This is exactly the same as (d) above (rolling a forward deal) except that a new deal is not substituted for the old maturing deal.

2 Currency options

Currency options are a valuable tool for the treasurer in protecting the company against adverse foreign exchange movements. The major differences between options and forward foreign exchange contracts are:

- *forward contracts give the right and the obligation to fulfil that foreign exchange contract*
- *currency options, if purchased, give the right but not the obligation to fulfil the underlying foreign exchange contract.*

This guide is to be used only as a mechanical reference for undertaking currency options using the dealing system. The decision to use or not use currency options will rest with the group treasurer and director of finance, and will be recognized as a policy decision, the parameters for which will be outside the dealing system itself.

There are two different option types for which the system caters: simple option and cylinder option.

(a) Simple option

A simple option provides a fixed point protection against a particular currency's movements compared to the base currency (sterling).

Example
Consider the case where the company buys an option (for a consideration known as an 'option premium') to sell US$ at 1.50: the company will achieve a conversion exchange rate of no worse than 1.50. This is the fixed point of protection currently known as the 'downside rate' or the 'strike rate'. However, if the current exchange was lower than this, say 1.25, the company would rather convert its US$ at this rate in preference to the option rate of 1.50. In contrast to a forward deal, an option provides the right, not obligation, to contract currency flows at the particular rate. The company can ignore or lapse the option in preference to the rates currently available in the market, i.e., option to sell US$ 10 000 000 at $1.50 (GBP 6 666 666.66). The conversion rate available in the market is $1.25. Therefore sterling, which can be received by using the market rather than the option rate, is worth GBP 8 000 000 or GBP 1.3m higher than the option rate.

If the original option was 'sold' by the company rather than purchased as in the above example, the reverse would be true. In this case a counterparty would be exercising the option against the company, thus requiring the company to sell the US dollar at a rate of $1.50 even though the market rate of $1.25 is more attractive for conversion purposes. The reasons are obvious, in this example the company has sold the 'right' to exercise the option in return for a consideration known as option premium revenue.

(b) Cylinder option (fence or collar)

If the company is happy that the exchange rates for a particular currency will trace within a band either side of the current rates, it may decide to undertake a cylinder option. This is the combination of two simple options, one that is bought and another that is sold. The option that is bought will be purchased to protect a certain 'downside rate' ($1.50 in the last example). The other half of the option will be sold in order to earn some option premium revenue to offset the cost of the option that has been purchased. This will be bought at an exchange rate which fits the company's perception of where the currency will move against the sterling—say, a rate of $1.35.

In summary, the cylinder option (per the example) provides:

```
            THE  J O N A T H A N  R O B I N  C O M P A N Y  LIMITED
                  Foreign Exchange Dealing - Simple Option

+==================================+ +---------------------------------
|DEAL REF......     52             | |Co BANK CODE. DEM001
+==================================+ |BANK NAME.... Demo Banking Corp Ltd
|OPTION B/S.... B                  | |ADDRESS...... Demonstration House
|CURRENCY...... USD                | |       ...... Testing Lane
|BUY/SELL...... S                  | |       ...... London
|AMOUNT........     10,000,000.00  | |BANK DEALER.. Felicity
+----------------------------------+ +---------------------------------
|STRIKE RATE...       0.00000      |
|STER. VALUE...                    |
|STYLE.........                    |
+----------------------------------+
|SPOT RATE.....                    |
|PREMIUM(%)....                    |
|PREMIUM()....                    |
|EXERCISE DATE.                    |
|SET'MENT DATE.                    |
+----------------------------------+
```

Figure 22

```
            THE  J O N A T H A N  R O B I N  C O M P A N Y  LIMITED
                  Foreign Exchange Dealing - Simple Option

+==================================+ +---------------------------------
|DEAL REF......     52             | |Co BANK CODE. DEM001
+==================================+ |BANK NAME.... Demo Banking Corp Ltd
|OPTION B/S.... B                  | |ADDRESS...... Demonstration House
|CURRENCY...... USD                | |       ...... Testing Lane
|BUY/SELL...... S                  | |       ...... London
|AMOUNT........     10,000,000.00  | |BANK DEALER.. Felicity
+----------------------------------+ +---------------------------------
|STRIKE RATE...       1.90000      |
|STER. VALUE...       5,263,157.89 |
|STYLE......... American           |
+----------------------------------+
|SPOT RATE.....       1.88000      |
|PREMIUM(%)....   1.50000          |
|PREMIUM()....          78,947.37 |
|EXERCISE DATE. 27/12/90           |
|SET'MENT DATE. 31/12/90           |
+----------------------------------+

             Are the above entries correct ? (Y/N) Y
```

Figure 23

```
            THE  J O N A T H A N  R O B I N  C O M P A N Y  LIMITED
                  Foreign Exchange Dealing - Simple Option

+==================================+ +---------------------------------
|DEAL REF......     52             | |Co BANK CODE. DEM001
+==================================+ |BANK NAME.... Demo Banking Corp Ltd
|OPTION B/S.... B                  | |ADDRESS...... Demonstration House
|CURRENCY...... USD                | |       ...... Testing Lane
|BUY/SELL...... S                  | |       ...... London
|AMOUNT........     10,000,000.00  | |BANK DEALER.. Felicity
+----------------------------------+ +---------------------------------
|STRIKE RATE...       1.90000      |
|STER. VALUE...       5,263,157.89 |
|STYLE......... American           |
+----------------------------------+
|SPOT RATE.....       1.88000      |
|PREMIUM(%)....   1.50000          |
|PREMIUM()....          78,947.37 |
+----------------------------------+
|PREMIUM DATE.. 10/09/90           |
+----------------------------------+
```

Figure 24

```
          THE  J O N A T H A N  R O B I N  C O M P A N Y  LIMITED
                   Foreign Exchange Dealing - Simple Option

+==================================+ +----------------------------------
|DEAL REF......    52             | |Co BANK CODE. DEM001
+==================================+ |BANK NAME.... Demo Banking Corp Ltd
|OPTION B/S.... B                 | |ADDRESS...... Demonstration House
|CURRENCY...... USD               | |       ...... Testing Lane
|BUY/SELL...... S                 | |       ...... London
|AMOUNT........     10,000,000.00 | |BANK DEALER.. Felicity
+----------------------------------+ +----------------------------------
|STRIKE RATE...       1.90000     |
|STER. VALUE...       5,263,157.89|
|STYLE......... American          |
+----------------------------------+
|SPOT RATE.....       1.88000     |
|PREMIUM(%)....   1.50000         |
|PREMIUM()....          78,947.37 |
+----------------------------------+
|PREMIUM DATE.. 10/09/90          |
+----------------------------------+
```

Figure 25

```
          THE  J O N A T H A N  R O B I N  C O M P A N Y  LIMITED
                   Foreign Exchange Dealing - Simple Option

+==================================+ +----------------------------------
|DEAL REF......    52             | |Co BANK CODE. DEM001
+==================================+ |BANK NAME.... Demo Banking Corp Ltd
|OPTION B/S.... B                 | |ADDRESS...... Demonstration House
|CURRENCY...... USD               | |       ...... Testing Lane
|BUY/SELL...... S                 | |       ...... London
|AMOUNT........     10,000,000.00 | |BANK DEALER.. Felicity
+----------------------------------+ +----------------------------------
|STRIKE RATE...       1.90000     |
|STER. VALUE...       5,263,157.89|
|STYLE......... American          |
+----------------------------------+
|SPOT RATE.....       1.88000     |
|PREMIUM(%)....   1.50000         |
|PREMIUM()....          78,947.37 |
+----------------------------------+
|PREMIUM DATE.. 10/09/90          |
|----------------------------------+
```

Figure 26

```
          THE  J O N A T H A N  R O B I N  C O M P A N Y  LIMITED
                   Foreign Exchange Dealing - Simple Option

+==================================+ +----------------------------------
|DEAL REF......    52             | |Co BANK CODE. DEM001
+==================================+ |BANK NAME.... Demo Banking Corp Ltd
|OPTION B/S.... B                 | |ADDRESS...... Demonstration House
|CURRENCY...... USD               | |       ...... Testing Lane
|BUY/SELL...... S                 | |       ...... London
|AMOUNT........     10,000,000.00 | |BANK DEALER.. Felicity
+----------------------------------+ +----------------------------------
|STRIKE RATE...       1.90000     | |PREMIUM.....           78,947.37
|STER. VALUE...       5,263,157.89| +----------------------------------
|STYLE......... American          | |BANK........Demo Banking Corp Ltd
+----------------------------------+ |ADDRESS.....1 High Street
|SPOT RATE.....       1.88000     | |     .......New Town
|PREMIUM(%)....   1.50000         | |ACCOUNT.....The Corporate Limited
|PREMIUM()....          78,947.37 | |ACCOUNT NO..12345678
+----------------------------------+ |SORT CODE...01-02-03
|PREMIUM DATE.. 10/09/90          | |SECURITY....
+----------------------------------+ +----------------------------------

                  ** PLEASE CONFIRM WITH LOCAL BANK **
```

Figure 27

```
            THE  J O N A T H A N  R O B I N  C O M P A N Y  LIMITED
                   Foreign Exchange Dealing - Simple Option

+==================================+ +----------------------------------
|DEAL REF......      52            | |Co BANK CODE. DEM001
+==================================+ |BANK NAME.... Demo Banking Corp Ltd
|OPTION B/S.... B                  | |ADDRESS...... Demonstration House
|CURRENCY...... USD                | |        ...... Testing Lane
|BUY/SELL...... S                  | |        ...... London
|AMOUNT........     10,000,000.00  | |BANK DEALER.. Felicity
+----------------------------------+ +----------------------------------
|STRIKE RATE...       1.90000      | |PREMIUM.....          78,947.37
|STER. VALUE...       5,263,157.89 | +----------------------------------
|STYLE......... American           | |BANK........Demo Banking Corp Ltd
+----------------------------------+ |ADDRESS.....1 High Street
|SPOT RATE.....       1.88000      | |     .......New Town
|PREMIUM(%)....   1.50000          | |ACCOUNT.....The Corporate Limited
|PREMIUM()....          78,947.37  | |ACCOUNT NO..12345678
+----------------------------------+ |SORT CODE...01-02-03
|PREMIUM DATE.. 10/09/90           | |SECURITY....Code QSV513
+----------------------------------+ +----------------------------------

                    ** PLEASE CONFIRM WITH LOCAL BANK **
```

Figure 28

```
            THE  J O N A T H A N  R O B I N  C O M P A N Y  LIMITED
                   Foreign Exchange Dealing - Simple Option

+==================================+ +----------------------------------
|DEAL REF......      52            | |Co BANK CODE. DEM001
+==================================+ |BANK NAME.... Demo Banking Corp Ltd
|OPTION B/S.... B                  | |ADDRESS...... Demonstration House
|CURRENCY...... USD                | |        ...... Testing Lane
|BUY/SELL...... S                  | |        ...... London
|AMOUNT........     10,000,000.00  | |BANK DEALER.. Felicity
+----------------------------------+ +----------------------------------
|STRIKE RATE...       1.90000      | |PREMIUM.....          78,947.37
|STER. VALUE...       5,263,157.89 | +----------------------------------
|STYLE......... American           | |BANK........Demo Banking Corp Ltd
+----------------------------------+ |ADDRESS.....1 High Street
|SPOT RATE.....       1.88000      | |     .......New Town
|PREMIUM(%)....   1.50000          | |ACCOUNT.....The Corporate Limited
|PREMIUM()....          78,947.37  | |ACCOUNT NO..12345678
+----------------------------------+ |SORT CODE...01-02-03
|PREMIUM DATE.. 10/09/90           | |SECURITY....Code QSV513
+----------------------------------+ +----------------------------------

            Do you wish to record this deal ?(Y/N)
```

Figure 29

Demo Banking Corp Ltd
Demonstration House
Testing Lane
London

8 September, 1990 Our Ref : 52

Dear Sir,

We confirm our telephoned instructions for the purchase of the following foreign exchange option :-

Currency sold by us :-

Style	: American
Currency	: US Dollar
Amount	: *****10,000,000.00
Exchange Rate	: 1.90000
Sterling Value	: ******5,263,157.89
Exercise Date	: 27 December, 1990
Settlement Date	: 31 December, 1990
Premium %	: 1.50000000
Premium Cost	: *********78,947.37
Premium Date	: 10 September, 1990

Premium to be paid to your instructions as follows :-

Bank : Demo Banking Corp Ltd
1 High Street
New Town

Account : The Corporate Limited
A/C No. : 12345678

Yours faithfully,

S Smith
Finance Director

T Taylor
Group Treasurer

Figure 30

Own Clearing Bank Ltd
1 Victoria Street,
Westminster,
London SW1

8 September, 1990 Our Ref : 52

Dear Sir,

This is to confirm our telephoned instructions of today to make the following transfer :-

Amount	:	£*********78,947.37
Bank	:	Demo Banking Corp Ltd Demonstration House Testing Lane London
Sort Code	:	01-02-03
Account	:	The Corporate Limited
A/C No.	:	12345678
Security Ref	:	Code QSV513
Date	:	10 September, 1990

Yours faithfully,

S Smith
Group Treasurer

T Taylor
Group Treasurer

Figure 31

- a conversion rate of currency to sterling of no worse than 1.50 ('downside' rate)
- a best conversion rate of 1.35 (known as the 'upside' rate).

If the exchange rate available in the market becomes better than $1.35 (say $1.30) the company will not benefit from the appreciation as it has sold its right to any further appreciation beyond a level of $1.35.

(c) Dealing routine

Once the need for currency option protection has been established, an option deal should be put in place using either the simple option screen (1.2.1) or the cylinder option screen (1.2.2).

Simple option screen (1.2.1)
(See Figures 22–31 for details of the transaction.)
Call up the screen. A new deal reference will appear automatically.

Option B/S The first question, option B/S, refers to whether the option is being bought or sold. It is important that this is correct. In most circumstances the company will be buying an option. See the comments in section 2 above if in any doubt. The next parts of the screen should be filled in as for an ordinary forward foreign exchange deal (see Chapter 4, section 1(a)) down to the dealer's name.

Strike rate The next part of the screen will now become visible. The strike rate (downside rate) should now be input ($1.50 in the previous example). The sterling value of the deal will be calculated automatically.

Option style The option 'style' refers to whether the option can be exercised on only one day of its existence (its exercise date) or at any time between the date of dealing and the exercise date. The former is known as a 'European' (E should be input) style option and the latter as an 'American' (A should be input) style option. As one would expect, the American style options are more expensive as they are more flexible. It is often thought appropriate for corporates to sell European-style options (since the potential liability can be planned for at least on a time basis) and to buy American (for greater flexibility).

Spot rate This refers to the current 'spot' rate available in the market for that currency. In the case of some banks the total premium payable on the option is determined by the currency amount dividend by the spot rate. This is true for example for Barclays Bank (bank code BBI001). Other banks use the strike rate as the denominator. The dealing system is automatically set up to determine which rate to use for which counterparty.

Premium % This is the price of the option quoted in terms of a percentage of the sterling equivalent of the option. The sterling equivalent can be worked out two ways (see 'spot rate' above). The rate will be quoted by the counterparty and should be input as a percentage, e.g., 1 per cent is input as 1.0.

Premium (£) This is calculated by the dealing system by multiplying the premium percentage by the sterling equivalent of the option (see above).

Exercise date This is the final date upon which the option can be exercised in the case of an American-style option. It is the only date for a European-style option. Agree date with counterparty and input.

Settlement date This is the date upon which the flow of the underlying foreign exchange deal will be made. This should be two business days after the exercise date. Whether any flows do occur will depend on the option being exercised. If the option is not exercised it will lapse and nothing will occur on the settlement date. Agree date with counterparty and input.

Check to see whether all above entries are correct before answering 'yes' to the next screen question.

Premium date Agree date upon which the premium value will flow. This is usually two business days from the dealing date. The dealing system will then call up the appropriate sterling delivery instructions which should be agreed with the counterparty dealer.

When all the above items have been agreed the deal should be saved.

Cylinder option screen (1.2.2)
(See Figures 32–41 for details of the transaction.)

THE J O N A T H A N R O B I N C O M P A N Y LIMITED

Foreign Exchange Deal – Cylinder Option

```
+===================================+ +------------------------------------
|REF1...     53      REF2...     54  | |Co BANK CODE.
+===================================+ |BANK NAME....
|CURRENCY......         BUY/SELL...  | |ADDRESS......
|AMOUNT........                      | |        ......
+-----------------------------------+ |        ......
|BUY  STYLE....                      | |BANK DEALER..
|SELL STYLE....                      | +------------------------------------
|BUY  RATE.....                      |
|SELL RATE.....                      |
|SPOT RATE.....                      |
|BUY  VALUE().                      |
|SELL VALUE().                      |
+-----------------------------------+ +------------------------------------
|BUY  PREM. %..                      | |BUY  PREM()..
|SELL PREM. %..                      | |SELL PREM()..
+-----------------------------------+ +------------------------------------
```

Figure 32

THE J O N A T H A N R O B I N C O M P A N Y LIMITED

Foreign Exchange Deal – Cylinder Option

```
+===================================+ +------------------------------------
|REF1...     53      REF2...     54  | |Co BANK CODE. DEM001
+===================================+ |BANK NAME.... Demo Banking Corp Ltd
|CURRENCY...... USD    BUY/SELL...S | |ADDRESS...... Demonstration House
|AMOUNT........       10,000,000.00 | |        ...... Testing Lane
+-----------------------------------+ |        ...... London
|BUY  STYLE.... American             | |BANK DEALER.. Felicity
|SELL STYLE.... European             | +------------------------------------
|BUY  RATE.....           1.90000    | +------------------------------------
|SELL RATE.....           1.80000    | |NET  PREMIUM..               0.0000000
|SPOT RATE.....           1.88000    | |EXERCISE DATE.
|BUY  VALUE().        5,263,157.89  | |SET'MENT DATE.
|SELL VALUE().        5,555,555.56  | +------------------------------------
+-----------------------------------+ +------------------------------------
|BUY  PREM. %..  1.5000000000000     | |BUY  PREM()..
|SELL PREM. %..  1.421052631578947  | |SELL PREM()..
+-----------------------------------+ +------------------------------------
```

Figure 33

THE J O N A T H A N R O B I N C O M P A N Y LIMITED

Foreign Exchange Deal – Cylinder Option

```
+===================================+ +------------------------------------
|REF1...     53      REF2...     54  | |Co BANK CODE. DEM001
+===================================+ |BANK NAME.... Demo Banking Corp Ltd
|CURRENCY...... USD    BUY/SELL...S | |ADDRESS...... Demonstration House
|AMOUNT........       10,000,000.00 | |        ...... Testing Lane
+-----------------------------------+ |        ...... London
|BUY  STYLE.... American             | |BANK DEALER.. Felicity
|SELL STYLE.... European             | +------------------------------------
|BUY  RATE.....           1.90000    | +------------------------------------
|SELL RATE.....           1.80000    | |NET  PREMIUM..            5,497.0800
|SPOT RATE.....           1.88000    | |EXERCISE DATE.          27/12/90
|BUY  VALUE().        5,263,157.89  | |SET'MENT DATE.         31/12/90
|SELL VALUE().        5,555,555.56  | +------------------------------------
+-----------------------------------+ +------------------------------------
|BUY  PREM. %..  1.5000000000000     | |BUY  PREM()..(          78,947.37)
|SELL PREM. %..  1.520000000000000  | |SELL PREM()..           84,444.44
+-----------------------------------+ +------------------------------------
```

Figure 34

THE J O N A T H A N R O B I N C O M P A N Y LIMITED
Foreign Exchange Deal – Cylinder Option

```
+===================================+ +------------------------------------
|REF1...    53     REF2...    54    | |Co BANK CODE. DEM001
+===================================+ |BANK NAME.... Demo Banking Corp Ltd
|CURRENCY...... USD    BUY/SELL...S | |ADDRESS...... Demonstration House
|AMOUNT........     10,000,000.00   | |       ...... Testing Lane
+-----------------------------------+ |       ...... London
|BUY  STYLE.... American            | |BANK DEALER.. Felicity
|SELL STYLE.... European            | +------------------------------------
|BUY  RATE.....        1.90000      | +------------------------------------
|SELL RATE.....        1.80000      | |NET  PREMIUM..           5,497.0800
|SPOT RATE.....        1.88000      | +------------------------------------
|BUY  VALUE().     5,263,157.89   | |PREMIUM  DATE.      10/09/90
|SELL VALUE().     5,555,555.56   | +------------------------------------
+-----------------------------------+ +------------------------------------
|BUY  PREM. %..   1.5000000000000   | |BUY  PREM()..(        78,947.37)
|SELL PREM. %..   1.520000000000000 | |SELL PREM()..         84,444.44
+-----------------------------------+ +------------------------------------
```

Figure 35

THE J O N A T H A N R O B I N C O M P A N Y LIMITED
Foreign Exchange Deal – Cylinder Option

```
+===================================+ +------------------------------------
|REF1...    53     REF2...    54    | |Co BANK CODE. DEM001
+===================================+ |BANK NAME.... Demo Banking Corp Ltd
|CURRENCY...... USD    BUY/SELL...S | |ADDRESS...... Demonstration House
|AMOUNT........     10,000,000.00   | |       ...... Testing Lane
+-----------------------------------+ |       ...... London
|BUY  STYLE.... American            | |BANK DEALER.. Felicity
|SELL STYLE.... European            | +------------------------------------
|BUY  RATE.....        1.90000      | +------------------------------------
|SELL RATE.....        1.80000      | |NET  PREMIUM..           5,497.0800
|SPOT RATE.....        1.88000      | +------------------------------------
|BUY  VALUE().     5,263,157.89   | |PREMIUM  DATE.      10/09/90
|SELL VALUE().     5,555,555.56   | +------------------------------------
+-----------------------------------+ +------------------------------------
|BUY  PREM. %..   1.5000000000000   | |BUY  PREM()..(        78,947.37)
|SELL PREM. %..   1.520000000000000 | |SELL PREM()..         84,444.44
+-----------------------------------+ +------------------------------------

              ** PRESS ANY KEY FOR PREMIUM BANK DETAILS **
```

Figure 36

THE J O N A T H A N R O B I N C O M P A N Y LIMITED
Foreign Exchange Deal – Cylinder Option

```
+===================================+ +------------------------------------
|REF1...    53     REF2...    54    | |Co BANK CODE. DEM001
+===================================+ |BANK NAME.... Demo Banking Corp Ltd
|CURRENCY...... USD    BUY/SELL...S | |ADDRESS...... Demonstration House
|AMOUNT........     10,000,000.00   | |       ...... Testing Lane
+-----------------------------------+ |       ...... London
|BUY  STYLE.... American            | |BANK DEALER.. Felicity
|SELL STYLE.... European            | +------------------------------------
|BUY  RATE.....        1.90000      | |PREMIUM.....               5,497.08
|SELL RATE.....        1.80000      | +------------------------------------
|SPOT RATE.....        1.88000      | |BANK........ Own Clearing Bank Ltd
|BUY  VALUE().     5,263,157.89   | |ADDRESS..... 1 Victoria Street,
|SELL VALUE().     5,555,555.56   | |      ...... Westminster,
+-----------------------------------+ |ACCOUNT..... The Corporate Limited
|BUY  PREM. %..   1.5000000000000   | |ACCOUNT NO.. 12345678
|SELL PREM. %..   1.520000000000000 | |SORT CODE... 01 04 06
+-----------------------------------+ +------------------------------------
```

Figure 37

```
          THE  J O N A T H A N   R O B I N   C O M P A N Y  LIMITED
                      FOREIGN EXCHANGE DEAL - CYLINDER OPTION
+==================================+ +-----------------------------------
|REF1...    53     REF2...    54   | |Co BANK CODE. DEM001
+==================================+ |BANK NAME.... DEMO BANKING CORP LTD
|CURRENCY...... USD    BUY/SELL...S | |ADDRESS...... DEMONSTRATION HOUSE
|AMOUNT........      10,000,000.00  | |        ...... TESTING LANE
+----------------------------------+ |        ...... LONDON
|BUY  STYLE.... AMERICAN           | |BANK DEALER.. FELICITY
|SELL STYLE.... EUROPEAN           | +-----------------------------------
|BUY  RATE.....        1.90000     | |PREMIUM.....              5,497.08
|SELL RATE.....        1.80000     | +-----------------------------------
|SPOT RATE.....        1.88000     | |BANK........  OWN CLEARING BANK LTD
|BUY  VALUE().      5,263,157.89  | |ADDRESS.....  1 VICTORIA STREET,
|SELL VALUE().      5,555,555.56  | |      .......  WESTMINSTER,
+----------------------------------+ |ACCOUNT.....  THE CORPORATE LIMITED
|BUY  PREM. %..  1.5000000000000   | |ACCOUNT NO..  12345678
|SELL PREM. %..  1.520000000000000 | |SORT CODE...  01 04 06
+----------------------------------+ +-----------------------------------

          DO YOU WISH TO RECORD THIS DEAL ?(Y/N)  Y
```

Figure 38

```
          THE  J O N A T H A N   R O B I N   C O M P A N Y  LIMITED
                      FOREIGN EXCHANGE DEAL - CYLINDER OPTION
+==================================+ +-----------------------------------
|REF1...    53     REF2...    54   | |Co BANK CODE. DEM001
+==================================+ |BANK NAME.... DEMO BANKING CORP LTD
|CURRENCY...... USD    BUY/SELL...S | |ADDRESS...... DEMONSTRATION HOUSE
|AMOUNT........      10,000,000.00  | |        ...... TESTING LANE
+----------------------------------+ |        ...... LONDON
|BUY  STYLE.... AMERICAN           | |BANK DEALER.. FELICITY
|SELL STYLE.... EUROPEAN           | +-----------------------------------
|BUY  RATE.....        1.90000     | |PREMIUM.....              5,497.08
|SELL RATE.....        1.80000     | +-----------------------------------
|SPOT RATE.....        1.88000     | |BANK........  OWN CLEARING BANK LTD
|BUY  VALUE().      5,263,157.89  | |ADDRESS.....  1 VICTORIA STREET,
|SELL VALUE().      5,555,555.56  | |      .......  WESTMINSTER,
+----------------------------------+ |ACCOUNT.....  THE CORPORATE LIMITED
|BUY  PREM. %..  1.5000000000000   | |ACCOUNT NO..  12345678
|SELL PREM. %..  1.520000000000000 | |SORT CODE...  01 04 06
+----------------------------------+ +-----------------------------------

          DEAL HAS BEEN ADDED TO DATABASE - PRESS ANY KEY -
```

Figure 39

Demo Banking Corp Ltd
Demonstration House
Testing Lane
London

8 September, 1990 Our Ref : 53

Dear Sir,

We confirm our telephoned instructions for the purchase of the following foreign exchange option :-

Currency sold by us :-

Style	:	American
Currency	:	US Dollar
Amount	:	*****10,000,000.00
Exchange Rate	:	1.90000
Sterling Value	:	******5,263,157.89
Exercise Date	:	27 December, 1990
Settlement Date	:	31 December, 1990
Premium %	:	1.50000000
Premium Cost	:	*********78,947.37
Premium Date	:	10 September, 1990

Please refer to the confirmation for our deal reference 54 for premium payment details.

Yours faithfully,

T Taylor
Group Treasurer

B Bloggs
Financial Controller

Figure 40

```
Demo Banking Corp Ltd
Demonstration House
Testing Lane
London

 8 September, 1990                                    Our Ref :      54


Dear Sir,

We confirm our telephoned instructions for the sale of the following
foreign exchange option :-

Currency sold by us :-
Style                : European
Currency             :  US Dollar
Amount               :  *****10,000,000.00
Exchange Rate        :           1.80000
Sterling Value       :  ******5,555,555.56
Exercise Date        :  27 December, 1990
Settlement Date      :  31 December, 1990
Premium %            :           1.52000000
Premium Revenue      :  *********84,444.44
Rel. Deal Premium    :  *********78,947.37            Our Ref :      53
Net Premium          :  **********5,497.07
Premium Date         :  10 September, 1990

Premium to be paid to our instructions as follows :-
Bank     :       Own Clearing Bank Ltd
                 1 Victoria Street,
                 Westminster,

Account :        The Corporate Limited
A/C No. :        12345678



Yours faithfully,



T Taylor                                                 B Bloggs
Group Treasurer                                          Financial Controller
```

Figure 41

In many respects the cylinder option is similar to the simple option dealing procedure. However, the difference here is that two option deals are being dealt with simultaneously. One option is being bought and the other sold (see earlier explanation of cylinder option, section 2(b) above). In this respect it is not necessary to have the option B/S, as seen in the simple option screen, as these are both included in the deal.

Other minor changes seen in the cylinder screen are as follows:

Buy style/Sell style These refer to the option styles of the two separate components of the cylinder. The option that the company buys has an option style as well as the half that is being sold (see above for option style definition).

Buy rate/Sell rate Again, buy and sell refer to the underlying options that are being bought and sold. The buy rate refers to the 'strike rate—downside' of the option that is being bought. Similarly, the sell rate refers to the 'strike rate—upside' that is being sold.

Buy value/Sell value Both refer to the sterling equivalent of the currency amount divided by the buy or sell rate above. This is calculated automatically.

Buy premium % This is identical to the 'premium %' seen in the simple option. This should be input by the user after agreeing the price with the counterparty.

Net premium This is the total net premium that the company expects to pay. At this stage the screen defaults to 0.00. If the enter key is now chosen the 'sell premium%' box will display the per cent premium that would be receivable on the option sold to give a cylinder that would have a net premium of GBP 0.00. This is known as a 'zero cost cylinder' and is where the premium received on the option being sold is matched by the cost of the option that has been bought.

If a round sum premium is going to be paid, e.g., 50 000, this should be input into the 'net premium' field. The appropriate 'sell premium %' will then be entered and automatically recalculated. A net premium payable of GBP 50 000 would be input as a positive number in this field.

If the net premium is not known at this stage and just both

halves of the 'premium %' are known the enter key should be pressed to take the cursor to the 'sell premium %' field. The appropriate 'premium %' can then be input (again as a positive number). Once input, the net premium current, displayed 0.00, will be recalculated to show the true net premium payable or receivable as a result of the cylinder. The appropriate buy and sell premia will then appear on the screen (for a zero cost cylinder they would be identical but opposite in sign).

The premium delivery instructions of the deal can be completed in the usual way, and the deal ultimately recorded.

(d) Exercising an option

Options are usually dealt for an exercise date that is up to one year in the future. During this time, or on the exercise date (depending on the option style), the option will be exercised or will lapse.

If the option was originally purchased and the current rates are better than the option rates, it will not be beneficial for the company to exercise the option (see 2(a) above). If the original option was sold the option will be exercised if the counterparty considers the current rates beneficial.

Exercising an option bought is not necessarily a good thing for the company. The original option was bought to protect a position worse than was currently available in the market when the option was bought. This 'slack' away from the rates available in the markets when the option was purchased is the 'opportunity cost' or going 'out of the money'. This is akin to an 'excess' on a car insurance policy. The insuree promised to suffer, say, the first GBP 100 of loss, but thereafter losses are sustained by the insurance policy. If the insurance is used it therefore follows that the insuree has lost GBP 100. This is similar to exercising an option. If the option is exercised the 'out of the money' movement is equivalent to suffering the excess on the insurance policy.

Example

Current rate at time of deal US$: $1.65. Option bought to sell US$ currency at $1.70 (i.e., 5 cents 'out of the money').

Exchange rate at time of exercising the option is $1.75. The company will exercise the option to sell at a rate of $1.70. Sterling received on $5 000 000 sold would be GBP 2 941 176.47. This is better than the GBP 2 857 142.86 that is currently available in the market at $1.75, but is not as good as selling at the rate of $1.65 that was available when the option was bought. In fact, this would have yielded GBP 3 030 303.03 (GBP 89 126.56 more than the company will actually receive).

Exercise routine

Decide whether an option is coming to maturity. Review the FX maturity ladder to see whether any SIM or STR deal types are coming to maturity (i.e., is the exercise date the current date?).

Call up screen 1.2.3. If the company is exercising an option, type in the deal reference. The screen will then ask a question about the current exchange rate for the currency that is the subject of the option to decide if the option is worth exercising. If it is worth exercising, the screen will ask for a deal type (T/L). Answer as appropriate (usually T—trading deal).

The screen will now pull up the relevant details of the option. Once exercised the option will become a normal foreign exchange deal indistinguishable from any other.

The question 'deal close' should then be answered. If, as is likely, the amount of currency concerned in the option is not readily available, a 'no' answer should be chosen. Appropriate reversing of foreign exchange deals can then be undertaken to mature this foreign exchange deal that has just been created.

Example

Option bought to sell DM 30 000 000 at 3.00 for 1 December

Current rate at exercise date = 3.10

No deutschemarks available to fulfil deal at 1 December

Two business days prior (29 November): Exercise option

Treat as 'N' for deal close

Purchase DM 30 000 000 at 3.0 to match with currency sold for 1 December settlement date

Receive sterling into the company's home bank account.

If cover is still required a simultaneous deal to see DM 30m would be struck for delivery on a later date, e.g., 31 December.

The option exercise screen just converts an option to undertake a foreign exchange deal into the actual underlying deal. After being exercised the 'deal' performs in exactly the same way as all other foreign exchange deals.

The above concepts relate to both simple and cylinder options. While the option is on the system unexercised, the rate at which the deal is evaluated in the TEM report, foreign exchange maturity ladder and month-end journal will depend on the relationship of the current/month-end rates to the strike rates of the options. If the rates are worse then the strike rate will be used. If, in the case of the simple option, the current rates are better than the 'downside' strike rate, the current rate would be used. The principle to apply here is to ask the question at this stage 'Would the company exercise the option?'. If the answer is 'yes', the strike rate will apply; if 'no', then the current rate would apply. In the case of a cylinder option this relationship also holds except that if the current rate improves beyond the best possible rate of the cylinder (upside strike rate) only the upside rate is used for evaluation purposes. This is because at that moment the option would be exercised against the company with the counterparty accruing the extra advantage of the current rates.

Example

Assume 10 deals as follows:

Deal Ref.	*Currency*	*Bank*	*Deal date*	*Settlement*
1	USD	BBI001	24/04/90	26/06/90
2	USD	LYD001	28/05/90	31/10/90
3	USD	BBI001	29/05/90	03/06/90
4	AUD	ANZ001	29/05/90	31/05/90
5	JPY	SBC001	15/06/90	30/06/90
6	JPY	BBI001	18/06/90	30/06/90
7	DEM	DEB001	18/06/90	31/07/90
8	USD	SBC001	30/06/90	31/07/90
9	AUD	BOS001	18/07/90	22/07/90
10	FRF	LYD001	18/07/90	30/09/90

Obviously the individual details of the deal, e.g., sold, bought amounts, etc., would also be sorted and printed; but for illustration purposes, only the key sort fields above are shown.

Options selected: A —All
Sort criteria: B —Bank
S —Settlement date
* —Ignore

The report printed would be as follows:

4	AUD	ANZ001	29/05/90	31/05/90
3	USD	BBI001	29/05/90	03/06/90
1	USD	BBI001	24/04/90	26/06/90
6	JPY	BBI001	18/06/90	30/06/90
9	AUD	BOS001	18/07/90	22/07/90
7	DEM	DEB001	18/06/90	31/07/90
10	FRF	LYD001	18/07/90	30/09/90
2	USD	LYD001	28/05/90	31/10/90
5	JPY	SBC001	15/06/90	30/06/90
8	USD	SBC001	30/06/90	31/07/90

The primary sort key determined the overall order of the report with the second option becoming the subcategory.

If the sort criteria had been reversed, e.g.,

S—Settlement
B—Bank
*—Ignore

then the deal reference order would have been as follows:

4, 3, 1, 5, 6, 9, 7, 8, 10, 2

A further feature of the report is that when the settlement date or reference sort options are selected, the report enables the user to select a time period: e.g.,

Reference selected for sort function.

Start and End dates appear on the screen. These should be overtyped to the user's chosen parameters. When the 'reference' sort option is chosen the date parameters refer to the dealing dates. When the settlement date option is chosen the start and finish dates refer to the settlement dates. This will result in practical differences appearing in the reports. The reference sort option is particularly useful when finding the deals that have actually been dealt with in a month. This is necessary when computing the 'position change report' for the monthly board papers. The settlement date sort is useful when determining the maturities of particular deals as opposed to the date they were actually dealt. It should be noted that if this option is selected and the dates chosen are not wide enough to cover all deals in the system, such deals outside the dates chosen will be excluded from the report.

In the previous examples if the settlement date range chosen had been:

Start date: 01/06/90 End date: 30/06/90

then deals 4, 9, 7, 10, 2 and 8 would have been excluded.

3 Confirmation exception reports

Confirmation exception reports enable the user to determine whether a third party confirmation has been received or whether the company has printed and sent its own confirmations. Prior to implementation of the system it was not feasible to ensure that all confirmations of deals were exchanged by the company and the relevant counterparty. The dealing system has a database, which is updated when third party confirmations are received or company confirmations are sent, so that it is possible to print a number of reports showing the cross confirmation position. The ability to print these exception reports enables the company to track and chase any unprinted or unreceived confirmations. In addition, this management report can determine how quickly the treasury section is receiving and matching third party confirmations as well as sending the company's own copy. This is crucial in ensuring that both parties' perceptions of a deal are correct.

The two true 'exception reports' are found using screens 7.3.2 and 7.3.3 and can be run using the procedure outlined in Chapter 4, section 4). In addition, there is a report 7.3.1 that will print all deals (within selected deal reference parameters), showing the relevant matching confirmation reference received from the counterparty. This, and the two other exception reports, can be used by internal audit to ensure that adequate internal controls are maintained within the treasury area.

Report 7.3.1 prints all deals to date in deal reference order together with the bank references that were received on their matching confirmation. A reference cannot be input into the system until the deal has been matched with the company's own perception. This report could be used by internal audit to test check confirmations received by the company (direct to internal audit prior to being passed to treasury).

CHAPTER 7

Management reporting

There are a number of reports available from the dealing system which will give the following information:

(1) Evaluate complete dealing performance by currency for the year against plan and market rate criteria (TEM reporting).
(2) List deals that were/are outstanding and compare these deals with current forward market rates to evaluate whether they are in a profit or loss position (FX maturity ladder).
(3) A list of all deals year-to-date (or for a selected time period) sorted and analysed by a number of different criteria. These include bank, currency, settlement date and deal reference order.
(4) Confirmation exception reports to indicate which confirmations have not been sent by the company or not received from third parties.
(5) A list of all deals year-to-date together with the appropriate matching deal reference quoted on the counterparty confirmation.

It is recommended that the next section should be read in conjunction with the corresponding report. Examples of each report can be found in the screen detail section as specified:

TEM report (7.1.3)
FX maturity ladder (7.1.1)
Deals to date (7.1.2)
Deals with no confirmation printed (7.3.2)
Deals not confirmed by counterparty (7.3.1)

1 Treasury exposure management (TEM) report: description

The TEM report gives the reader a better understanding of how the treasury foreign exchange deals undertaken year-to-date relate to the total foreign exchange exposure for the year.

The report concentrates only on trading or TRAN-saction deals. Those which relate to liquidity or LIAB-ility management are not included. The report evaluates the deals undertaken against two parameters: plan rate and spot rate.

(a) Plan rate

Each deal is evaluated against a certain plan rate for the currency, which is established once a year.

At the beginning of the year, when the total exposure to a currency is known, a plan rate is set. This is generally equivalent to the six month forward rate achievable for a particular currency on the date the plan is set. Once this rate is known, it therefore follows that the total sterling value that is expected to be received for a particular currency is also known, i.e.,

Australian dollar: Exposure for 1990/1	=	6m A$
Plan rate	=	2.30
Plan sterling value expected	=	GBP 2 608 695.65

The TEM report totals the sterling value from deals transacted so far during the year, and project forward on a forecast basis the additional currency that should be sold to match the total forecast currency exposure for the year, at the current rates achievable, e.g.,

Australian dollars

A$	GBP
Total currency sold YTD: 3 000 000	Total sterling achieved so far: 1 333 333.33
Future currency to sell: 3 000 000	Sterling value at current rate of 2.35: 1 276 595.74
Total planned currency: 6 000 000	Total sterling expected to date of TEM report: 2 609 929.02

Comparison:

Total sterling expected for year:	2 609 929.07
Plan sterling expected:	2 608 695.65
Gain against plan:	1 233.42

Expressed in report as GBP 1.2K

(b) Spot rate

Each deal is compared to the rate that would have been attained if all the currency received during the year was sold only as it came in, i.e., for Spot. Treasury, however, normally sell currency in advance of it arriving in the UK. The rate for which it has been sold on, say, Day 0 will be different from the ultimate rate that would have been achieved if it was sold just as it arrived, which is, say, Day 91. The sterling value achieved by selling the currency forward (i.e., in advance) is compared with the sterling value that would have been achieved by selling on Day 89 (the spot date for Day 91). If the forward sterling value is greater than the spot sterling value, a gain has been made against 'spot'.

The total of all these gains and losses for each currency are shown in the last column of the TEM report. Other items included on the TEM report are explained as follows:

Total currency exposures (M) These are calculated annually with revisions at each quarter forecast for known variations from plan. For input to the computer, see Chapter 9. The total exposure to a particular currency is made up of the following components:

Third party sales of overseas subsidiaries/distributions (net of any commission payable)	X
Overseas third party controllable costs of subsidiaries	(X)
Net profit after tax	X
Third party currency purchases made by parent company	(X)
Total net exposure	X

Treasury then undertake to manage the total net exposure for that currency. Broadly, the TEM report mimics the foreign exchange accounting risk that the company has for a particular year. It is worth noting, however, that the currency that actually flows from subsidiaries/distributors is only the ex-parent company invoice value of sales, together with any dividends.

The flows are thus different from the actual exposure (lower in most cases) and it is therefore important to review the exposure regularly to ensure that the 'non-flowing' exposure is closed out as the year progresses. This is particularly important in subsidiaries where a low transfer price gives large profits overseas earned on a monthly basis, and which are not remitted back to the parent except possibly at year-end when a dividend might flow. This could potentially lead to an overcovered position, particularly as the year draws to a close. The reverse is also true.

Although treasury manages the total risk it does not control the timing of the individual components making up the currency exposure. The TEM report should therefore be seen as only a guide to the forecast foreign exchange out-turn for the year. Many other accounting problems could be affected by this out-turn.

Residual cover (months) This column informs the reader of the report of the total number 'months worth' of cover (foreign exchange deals outstanding) in existence for the year. For example:

Deutschemark	DM
Currency exposure for year 1990/1 (equivalent to 12 months)	61 400 000
DM FX deals outstanding at date of report	35 000 000

Therefore, by calculation, the residual cover is:

$$\frac{35\ 000\ 000}{61\ 400\ 000} \times 12 = 6.8 \text{ months}$$

AOP These are the individual plan rates set for a currency. See Chapter 9 for instructions on input.

Cover taken This is the composite rate that has been achieved on all FX deals for a particular currency year to date, e.g.,

DM 1 000 000 @ 2.5	GBP 400 000.00
DM 3 000 000 @ 3.0	GBP 1 000 000.00
DM 4 000 000	GBP 1 400 000.00

'Cover taken' composite rate is therefore

$$\frac{4\ 000\ 000}{1\ 400\ 000} = 2.857$$

Expressed in the report as 2.86.

Current spot These are the rates held by the system as the current spot rates achievable for a particular currency in the foreign exchange market. They should be changed regularly to reflect market rate changes. They are changed using the procedure in Chapter 9.

Gain/loss v plan and *Gain/loss v spot* have been covered earlier in TEM description.

2 Maturity ladder: description

Reading from top to bottom and left to right the FX maturity ladder is made up of the following components:

Date At 8 August 1990 describes the date up to which the maturity ladder is made. Obviously, if a deal is not dealt until 15 August it will not be on a report showing outstanding deals as at 8 August. This date can be changed when requesting the maturity ladder by simply typing over the new date required. This is not normally necessary as the function of the maturity ladder is to provide details of deals that are outstanding (i.e., not yet delivered) at present.

Settlement date This date refers to the date for which foreign exchange deals actually mature, i.e., US dollars sold for 30 September would have a settlement date of 30 September 1990. Practically, this would mean that the US dollars sold would be delivered to the purchaser and the company would take delivery of the sterling proceeds gained from the sale. The deals on the maturity ladder are shown in chronological order. Normally a deal that has a settlement date within two business days from the present date will have to be addressed to ensure that both the currency and sterling elements are being delivered for the correct fulfilment of the contract.

Reference number This is the unique deal reference number that is given to each new deal in the database. There should be no gaps in this sequence, nor duplications.

Currency The type of currency corresponding to the three-letter code can be found by looking at the key on 5.3.5.

Type Under 'type' in the report it will state New, Sim or Cyl. New is a straight foreign exchange contract. Sim or Cyl correspond to simple and cylinder currency options which may or may not be exercisable. This will depend on the current market rates. See Chapter 6 for the section on options.

The S and B indicators in the 'type' column of the report indicate whether currency (i.e., other than sterling) has been sold or bought. This is further emphasized by the 'currency amount' column which shows a figure in brackets if the currency has been sold and without brackets if it has been bought.

TRAN or LIAB correspond to whether the deal is covering a trading (TRAN-saction) exposure or liquidity (LIAB-ility) exposure. The latter are only used when taking hedging action on deposits/borrowings the parent company has with its subsidiaries. These deposits are made in currency and therefore there is a currency risk for the parent company.

The counterparty refers to the bank that was dealt with.

If the letters CL (which stand for 'closed') appear after the deal type TRAN or LIAB, this means that the particular deal or deals have been addressed and no further action is required. They only remain on the maturity ladder because the sterling and currency funds, which are moving as a result of the deals, have still to move, e.g., two business days away.

Counterparty The code shown under this column refers to the bank against which the particular foreign exchange deal was struck.

Currency amount The currency amount always refers to the currency denoted in the 'currency' field of the report.

Exchange rate The exchange rate is the all-in rate for which the deal was struck. This rate is made up of two components:

(1) the 'spot rate' for the currency, which is expressed as the value of one currency in terms of another for a delivery of that currency two business days away;
(2) an interest rate adjustment (known as forward points) to correct for the disparity between the interest rates for pound sterling and the interest rates of another currency.

The interest rate adjustment will always be necessary if a deal has been struck for other than two business days hence.

Sterling value The sterling value is the amount of sterling (currency amount divided by exchange rate) that will be paid or received on the settlement date of the deal.

Profit/loss on current rate The profit/loss on current rate is the valuation of the deals already outstanding against a market rate valuation. Thus, if the currency has been sold, and therefore sterling will be received, this column values how much it would be to reverse this deal, i.e., buy the currency and sell sterling. In doing so it mimics how much it would cost/gain if all the present FX contracts were removed. This column uses the 'current and forward rates' that are currently in the system.

To check whether these rates are approximately correct, go back to the main menu (0.0) and input 5 enter 3 enter 5 enter A enter ZZ enter. This will print out the current rates for each currency in the system. These can then be checked against daily rates in a newspaper or up-to-the-minute rates using Telerate screens 3851 and 3814, or Reuters screens ASAP and ASAQ.

Forward rates are also used in the calculation of the profit/loss column. These can be checked by each currency by typing from the main menu (0.0) the following: 1 and 4 enter 3 enter, and then the appropriate currency code (see 5.3.5). The buy and sell forward points should then be checked and adjusted against, for example, Telerate screens 3851 and 3814, or Reuters screens BAST and BASU. (See Chapter 4 for the forward rates screen adjustment procedure.)

3 Deals to date report

This report enables the user to obtain information about the deals in the dealing system analysed and sorted by using a number of different criteria. The report is particularly useful when determining all the deals for a particular currency or all deals made with a particular bank. In addition, the facility to print out the report within different time parameters enables the user to track a few days, a whole month or the complete year for the criteria selected. This feature is a particularly useful aid when producing the 'position change report' for the monthly board and executive committee papers.

The report should be requested using screen 7.1.2. The first screen asks the user to select the type of deals required to be reported upon. The options are 'all' (everything), 'new' (just forward and spot contracts), or 'simple options' and 'cylinder options'. The usual request is for 'all'.

After the correct option has been chosen, a further level of criteria appears. These criteria determine the order in which the report is sorted. There are four different sort keys of which any three can be selected for the report at one time. The option chosen first will be the primary sort function and will override any others chosen. Supplementary options chosen will only affect the order of the report as a subcategory within the overall primary sort order.

A further feature of the report is that when the settlement date or reference sort options are selected, the report enables the user to select a time period.

Start and end dates appear on the screen. These should be overtyped with the chosen parameters. When the 'reference' sort option is chosen, the date parameters refer to the dealing dates. When the settlement date option is chosen, the start and finish dates refer to the settlement dates. The reference option is particularly useful when finding the deals that have actually been dealt within a month. This is necessary when computing the 'position change' report for management reporting purposes. The settlement date sort is useful when determining the maturities of particular deals as opposed to the deal date. *Note*: Should this option be chosen, and the dates do not cover all the deals in the system, deals outside the dates chosen will necessarily be excluded from the report.

4 Confirmation exception reports

These enable the user to determine whether a third party confirmation has been received or whether the company has printed and sent its own confirmations. The dealing system database is updated when third party confirmations are received, so that the cross-comparison of confirmations can be checked. The ability to produce exception reports enables the company to track unprinted or unreceived confirmations, as well as the relative efficiency of banks in this area.

The exception reports are found using screens 7.3.2 and 7.3.3

and can be run using the procedure outlined in Chapter 4 (section 4). There is also report 7.3.1 which will print all company deals (within selected parameters), showing the relevant matching confirmation reference received from the counterparty. These reports can be used by internal audit to ensure that adequate internal controls are maintained within the treasury area.

Report 7.3.1 prints all deals year-to-date in deal reference order together with the bank references that were received on their matching confirmation. A reference cannot be input into the system until the deal has been matched with the company's own record. This report can also be used as a direct check on the effectiveness of the cross-checking function.

CHAPTER 8

Internal controls

Detail The treasury dealing system helps to create the correct environment for proper internal controls. However, any number of complicated passwords and levels of systems controls would not stop unauthorized dealing. It should therefore be stressed that the controls provided by the system only supplement what should already be good working internal controls. The most important internal control in any system is segregation of duties. This is possible within treasury only to a certain extent as it is a small section. However, the use of other corporate personnel should provide adequate control. The major internal controls for the treasury area are:

(1) third party bank confirmations directed initially to person(s) external to the treasury area;
(2) company bank confirmations signed by two finance (list B) signatories;
(3) company confirmations dispatched by persons external to the treasury area; signed copies being returned to treasury for filing.

If the above controls are not adopted rigorously, any degree of control placed within the dealing system will not prevent unauthorized dealing. As an aid to maintaining this 'control' environment the dealing system provides a disciplined structure and eases what used to be tedious but necessary manual procedures. Within the dealing system there are a number of controls that help to create the right framework.

These controls are written into the system program and are not immediately obvious to the user.

Currency The system checks, before allowing a deal, that it is a designated currency on the system.

Counterparty bank Same as above, but for the bank.

Screen colour Currency and sterling flows are highlighted on the screen using red and blue coloured backgrounds to denote whether funds are travelling out of (red) or into (blue) the group. This helps the user strike the deal the correct way round.

Deal reference Each deal reference is numerically in sequence with no gaps.

Base currency This is calculated by the system so that the user can agree with the counterparty dealer at the time of dealing.

Related deals These are deals which net with other deals (same settlement date, currency and sterling funds flowing just by reading from the screen).

Counterparty details The normal place that a counterparty takes his funds (sterling or currency) is displayed at the time of dealing enabling timely agreement with the bank's dealer.

Options Premia or net premia calculated by either using spot or strike rate data.

Option exercise Current exchange rate must be input to stop company exercising an option that is not beneficial.

Co-confirmation signatories Two must be selected from a predesignated list.

Maturity ladder Daily production enables a track to be kept of deals which are maturing and need to be addressed.

TEM report Management can keep track of dealing year-to-date performance versus a number of set parameters all of which are displayed on the face of the report (e.g., plan and current rates).

Month-end journal Produced automatically by the system. The user need only input month-end rates and month-end debtors by currency.

Accounts coding The user types the minimum information to correctly code treasury deals. All the coding information is held within the system. The user needs only to input the correct currency or sterling amount. The system automatically codes it to the correct account together with the appropriate exchange differences thereon. All parts of sterling and currency movements need to be coded before the system accepts the posting.

Counterparty Confirmations received from counterparties are verified automatically by the system with the appropriate bank reference being keyed in by the user for production of subsequent matching company confirmations.

Company confirmations Produced automatically, no user input. Reprints can be requested if for any reason a third party does not receive a copy.

Most of the above 'controls' can be changed within the system but it should be stressed that once set up these 'aids' enable a user to deal in a correct and accurate manner, with the results of that deal being accurately reflected in the ledgers of the company. The strength of the dealing system lies here, not in creating the overall internal control environment. That can only be achieved by proper segregation of duties. The dealing system will, however, aid that environment if in place by using physical controls and by printing a number of 'control' reports. These are outlined below.

1 Password/user ID

Before a user can access the dealing system it is necessary to have the following items:

- a key to unlock the security keyboard if lock fitted
- details of the system user ID
- the current password.

All of these are obtainable from the senior finance or treasury staff. The password can be changed by overtyping the current password with a new word and saving the result. This is only recommended if appropriate action is taken to secure the new name in a place known only to the registered system users.

2 Confirmation exception reports

These reports (7.3.1, 7.3.2, 7.3.3) have been discussed in Chapter

4 (section 4) and Chapter 7 (section 4). Use of these reports by the staff external to the treasury area will enable a correct check of dealing confirmations. In practice, the strongest internal control is that counterparty confirmations are routed external to the treasury area for logging prior to being sent to the dealing area. Matching of this log against company confirmations will determine whether there have been any unauthorized deals.

Report 7.3.1 can also be used to check the position change report printed in the monthly board papers. This report ultimately gives formal approval to FX deals above the group treasurer's and director of finances' level of approval (example, GBP 3m and GBP 5m). For this purpose the GBP 3m and GBP 5m are taken to be 'position changes' and do not refer to deals originally approved then subsequently rolled. The practice of rolling deals does not present a large risk to the company. In fact, the 'non-rolling' of a deal would in most cases have dire consequences. This is akin to allowing an insurance policy on a rolling monthly renewal to lapse.

3 Cash office/sales ledger reports

Any large amounts of sterling that pass through the bank account are noted by the cash office (external to treasury). This means that any significant payments or receipts are first flagged up by the cash office. As part of the dealing routine reports are printed for the cash office and sales ledger to register the impact of treasury deals on the company's ledger. The cash office uses these reports to post the sterling flowing through the company's bank account. Any discrepancies arising, e.g., cash not received on the correct day or slightly different amounts will be brought to treasury's attention for investigation.

In practice, any payments/receipts that are made later are picked up by the treasury cash manager when reconciling the company's cleared overdraft every morning with the local bank.

The sales ledger report is used in a similar way and is a truncated version of the cash report. This is sent to the sales ledger area as advance warning of the posting to be made by the cash office into the ledger.

4 Bank confirmations

These are produced daily after treasury foreign exchange dealing has been completed. They are printed onto company headed notepaper automatically. The user need only select which two signatories are required from the current finance (list B) signatory list for inclusion at the bottom of the letter. A copy of the relevant dealing screens used for the processing of a particular deal, together with the dealer's signature, should be clipped to the confirmation for signing. All confirmations should be kept in a zipped plastic folder to ensure that all confirmations are signed and sent.

Company confirmations should be physically dispatched by the departmental secretary who then returns any dealing back-up papers, together with a copy of the signed confirmation, to the treasury area for filing.

CHAPTER 9

'Change'

Detail In all systems it is necessary to change standing or master file data occasionally. The treasury dealing system is no exception. The master file data are stored as a number of separate databases which may be accessed as a program is run. It is important that the standing data are reviewed regularly to ensure that they are accurate.

This chapter will outline the procedures that should be used to change different components of the master file data (commonly known as 'maintenance').

1 Signatories

The list of signatories held in the system should reflect the current financial (list B) signatory list. Only these personnel are authorized to sign AI bank confirmations. The user can find the current signatories held by printing them out using screen 5.7.5 and selecting the parameters A to ZZZ.

Each signatory is accessed in the confirmation printing screen by inputting the three-lettered code noted on the left-hand side of the report (each code relates to the initials of the signatory).

Signatories, together with their respective job titles (up to 25 letter characters in length), can be input using screen 5.7.3. Changes or deletions to existing signatories can be accomplished by using 5.7.2 or 5.7.4 respectively.

2 Subsidiaries

To ensure that the correct description appears in the sales ledger report for subsidiaries or distributors remitting cash, the subsidiary master file should always be current.

New subsidiaries can be added using screen 5.6.3 while existing names can be changed by using screen 5.6.2. The procedure for printing the current list held by the system is similar to 1 above except that screen 5.6.5 is used.

3 Deals

Adjustments to deals held in the database should only be necessary in exceptional circumstances as adequate checking should have been carried out before the deal was saved. However, there may be occasions when this is necessary, e.g., if a settlement date has been incorrectly input. This may happen when it becomes apparent, subsequent to the deal having taken place, that there is a bank holiday in the currency dealt.

The dealing system provides the facility to adjust individual parts of the deal using the modify deal screen (5.4.2). Simply type in the deal reference concerned, and the original deal will be displayed on the screen for amending. The deals in the database can only be changed if they are currently 'open', i.e., no delivery instructions for the flows of currency and sterling in the deal have been agreed. This ensures that the database remains accurate once flows have been fixed, agreed and coded.

Deals that are currently 'open' can have the following fields modified:

T/L	A change from a trading to a liquidity exposure deal
Bought/sold	Direction of the deal
Spot Forward point Forward rate Sterling value	Currency amounts cannot change. Ensure if changing the rates that the field's sterling value is also adjusted. This is not automatic in the modify dealscreen.

When the appropriate changes have been made to the deal the deal will be resaved. At this point the original confirmation sent will be deleted. A new confirmation should then be printed and sent to the counterparty concerned if necessary.

Screen 5.4.1 (display deal) can be used as a quick reference as to the individual parts of a deal already on the system. By pressing 'shift print screen' (PRTSC) a hard copy of the deal detail screen can be obtained. This function is useful if a hard copy of the deal was not taken as the deal was struck.

The print deal screen (5.4.3) is identical to the deals-to-date report screen (7.1.2) and therefore should be used as an alternative.

4 Foreign exchange exposures

At the start of each year, or as part of the quarterly forecasting process, the net currency exposures that the group will suffer over the next year should be reviewed and adjusted. Currency exposures are displayed in the treasury exposure report (TEM) and are explained in Chapter 7, section 1. It is important that they are updated regularly because the total exposure determines the level of the foreign cover that treasury undertakes. An understatement of the currency exposures will cause the group to be 'exposed' and any strengthening of the pound sterling against the currency in question will undermine the group's profitability. Screen 1.5.3, currency exposures (AOP), should be used to input the total currency exposure evaluated when the AOP is completed. As explained in Chapter 7, section 2, the exposure is made up of four components. These individual components should be inserted into the displayed screen as straight whole currency units—i.e., 5 million is inserted as 5 000 000 not 5. The net exposure (columns 2 and 4 automatically subtracted from columns 1 and 3) will be calculated and shown at the bottom of the screen. This exposure figure, expressed in millions, is shown on TEM report 1.5.1.

If significant changes to exposures occur throughout the year as part of the quarterly review process (e.g., sales in one country/currency fall below plan) these should be amended by inserting them in the 'latest forecast' (screen 1.5.4) using the same process as above. It is now possible to run both the original TEM report (1.5.1), using AOP figures, and a further report (1.5.2) using the latest forecast figures.

5 General ledger codes

Occasionally changes need to be made in the general ledger coding system to reflect changes in business reporting lines. These may affect treasury coding of exchange differences, but this is unlikely.

The accounts coding screen previously described in Chapter 4 draws on a master file when coding up individual deals for the general ledger. The dealing system has the ability to change the accounts codes that the system uses to make the relevant deal postings. Two major areas can be changed: subsidiary codes and treasury codes.

(a) Subsidiary codes

These are the accounts codes used when posting individual sales ledger remittances from subsidiaries or distributors. They can be changed by using screen 5.5.1.

If a new subsidiary is being added this must first be set up by using the add subsidiary detail screen 5.6.3 mentioned in section 2 above prior to adding the general ledger codes.

When screen 5.5.1 is called up, the screen asks for a currency to be input. Use the usual three-letter code found on 5.3.5. A subsidiary will now be displayed if previously set up together with accounts fields for current, materials and deposit accounts.

The ledger codes consist of three fields: budget holder, accounts code and a descriptive third field. These should be adjusted to reflect the new ledger codes. At the end of each line is a calculation basis. This can either be budget or forward (select B or F and type enter). This represents the basis that the system will use when determining how much of a particular deal is allocated to that account.

Example

Sales ledger remittance US$5 000 000. This can be posted as sterling in the ledger at the budget rate for the year at, say, $1.90 for 1991, or at the actual rate of the underlying deal. The present convention is that such sales ledger and current account remittances are posted at budget rate. If the forward rate had been selected the remittance would have been posted at the rate of the last FX deal that provided that currency flow. This rate approximates to the 'spot rate'. This is used for deposit account remittances and all other types of remittance not specifically relating to subsidiaries or distributors.

A list of all the subsidiary codes in the system can be obtained by using screen 5.5.6.5.

(b) Treasury codes

This refers to the treasury exchange difference codes used with the general ledger. There are five different types of exchange difference. These can be seen using screen 5.5.2, and arise in the following manner:

Code type

Transaction Difference between treasury deals and underlying currency delivered at a spot rate, i.e., a comparison of treasury action taken with no action.

Group liability All payments or receipts relating to closing liquidity hedging deals.

Option All option premia paid or received.

SLC Difference between currency received or paid on subsidiaries. Current account converted at plan rate and at the 'spot rate'. This difference would have arisen without treasury action.

SLM As for SLC, but for sales ledger materials account currency movements.

As for the codes for subsidiaries, there is a calculation basis of forward or budget for each component. At present the first three are at actual/forward rate and the latter two at budget rates.

Only one set of five treasury codes need to be set up. When deals are actually coded a suffix of /USD, or whatever is the appropriate currency, will be added to the exchange difference treasury code to enable quick posting and analysis of the general ledger at the month-end.

6 Month-end rates

These need to be input every month to enable the month-end journal revaluation of foreign exchange deals to take place. Screen 1.4.2 should be used. The screen should be called up and the user should insert the current month displayed.

7 Adding or changing bank details

(a) Sterling bank details

Each time a new bank is to be added to the system the following procedure should be adopted.

Set up new bank code using screen 5.1.3. The code chosen should be of alphanumeric form, e.g., BBI001 or LYD001. Once the screen has been displayed the rest of the details can be inserted. These will be used by the system in the following ways:

Counterparty name/address Displayed at top of dealing screens 1.1, 1.2.2, 1.2.2, 1.2.3, 1.3 every time that bank code is inserted. Will be used as the address on the confirmation letter that the company sends out.

Settlement details Here SP or ST should be input. Once input, the spot rate or strike rate will appear. This is used in the options screen when determining the method by which the bank calculates the option premia or option deals. Most banks use the strike rate. A notable exception is Barclays Bank BBI001. An explanation of this point can be seen in Chapter 6, section 2, under 'spot rate'.

Cheque FOA This is used on the dealing screens when a sterling settlement under 10 000 needs to be made to a counterparty. This is too low to be handled by the CHAPS system; therefore a cheque needs to be raised by the company. Such cheques are sent to a designated person at the counterparty concerned and these details will appear on the company's confirmation letter.

Transfer This gives the usual sterling bank details which, when displayed on the dealing screens, allow a transfer to be made in sterling (i.e., >GBP 10 000) to a counterparty. These details will appear on the confirmation letter and should be used by treasury personnel when transferring such monies unless otherwise informed by the counterparty dealer.

Facility This section is associated with borrowing lines and will be activated on completion of the lending module.

A list of the sterling bank details can be obtained using screen 5.1.

Press ESC when screen is complete; the database is automatically updated.

(b) Correspondent bank details

Once a bank has been added to the system as above the individual currency delivery instructions should be inserted for each currency with which the company deals. To achieve this, the currency needs to be on the system (by using screen 5.3.3.). Then by using screen 5.2.3 (correspondent bank maintenance—add detail) the individual names, addresses and account number details (if available) can be added to the system for each correspondent bank of the counterparty bank. Each currency added to the system should have correspondent details for each counterparty on the system.

A list of the correspondent banks can be obtained using screen 5.2.5. There is a bank on the system called HOMEBK. This refers to the company's own clearing bank details. This is accessed each time sterling is being paid into the company's account as a result of a deal. Also, if the dealing counterparty is the same bank (e.g., Lloyds Bank) payments will be made from the company's account in settlement of deals (even under GBP 10 000) using the Lloyds Bank system. This will be reflected in the dealing screens at the time of the deal and also on confirmations resulting therefrom.

8 Current and forward exchange rates

Adjustments to these are necessary to ensure that the FX maturity ladder and the TEM reports are accurate. Procedures for changing the 'current rates' are outlined in Chapter 3, section 1. Chapter 4, section 2, outlines the procedure for forward exchange rates.

CHAPTER 10

Export data to Lotus 1-2-3

1 The export data function

This function will enable the user to use all of the facilities available in Lotus 1-2-3 without having to rekey the deal information. It is envisaged that this function will be used when wishing to reflect graphically the performance of a particular currency. This function should also be used to determine total dealing turnover in sterling terms. The following notes take the user through the steps that are required to export the data to Lotus 1-2-3 using screen 7.2.

Notes on exporting data from dealing system

To transfer data:

1. Select export data option from reports menu.
2. Enter dates to print from and to (these are DEAL dates).
3. Select the correct type of data to export (i.e., Lotus or ASCII). (The ASCII option should be used for word processors, the Lotus option for all spreadsheets or databases capable of importing 'comma delimited' files.)
4. In either case, the data will be written to a file (in the same directory as the dealing system) called DEALEXP.TXT.
5. The next stages depend on the software being used to access the data. The process described here is the procedure to be followed for importation by Lotus 1-2-3.
6. Load Lotus 1-2-3.
7. SELECT/File directory.
8. Change the directory to C:\DEALING.SYS.

9 SELECT/File import numbers.
10 C:\DEALING.SYS\should now be seen on the screen.
11 Type in DEALEXP.TXT <enter>
12 The file will now be imported into Lotus as a worksheet.
13 The file may be saved with any given name; it will now be treated as a standard 1-2-3 WK1 file.
14 The data in the columns imported are (from left to right):

Reference number.
Currency key (i.e., DEM, USD, etc.).
Whether OPTION bought or sold. (Blank if Deal not an option).
Whether CURRENCY bought or sold.
Whether DEAL is TRAN or LIAB.
Currency amount.
Strike rate (zero if not an option).
Forward rate.
Sterling amount.
Premium percentage (zero if not an option).
Premium amount.
Bank code (e.g., LYD001).
Exercise date (only relevant in OPTIONS).
Settlement date.
Premium settlement date (only relevant in OPTIONS).
Deal date.
Deal close flag ('Y' if it is).
Net currency flow.
Net sterling flow.
Deal type (1 = NEW DEAL, 2 = SIMPLE OPTION, 3 = CYLINDER OPTION).

15 One final point. Some of the numeric fields above are 15 places wide. The global format in Lotus must be set accordingly in order to avoid field overflows.

CHAPTER 11

Programming changes

Detail As any system is developed, changes to the program may become necessary, whether to correct a logic fault or to reflect new developments within the treasury function.

Before any program changes are made a back-up of the dealing system should be taken and stored (never to be overwritten). See Chapter 3, section 3, for back-up procedure. This is necessary to ensure that changes made do not corrupt other parts of the database previously uncorrupted. All program changes should be undertaken by competent personnel from the Jonathan Robin User Support Group. If there is any doubt as to the cost effectiveness of the proposed changes, it might be best to work with a system that is performing well but suffering from a few minor problems rather than suffer doubt and uncertainties during a development phase. Remember: the user depends on the system to effect dealing in a quick, efficient and accurate manner. Test all system changes on the test system thoroughly before running with the changes on the live system.

The Jonathan Robin Company Limited
18 High Street
BLAKESLEY
Northants NN12 8RE
United Kingdom

Index